Human Values and Natural Science

CURRENT TOPICS OF CONTEMPORARY THOUGHT

A series devoted to the publication of original and thought-evoking works on general topics of vital interest to philosophy, science and the humanities.

Edited by **Rubin Gotesky** and **Ervin Laszlo**

Volume 1

SYSTEM, STRUCTURE, AND EXPERIENCE. Toward a Scientific Theory of Mind
Ervin Laszlo

Volume 2

VALUE THEORY IN PHILOSOPHY AND SOCIAL SCIENCE
Proceedings of the First and Second Conferences on Value Inquiry
Edited by **Ervin Laszlo** and **James B. Wilbur**

Volume 3

INTEGRATIVE PRINCIPLES OF MODERN THOUGHT
Edited by **Henry Margenau**

Volume 4

HUMAN VALUES AND NATURAL SCIENCE. Proceedings of the Third Conference on Value Inquiry
Edited by **Ervin Laszlo** and **James B. Wilbur**

Volume 5

HUMAN DIGNITY: THIS CENTURY AND THE NEXT
Edited by **Rubin Gotesky** and **Ervin Laszlo**

Human Values and Natural Science

Proceedings of the Third Conference on Value Inquiry
State University of New York, College at Geneseo

Edited by

ERVIN LASZLO and JAMES B. WILBUR

GORDON AND BREACH SCIENCE PUBLISHERS
New York   London   Paris

Copyright © 1970 *by*

Gordon and Breach, Science Publishers, Inc.
150 Fifth Avenue
New York, N.Y. 10011

Editorial office for the United Kingdom

Gordon and Breach, Science Publishers Ltd.
12 Bloomsbury Way
London W.C.1

Editorial office for France

Gordon & Breach
7–9 rue Emile Dubois
Paris 14ᵉ

Editors' Preface

The present volume contains the Proceedings of the Third Conference on Value Inquiry, *Human Values and Natural Science*, held at the State University of New York's College of Arts and Science at Geneseo, on April 25 and 26, 1969. The Conference addressed itself to one of the central issues on the contemporary scene: the relevance of the natural sciences to the area of human values. The topic is multifaceted and the contributors were asked to undertake a frontal attack on each of its many sides. The result is not a systematic presentation of one delimited aspect or problem-area, but a wide-ranging and challenging discussion of the full spectrum of problems elicited by the topic at hand. With the publication of the proceedings the editors hope to put into the hands of all persons interested in exploring this urgent and essential problem a text of readings which can be readily developed in any one, or all, of a dozen specific but related ways, depending on the interests and purposes of the reader or educator. The aspects under discussion range from the specific problems of philosophy, such as the logical and semantic gap between statements of value and statements of fact, to the practical interface studies of working scientists concerning the applicability of their specialities to human value-situations. The editors are conscious of proposing herewith a dozen concise volumes in one extensive set of readings, but feel that nothing less than this total-view approach can eliminate the dangers of too-specific spectacles, which would present a sharp and detailed but misleadingly one-sided picture of the complex syndrome of issues at hand. The Conference attempted to face these issues in a spirit of collaboration and mutual consultation between scientists, humanists, educators, and philosophers, and to discuss them without any preselection or preconception of conceptual orientation and framework. The proceedings are herewith offered in the same open and constructive spirit, in the hope that further discussions will be elicited, both by the accomplishments and the shortcomings of those presented at the Conference.

The present volume contains articles based on the papers formally read at the Conference. The formal papers were presented partly by eminent scientists and thinkers whose past work justified belief in the quality of their present contribution, and partly by workers in any of the relevant fields who responded to the Call for Papers circulated some nine months before the Conference. The former class of contributors made up the roster of invited speakers, and the latter that of the selected symposia-participants. In order to obtain the unqualified insight of leading minds nothing but the general topic of the Conference was suggested as guideline to the invited speakers, while the Call for Papers asked that the submitted papers consider one or more of the following questions: (i) The relevance of the methods of natural science for the recognition and description of human values; (ii) The values obtained by placing man as a natural entity into the universe described and pre-supposed by natural science; and (iii) the possibility and desirability of preserving or inducing values by means of the techniques and appli-cations of natural science in the light of its cognitive results. As a result, we are fortunate in having, in Part I, four articles by leading natural scientists: Harvard geologist Kirtley F. Mather, Yale physicist Henry Margenau in collaboration with his philosopher colleague Fred Oscanyan, English physicist and humanist Lancelot Law Whyte, and Nobel Prize winning biochemist Albert Szent-Györgyi. Part II presents contributions by Sorbonne value philosopher Raymond Polin, philosopher and logician Rubin Gotesky, W. Ray Rucker, Dean of the United States International University's Graduate School of Leadership, philosopher of science and nature Errol E. Harris, and by Stephen C. Pepper, renowned philosopher of value and author of *World Hypotheses*. Their articles display a wide spectrum of approaches anchored in a shared feeling of urgency in gaining insight into the dynamics of human value by exploring the remarkable storehouses of scientific knowledge. Each presents the nucleus of an embracing theory and provides food for thought for all concerned with the issues.

The majority of the articles in this volume fall under one of three broad headings: Naturalistic Facts and Human Values; Science, Free-dom and Determinism, and Toward a Science of Values. Each of these topics formed the context of a Symposium, wherein the participants presented their views. And since dialogue rather than unqualified agree-ment was sought, the method of the Symposia was dialectical, with the Socratic summation (usually missing in Plato) supplied by the respective Chairmen. Although these Symposia addressed themselves to different specific issues and ideas, the aim and motivation of all three is unmistakably the same: to delineate and suggest how to bridge the multiple chasms between the worlds of human value and of natural phenomena, produced by the extreme analytic and positivistic methodologies and techniques of our recent past. Not only is value excluded from nature and the relevance of natural factors in originating and guiding value assessments denied, but in the general dichotomy of this view man is conceived as a non-naturalistically intuiting, non-cognitively expressing evaluator, as an extra-natural agent isolated from the realm of physical, biological, ecological and sociological fact. If this be correct, a conference on human values and natural science could have but one task: to point out that natural science is irrelevant to human value. But if the contributions to this conference dispose over any cogency and truth, natural science and human values are *not* mutually irrelevant. Divergent as their particular ideas may be, all contributors were unanimous in their attempt to 'close the gap' between man and nature. In general, all agree that man is and must be considered to be a natural being, that he is the product of unbroken evolutionary development and that his world is the natural environment, in which he lives, with which he interacts and within which he values. Such valuing is not convincingly viewed as non-naturalistic nor is the expression of it entirely devoid of cognitive meaning.

Symposium I begins with a frontal criticism (Walter) of the basis of the Humian distinction between fact and value, leads to an affirmation of evaluative principles as empirical generalizations (Leavenworth) and comes to specify values in nonsubjective terms in reference first to socio-anthropological, then biocultural norms (Orenstein, Fay). The four articles suggest that values are immanent in society, and as such are capable of uniting men by counteracting the subjectivism and anarchy of our time in the value areas. The summary and evaluation of the Chairman (Wisdom) introduces a brilliant twist: although admitting the validity of these aims, he refuses to remove the 'fallacy' from 'naturalistic fallacy,' suggesting instead under what conditions non-naturalistic ethical subjectivism is capable of meeting the contemporary need for the interpersonal reliability and reasonableness of value assessments.

Symposium II faced the consequences of the assumed relevance of natural science to human agents. The concept of free will is examined as an hypothesis for verification and the canon of classical empiricism is found to need enlargement (Rose). The compatibility of determinism in the sciences with morality in human agents is argued for next (O'Connor), followed by the striking Stoic thesis that scientific determinism actually enhances and broadens the concept of human responsibility, rather than precluding it (MacGill). No insoluble opposition is recognized between the conceptual determinism characterizing contemporary scientific theories and the human experience of freedom required for morally responsible decisions.

The task of Symposium III presupposed the success, at least as a working hypothesis, of the foregoing Symposia. Facts and values, scientific determinism and human freedom, are presumed to be undivided by categorical gaps, and the possibility of constructing a science of values, similar to that of other phenomena, is envisaged. The formal problem of offering a mathematically manipulable definition of 'good' is considered first (Gill), followed by the attempt to elucidate the complex strands of interdependence among the principle kinds of intrinsic value (Bahm). Operational-factual analyses succeed formal theories and man is held to be not only a natural entity operating on and controlling nature, but part of the nature he controls. His total ecosystem role, given scientific formulation, provides the normative model for grounding human values in nature (Colwell). The proposed science of value acquires a Whiteheadian process-organismic metaphysical framework in the article by Hirst, which argues that values are expressions of emergent types of order in the historical evolution of structured societies, and that scientific axiology must be based on a combinatory logic which replaces intuitive notions with formal ones. The Chairman's closing summary and evaluation (Kuntz) elaborates on an organic, many-dimensional concept of order which must be available to those who seek a science of values, and argues that the Whiteheadian and ecosystem views expressed in the Symposium set a most important challenge to past theories that abstract living beings from their environments.

It is the hope of the editors that this volume, the third of a projected annual series of interdisciplinary conferences on the general area of value, will prove to be challenging and provocative reading for all those who have doubts about the wisdom of basing statements of value on statements of natural fact, as well as for those who, like the undersigned, are deeply concerned about the breakdown of traditional value systems in contemporary society and the grave difficulties encountered by attempts at a new synthesis, and who look to the accumulated storehouses of information in the sciences for clarification and suggestion.

Ervin Laszlo
James B. Wilbur

Acknowledgement

The editors wish to thank the editors and publishers of *Main Currents in Modern Thought* (New York), *Zygon* (Chicago), and *The Journal of Value Inquiry* (The Hague) for publishing several of the contributions to the Conference and making the appropriate copyright arrangements for their inclusion in this volume.

Contents

Editors' Preface v

PART I

The Emergence of Values in Geologic Life Development
Kirtley F. Mather **3**

A Scientific Approach to the Theory of Values
Henry Margenau and **Frederick Oscanyan** . . . **15**

Recover Values in a New Synthesis: a Manifesto
Lancelot Law Whyte **27**

The Mind, the Brain, and Education
Albert Szent-Györgyi **45**

PART II

Values Beyond Science
Raymond Polin **53**

What Criteria for Scientific Choice?
Rubin Gotesky. **65**

A Value-Oriented Framework for Education and the Behavioral
Sciences
W. Ray Rucker **81**

Reason in Science and Conduct
Errol E. Harris **95**

Survival Value
Stephen C. Pepper **107**

Recommended Reading—Parts I and II **115**

SYMPOSIUM I

Naturalistic Facts and Human Values

The Rationality of Facts and Values
  Edward F. Walter **119**

On Bridging the Gap Between Fact and Value
  May Leavenworth **133**

A Preliminary Application of Ethnological Analysis to Ethical and
Meta-Ethical Theory
  Henry Orenstein **145**

Ethical Naturalism and Biocultural Evolution
  Charles Fay **159**

Why the Gap is Under Attack
  J. O. Wisdom **169**

Recommended Reading **177**

SYMPOSIUM II

Science, Freedom, and Determinism

The Verification of the Free Will Hypothesis
  Mary Carman Rose **181**

Psychology, Moral Philosophy, and Determinism
  John O'Connor **193**

Determinism, Responsibility, and the Person
  Neil W. MacGill **203**

Responsibility, Freedom, and Statistical Determination
  George L. Kline **213**

Recommended Reading **221**

SYMPOSIUM III

Toward a Science of Values

An Abstract Definition of the Good
  John G. Gill **225**

How Intrinsic Values Interdepend
   Archie J. Bahm **237**

Some Implications of the Ecological Revolution
for the Construction of Value
   Thomas B. Colwell, Jr. **245**

Some Thoughts on Scientific Axiology: Its Metaphysical
Basis and Prerequisite Variables   .
   Norman F. Hirst **259**

The Serial Order of Values: An Argument Against
Unidimensionality and for Multidimensionality
   Paul G. Kuntz **267**

Recommended Reading **287**

Index **289**

PART I

The Emergence of Values in Geologic Life Development

KIRTLEY F. MATHER

Harvard University

The concept of survival values as an all-important factor in the process of natural selection has long been prominent in the thinking of students of organic evolution. Such values are considered in relation to all kinds of life, pre-human as well as human, plants as well as animals. Like all values, when that term is used in its philosophic sense, survival values are future-oriented. They carry a connotation of an objective, a goal, even a purpose. All living creatures, whether known only from their fossilized remains or by their presence today, seem to share one common purpose: to maintain as long as possible the continuing existence of their kind of life. This is by no means the equivalent of maintaining the existence of the species to which a creature belongs. When the last of the dinosaurs became extinct, near the end of the Mesozoic Era about 75 million years ago, a kind of life that had been maintained for more than 100 million years by countless successive saurian species came to an end. When the three-toed horse became extinct, fairly early in the Tertiary Period of the Cenozoic Era about 40 million years ago, the kind of life it represented was continued by its lineal descendants through successive equine species to the one-toed horse of Pleistocene and Recent times.

Extinction of a species does not necessarily mean that its survival values were inadequate. A species is a man-defined segment of what may be a long-continuing sequence of a particular kind of life. Such a sequence of lineally related species and genera is now designated as a taxa. In any consideration of survival values, it is the taxa that must be foremost in mind, although the survival value of a species may be temporarily appraised as involving one step on a long road. Such an appraisal is, however, a tricky business. What may seem good for one species may prove fatal for its descendants a few species later in the taxanomic lineage. Relatively huge bulk may have had great survival value for certain species of saurischian dinosaurs in the Mesozoic Era and for the megatheres among the mammals in early Cenozoic time, but both of those taxa were soon—geologically speaking—defunct. The skeletons of many victims of megalomania are strewn in considerable abundance along the path of life.

Survival values have been significantly different for different taxa and for successive species within a taxa at different times. Many of the strains of evolving animals and plants display a cyclical development. The new kind of life arises in some relatively small geologic niche: for example, an embayment of an epicontinental sea at the margin of a continent for a marine invertebrate fauna, or a small land area nearly or quite surrounded by epicontinental seas and with its own particular climatic conditions for a terrestrial vertebrate fauna. In each more or less isolated province the competition for survival leads to the natural selection of the local champion in terms of their survival values. Comparative isolation tends toward many experiments with previously untried organs, structures, or habits, and favors the development of gene pools that give viability to the new species or genera. Then comes one of the far-reaching geographic changes that have occurred so often in earth history. If the marginal embayments are extended to the continental interior by sea transgression, their marine faunas may mingle; if so, the local champions will be pitted against each other in the continental sweepstakes. Survival values that were adequate for continuing existence in each of several different provinces are tested under the new cosmopolitan conditions. Later withdrawal of the seas will return the more successful to marginal provinces, similar to those inhabited by their progenitors in the earlier geologic epoch. This cyclical alternation between provincialism and cosmopolitanism seems to have played an important role in the geologic life development.[1] I will comment later upon its significance with respect to human values. In a certain sense the cycles are rhythmic, but they are quite irregular in duration. The cycles for land animals are out of phase in relation to those for marine creatures; obviously a time of provincialism for the inhabitants of shallow epicontinental seas is a time of cosmopolitanism for the creatures of the land, and vice versa.

The survival values to which I have thus far directed your thoughts pertain to organic structures and forms and to the behavior made possible or necessary by those anatomical features. They are characteristic of the biology of the species or taxa with which the scientist is concerned. Let me take time for just one example. The brachiopods are shallow water, marine, bivalved invertebrates, quite distinct from the clams and oysters which might also be included in that designation. Their fossils are especially abundant in sedimentary rocks throughout the Paleozoic Era, 600 million to 225 million years ago, but they constitute only a minor fraction of the marine faunas living today. The great majority of the brachiopod fossils found in strata formed in the first 20 or 30 million years of that Era (Early Cambrian time) are indicative of inarticulate brachiopods—creatures whose two valves were held together only by the interior muscles, without articulation along a hinge line of projections from one valve into sockets in the other. Even held tightly shut by muscle contraction, the valves could be easily twisted apart by the tentacles of contemporary cephalopods, the most powerful creatures of the Cambrian seas. And the cephalopods presumably enjoyed 'brachiopods on the half-shell' as an item on their menu, even as we prize 'blue-points on the half-shell' today. There were, however, a small minority of articulate brachiopods in some of the Early Cambrian marine embayments. They were beginning to develop interlocking hinges, some of them of considerable length, such that the shell could not be twisted apart without breaking the shell. The survival value of such an apparatus is obvious; by the end of the Cambrian Period (about 100 million years in length) the great majority of brachiopods were articulates. It is but one example of the many episodes in geologic life development during which a small minority possessing superior survival values has become the majority among the creatures of its kind. Any paleontologist can cite scores, if not hundreds, of such events.

The example drawn from brachiopod history pertains to the value of defense mechanisms. There are also many examples of the survival value of organic structures that are useful in aggressive tactics, especially those involving the desire for food. In many of the phylogenetic lineages now known within the more complexly organized branches of the animal kingdom, increased mobility has had obvious survival value, whether the creatures swim freely in water, crawl or creep on the floors of sea or lake, or perambulate on the surface of the land. This involves the ability of the nervous system to coordinate the movements of the various segments of the body of segmented animals and of the paired appendages characteristic of so many orders of animal life. More significant for our present inquiry is the increased awareness of what is going on in their environment that is displayed by successive species in many an evolving taxa.

All unicellular protozoa and many of the more lowly multicelled animals are aware only of conditions and things in immediate contact with their cell walls. Cilia and, even better, antennae extend the awareness of creatures possessing such structures to distances of an inch or more from their bodies. Organs of sight, whether merely light-sensitive epidermal cells or single-lensed or compound eyes had obvious survival value by extending awareness to greater distances. The same is true for organs capable of detecting and identifying sounds or odors. The nature and degree of awareness displayed by any creature that lived in the past or is alive today is probably the best measure of progress as distinguished from mere change. That basis for appraisal is not necessarily equivalent to the measure of an extinct animal's resemblance to man or any other living animal. It simply asks the mathematical question: in how many different ways and to what measureable extent is an animal aware of its surroundings? The answer is found by investigating its anatomy and observing its behavior. This is the least anthropomorphic appraisal of evolutionary achievement we can apply to the various kinds of life we know.

Survival values accruing from anatomical structures may be designated as biological values. In addition there are spiritual values that can be recognized by the natural scientist. One such is the spirit of adventure that appears to have been influential in the evolution of certain taxa among animals that have achieved a considerable degree of awareness of their surroundings. To accept it as a reality is to acknowledge that mere continuity of existence is not the only objective of some forms of life. A description of certain events that happened during the Mesozoic Era, 225 to 70 million years ago, will clarify and sharpen what I have in mind.

The Mesozoic Era is often called 'The Age of Reptiles.' During almost all of that time-interval the dinosaurs were the dominant kinds of terrestrial animals. Some were herbivorous, others carnivorous; they gained temporary security for themselves in every habitat afforded by the surface of the land. Even while the saurians were becoming masters of the land, they also deployed into the sea and into the air. In the latter habitat there were two distinct groups of taxa: one, the earlier, included the flying reptiles or pterosaurs that became extinct at the close of the era; the other became the birds that have continued to the present day. We know fairly well how the terrestrial reptiles evolved into flying reptiles and birds but the question, why?, can be answered only by speculation. There is no evidence that the land was so over-crowded that some of its inhabitants, ever striving for continuing existence, were forced as a last resort to venture into the radically different and previously untried way of life. Rather, it seems more plausible that there was some kind of internal urge to launch out into the unknown, to try a new experiment—a spirit of adventure. The venture proved eventually to have survival value: about 100 million years of continuing existence for pterosaurs and at least 70 million years longer than that for birds.

Probably the most important of the spiritual values pertain to the spirit of cooperation and mutual aid. This cannot emerge until individuals in a species become organized to form societies. A colony of coral polyps is not a social organization, even though its members live in constant proximity to each other. There is no allocation of specific duties or responsibilities to particular individuals; none spring to the assistance of others whose welfare is endangered or whose lives are threatened; no communication is possible between individuals separated from each other by any appreciable distance. This last-mentioned item means that the minimum requirement for even the most primitive social organism is a nervous system capable of giving its possessor a considerable degree of awareness of its surroundings. It is highly probable that the first animals to attain that capacity were the trilobites. They constitute an extinct class of arthropods, the invertebrate phylum which includes among its many members the modern crustaceans and insects. They had segmented bodies, paired appendages, compound eyes, antennae, and a well-organized nervous system that must have made them the most intelligent denizens of the Cambrian seas. Their fossils are abundant in the Early Paleozoic rocks, reach a climax of diversity near the middle of that Era, and disappear completely from the record by its close. Whether or not any of the trilobites developed social organizations will probably never be known. They apparently had the potentialities for doing so and we are free to speculate that the spirit of cooperation may have emerged in them a half-billion years ago.

Be that as it may, we know definitely that this spirit has considerable antiquity—some fifty million years or so. Although certain kinds of insects appear in the record of Late Paleozoic life, the social insects—ants and termites and some bees and wasps—did not arise until much later. Their record begins early in the Tertiary Period (70 million to 2 million years ago) and continues throughout that Period and on to the present day. It is with the ants that social life has attained its highest expression among insects, and judging by their world-wide distribution the formicine ants display the most efficient social organization for that kind of life. There are fossil ants, preserved in amber and dating back to the Oligocene Epoch (40 million to 25 million years ago), that are scarcely distinguishable from *Formica fusca,* a widely distributed species in Europe and North America today. This is an extraordinary longevity for any complexly-structured species. The evidence suggests that the social insects, having climbed to their high state of evolutionary development more than 25 million years ago, have continued to exist on a dead level ever since. Even so, it is mute but conclusive testimony to the survival value of the spirit of cooperation.

Although the ants and termites display the ultimate development of social behaviour among insects, the wasps illustrate best the evolution of that way of life. The majority of their species are solitary in habit, others are incipiently social, and still others live in highly organized societies. There can be no doubt that social behavior began among insects with parental care of offspring. (Evidently human societies began the same way.) As it evolved, individualism was increasingly submerged for the welfare of the collectivized group. A rigid caste system was established, different for termites than for ants, but equally inflexible for all. Interestingly enough, social habits have arisen among insects no less than twenty-four times in as many different groups of solitary insects. Some of these have developed only the rudiments of social behavior, but all tend in the same direction. The caste system involves from three to five castes: the queens whose only function is egg-laying; the drones, males performing no function other than reproduction; workers, females whose sex organs are usually undeveloped and who are responsible for the manifold tasks of housekeeping and maintaining the food supply for all in the nest or hive; and warriors, also usually underdeveloped females, who defend the nest and occasionally sally forth to enslave workers from other nests or capture larvae to be reared in slavery. In some insect societies there is no separate warrior caste and that function is performed on occasion by the workers. In others there are two castes of workers, each performing special duties. These may run a wide gamut from excavating subterranean rooms and corridors, patroling the surrounding area to scavenge everything that might serve as food and tending the herds of domesticated aphid 'cows,' to farming beds of fungus or gathering nectar from flowering plants. This sounds like an exciting variety of occupations that might stimulate resourceful individual behavior. But not so; the inescapable regimentation of this instinctively established way of life has reduced the members of all insect societies to mediocrity of appearance and behavior. Brilliant individualism has vanished. The thrilling slogan of the Three Musketeers has been curtailed to 'one for all,' with no suggestion, except perchance with reference to the queens, of 'all for one.'

Societal organization, with its concomitant spirit of cooperation, is commonly displayed among vertebrate animals other than the more primitive members of this phylum. They all have a spinal cord and most have some sort of brain and nervous system as well as sense organs of greater or lesser efficiency. This permits a considerable degree of awareness of the various factors in their environments and makes them able to communicate with each other, at least in feeble ways. Among the vertebrate societies, some are loosely organized, others firmly structured. They range from a school of fish, a flight of birds, a flock of doves, to a herd of deer, a pack of wolves, a pride of lions, a troup of baboons, a nation of men. Organization of a group of individuals may be either for procuring food, for defense against predators, for attack upon other animals, or for construction of shelters. Coyotes, for example, customarily hunt in packs, and beavers join together to build their dams. In several mammalian taxa it is apparent that survival has depended primarily on the effectiveness of coordinated activities made possible by societal organization. Students of evolutionary processes have long recognized the value of the spirit of cooperation and the mutual aid it engenders.

But our conference is about *human* values. Where is man's place in the pattern of geologic life development? The scientist can now answer that question with great confidence. Man is certainly a part of the animal kingdom, a creature of the earth. He belongs in a taxa, a phylogenetic lineage, the historical development of which can be traced far backward in time. His morphologic and physiologic evolution has been in accordance with the same laws or principles as those to which all other animals are subject; and it will continue so to be.

The hominoid taxon branched away from the pithecine taxa (anthropoid apes) near the end of the Miocene Epoch, some ten million years ago. Its earlier members included the various species of the genus Australopithecus who lived in southern and eastern Africa during the Pliocene Epoch (the last epoch in the Tertiary Period which came to a close between one and two million years ago). The name Australopithecus means 'Southern Ape,' but the genus is a part of the hominoid taxon, not the pithecine taxa. Its members stood and walked erect; they were primitive hominoids with facial features of a somewhat simian cast; and their brain capacity was intermediate between that of modern man and that of anthropoid apes such as chimpanzees and gorillas. The break between them and the contemporary ancestors of modern apes is marked by their adjustment to a new way of life on broad savannas, tropical or subtropical grasslands with only scattered trees and shrubs, whereas the members of the pithecine taxa clung to the old ways of arboreal or semi-arboreal life in forests and jungles. In their new way of life, their social organization was even more essential to their survival than it was for their simian relatives in the much safer arboreal environment. Naked, unarmed, and alone, any member of the hominoid taxon is a rather helpless creature, no match for a carnivorous feline, scarcely able to secure adequate food for himself. The australopithecines must have organized themselves in small, tightly knits troups at least as well structured as are the troups of chimpanzees, investigated by modern students of animal behavior. Presumably they used clubs and stones for attack and defense, but no flaked stone tools or weapons or other artifacts are known in association with their fossil bones.

Representatives of genus Homo first appear in the known geologic record either near the close of the Tertiary Period or very early in the Pleistocene Epoch ('The Great Ice Age') of the Quaternary Period which continues to the present day. Paleontologists and anthropologists have recently revised the nomenclature of prehistoric hominids, discarding many of the names previously used for isolated fragmentary fossils and reflecting the modern consensus concerning the affinities of well-known fossil creatures to each other and to modern man. Thus, *Pithecanthropus erectus,* (the famous 'Ape-man of Java,' named by Du Bois in 1892) and several other creatures known or believed to have had closely similar characteristics are now known as *Homo erectus,* an extinct species in the genus to which modern man belongs, rather than a species in an extinct genus, closely related to, but separate from the one that includes us. Similarly, *Sinanthropus pekinensis* (the 'Man of China,' found in 1929 near Peking) is now known as *Homo pekinensis,* with the same implication of closer affinities to the other species in the genus than had earlier been inferred. Much the same changes in presumed relationship have overtaken the older nomenclature for extinct species earlier referred to genus Homo. The segments of the hominoid taxon for which the names *Homo heidelbergensis* and *H. neanderthalensis* were formerly used are now demoted to the rank of extinct varieties within the existing species: *Homo sapiens var. heidelbergensis* and *H. sapiens var. neanderthalensis.* Modern man becomes

Homo sapiens var. sapiens, compounding our self-aggrandizement by doubling the number of times we label ourselves as wise.

Chronologic overlap of australopithecines and members of genus Homo was definitely established by Leakey in the early 1960s when he found in Kenya the fossils of a hominid to which he gave the name *Homo habilis* (the 'handy man') because of the association with crudely fashioned artifacts. Depending on one of the radioactive time-keepers, he dated those fossils as 1.75 million years old, but that date is not unanimously accepted. Even so, *H. habilis* is probably the earliest known representative of the genus.

When asked how old is man, I cannot answer until I know what the questioner means by man: the variety of *Homo sapiens* to which we belong? the species as a whole, including its extinct varieties? the genus, including its extinct species? or the hominid family, including its extinct genera? My own predilection is to use 'man' for all varieties of *Homo sapiens,* 'mankind' for all members of genus Homo, and 'sub-human hominids' for earlier genera and species of the hominoid taxon (although in other contexts I may refer to all existing human beings as 'mankind').

Using that terminology, the record of the emergence of man, and of human values, may be briefly summarized. Subhuman hominids lived in Africa for several million years, prior to about one million years ago. There they were in direct and critical competition with the ancestors of anthropoid apes, 'old-world monkeys,' and predatory felines. It was a down-to-earth struggle for existence. Those that survived were doubtless the best killers'; they were also the ones best able to engage in collective and coordinated activities as they perfected their social organization in packs and clans. Appearing about two million years ago, or a little less than that, in eastern and northern Africa, mankind spread to South Africa and to the Eurasian continent. There the earliest records are found in Java; they are correlated with the first interglacial stage of the Pleistocene epoch and date back nearly a million years. (The Great Ice Age comprises four glacial and three inter-glacial stages.) The mankind fossils found near Peking, China, are correlated with the second interglacial stage and are therefore a half million years or so before the present. By that time Heidelberg man was living in what is now Germany. It was however the Neanderthalers who left the most extensive record of early man. They lived through-out the third interglacial stage and into the fourth glacial stage, an interval of at least 150,000 years, during which time they spread along the shores of the Mediterranean Sea and across the Eurasian continent from the Atlantic to the Pacific oceans. Their cultural development is shown in the progressive improvement of their stone tools and weapons, the artifacts they fashioned from the bones of slain animals, and the fact that some of them buried their dead. Modern man (*Homo sapiens var. sapiens*) first appears in the record shortly before the close of the third interglacial stage, fifty or sixty thousand years ago. The best-known type, Cro-Magnon man, entered Europe between 42,000 L.C. and 28,000 B.C., displacing or absorbing its earlier hominid populations.

All these various types of mankind and of man continued the competition with other animals that has been noted for their australopithecine ancestors. They were hunters and gatherers of food; not until ten or twelve thousand years ago, notably in Asia Minor, did any of the food-gatherers become food-producers to any significant extent. There must also have been considerable competition between various bands and clans as each 'staked out' its own territory to be defended against any and all intruders. Continuing improvement in the fashioning of tools and weapons had its obvious survival value. So also, and perhaps even more importantly, did improvement in the fine art of cooperation. Undoubtedly the acquisition of techniques for using fire was also of paramount value in the continuing struggle for existence. All these called for greater intellectual ability. Gradually the hominid brain became larger and more capable. To the ancient function of remembering experiences and observations, with the ability to retrieve needed items from its storehouse, were added the functions of thinking rationally and eventually abstractly, of designing patterns for things and for societal structures, and of becoming vividly aware not only of the physical and biological factors in the environment but of spiritual realities as well. The drawings and paintings in the caves of Lascaux in France and Altamira in Spain, dating from twenty to thirty thousand years ago, as well as the carved figurines found in anthropologist's digs cannot be overlooked by anyone concerned with the natural history of human values.

It is possible that aesthetic appreciation had no survival value, but awareness of ethical principles certainly did. With increasing necessity for effectively organized collective activities rather than idiosyncratic individual behavior, codes of approved and disapproved conduct were developed long before communication by means of pictographs or hieroglyphs had been achieved. Doubtless those codes stemmed from the 'law of the jungle' to which our pithecine progenitors—and some of our more recent ancestors as well—were subject. We must not be misled, however, by Kipling's or anyone else's equating of that 'law' with the supremacy of 'tooth and claw.' As Ardrey,[2] has expressed it in his vivid prose, that 'law' is a combination of 'enmity-amity'—enmity toward those outside one's own congregation, amity toward all within it. The history of the hominoid taxon, especially during the last quarter-million years, has been marked by increasingly efficient organization of individuals in societal groups on an amicable basis and by progressive expansion of the territories within which amity is sovereign. Families have banded together into clans, clans have united to form tribes, and tribes have joined together to create nations.

For thousands of generations, evolution within the hominoid taxon has been under the influence of provincial conditions, but provincialism has given way to cosmopolitanism during the last few hundred years. This radical modification is the result not of geologic or geographic changes but of human activities. Continuing improvement in means of transportation on sea or land or in the air and in methods of communication have made man the most cosmopolitan of all animals. Many of the values and consequent behavior that were adequate for survival under the old provincialism may be quite inadequate under the new cosmopolitanism.

Thanks to science and technology, we live today in a world of potential abundance and inescapable interdependence. The opportunity is ours to use the rich resources of the bountiful earth for the welfare of all mankind. In grasping that opportunity it will be necessary to engage in carefully planned collective action on a scale and in ways that were scarcely imaginable a century ago. Coordination of the activities of the individuals in a society may be accomplished in either of two ways: by coercion, externally applied through political, economic, or social pressure, with brute force and the threat of imprisonment or death, if necessary; or by cooperation, internally stimulated by education and persuasion and freely and intelligently given. If we choose the first-mentioned of these two ways, the future evolution of the hominoid taxon will parallel that of the social insects in the past. It is an experiment already tried and found wanting; social insects have existed on a dead level for at least ten million years. If we choose the second-mentioned way, we will be engaged in an experiment that seems never yet to have been tried.

It is however an experiment that has great appeal to many of us in spite of the disappointments and frustrations of these mid-century years. Actually there is much in its favour. As Wheeler[3] pointed out, many years ago, insect societies represent final and relatively stable accomplishments which have developed along purely physiological and instinctive lines. This instinctive basis, with consequent absence of education and tradition, constitutes a fundamental difference between them and human societies. Everything involved in the organization of human societies and in the endeavor to resolve the paradox of the individual and his social organization in ways that will enhance his unique personality is a part of the cultural evolution of modern man. Fortunately the tempo of cultural evolution, whether progressive or retrogressive, is much more rapid than that of biological evolution. Knowledge and values, ideas and ideals, acquired or developed in one generation, may be transmitted immediately and directly to the next, whereas changes in anatomy can be transmitted only if they are the result of prior changes in the genes, the 'carriers' of inheritable characteristics. Competent geneticists affirm that the 'gene pool' of existing populations is adequate to produce human beings who are aware of values in life that are essential to the attainment of a truly humane civilization.

The description and selection of the most noble human values are literally of cosmic significance today.

Notes and References

1. Kirtley F. Mather, 'Geologic Factors in Organic Evolution,' *Ohio Journal of Science*, **24,** pp. 117–145 (1924).
2. Robert Ardrey, *African Genesis*, New York, 1961.
3. W. M. Wheeler, *The Social Insects, Their Origin and Evolution*, New York, 1928.

A Scientific Approach to the Theory of Values

HENRY MARGENAU AND FREDERICK OSCANYAN

Yale University

The word *value* has an enormous variety of meanings which range all the way from the price of a commodity to the significance or the goals of human actions. The latter are called ethical values, and the discussion in this paper is restricted to them alone.[1]

Another word, often thought to denote the polar opposite or complement of value, is *fact*.[2] Its use is likewise extremely undisciplined, moving from what can be known through direct experience to what can be veridically certified by logical or any other means.

Recognition of this situation permits at once a dismissal of the popular claim that facts and values are in opposition; for what is not clearly defined can not be said to form a genuine contrast. A common extrapolation of the antithesis of facts vs. values is the allegation that science deals with facts and the humanities, notably ethics, study values. This, too, is logically indefensible because of the ambiguities just noted; it is furthermore contingently false because science is full of judgments involving goals of action, full of choices not based on facts in any sense, while the humanities surely address themselves to matter of truth in observation. These comments are meant to remove the *a priori* objections to the aim of this article, which attempts to exhibit similarities of a basic methodological sort between science and the study of ethical values.

That the two areas are outwardly different is of course a commonplace. Indeed when we first turn our attention to the question as to whether science can have a bearing upon the problems of ethical values, it seems as though the two fields of inquiry are so utterly distinct as to preclude any likelihood of establishing a common ground. Looking to natural science, we see that it strives to achieve an objective impersonal account of states of affairs which are thus independent of the scientific observer, while ethical norms appear in comparison to be intensely personal or subjective, and hence fundamentally closed off from an objective analysis in the scientific sense. Further, science is often said to achieve and to maintain a level of inquiry which is value-*free*; scientific knowledge is said to be ethically neutral, and only the use to which such knowledge is put may on occasion be considered morally right or wrong. In contrast, any study of ethics—whether purportedly scientific or otherwise—would seem by its very definition to provide ethically charged results, which are in that sense contrary to this ideal of the ethical neutrality of scientific knowledge.

However, the force of this initial distinction between science and ethics fades somewhat when we observe that scientific inquiry can itself be said to harbor certain ideal, nonempirical concerns regarding its product. As has been pointed out elsewhere, there are certain metaphysical requirements which cognitive constructs must fulfill in order to become genuine elements of a theoretical science; criteria such as internal consistency and fertility, simplicity, and elegance all serve in the evaluation of such constructs, as does the fundamental demand for some sort of empirical verification.[3] These criteria, however, are essentially either formal or pragmatic, and they do not in themselves relate to ethical norms *per se*. Hence, from a somewhat less naive standpoint we should say that natural science *does* involve the realization of certain values, but that these values are not intrinsically ethical, and that natural science does not contain in itself any *normative* principles regarding the ultimate goals of human actions.[4]

Granted that natural science is thus distinct from the study of ethics, we now ask whether or not the social or, more generally, *behavioral* sciences might not be a proper field for the pursuit of ethical norms and values. Here the objects of interest are far closer to particular human actions than is the case with natural science, so that we would at least appear to be approaching a proper standpoint for a scientific study of ethics. However, we wish to maintain that there are two aspects of behavioral science which preclude it from providing normative ethical principles. First, we suppose that behavioral science does not differ structurally from neutral science, so that the value neutrality ascribed to natural science can be said to hold for behavioral science as well, and, secondly, we maintain that behavioral science can in no case *provide* ethical norms unless it involves a fundamental error known in philosophy as the 'naturalistic fallacy.'[5]

Turning first to the relation of behavioral science to natural science, it is clear that on the level of their respective subject matters, there is no obvious common or unifying basis—the social behavior of human beings simply differs from physical or chemical phenomena. Nevertheless, from the point of view of their respective *methods,* behavioral science *is* formally analogous to natural science. In both disciplines, we find related aspects of theory construction and use as represented by the notions of models, various conceptual schemes, similar problems of definition and classification, as well as the need for distinguishing between theoretical and observational uses of terms, all of which indicate a functional or methodological isomorphism in terms providing consistent theories in response to the fundamental problems of explanation and prediction common to both areas of science.[6] Thus, insofar as the constructs of behavioral science compose elements of a theoretical science, they conform to the formal and pragmatic criteria mentioned above, and in this sense we maintain that while a theoretical behavioral science will conform to certain norms, the ethical neutrality ascribed to natural science holds of behavioral science as well, which is to say, the values realized by behavioral science are not in themselves ethical ones.[7]

However, while it can thus be maintained that behavioral science is or can be methodologically isomorphic with natural science, it nevertheless seems that the kind of knowledge provided by behavioral or social science differs in content from that of natural science, a difference which reflects their divergence in subject matter, in that the knowledge of human behavior given in social science embodies certain norms and values insofar as that behavior is normatively guided, seeks to attain certain values, or in a nutshell, is *purposive.* And this brings us to the so-called naturalistic fallacy.

If we suppose that social science uncovers general patterns of behavior which reflect certain values, as, e.g. has been claimed in regard to the importance of personal and social survival, then it simply does not follow that these values ought ethically to be the values toward which behavior is aimed. Indeed, even if we knew everything about the physical universe, about human physiology, about man's natural dispositions, his drives, his instincts and his normal reaction to all stimuli; even if we could predict how average men will behave under all specified circumstances at a given time of the evolutionary process, we should still have no basis for judging the moral quality of his actions. Even if the drive for survival or for individual happiness were absolutely universal we could still not prove, by using the laws of science, that man *ought* not to die or *ought* to be unhappy in certain situations. To use G. E. Moore's well-known expression, there is always an *open question* as to whether the resulting actions are *really* good; simply from the fact that they exist, it is fallacious to insist that they therefore *must* be ethically good or right.[8] It follows then that while social science may well throw light upon the principles actually employed in guiding human behavior, no social science will thereby provide us with ultimate ethical norms. We can, of course, choose to *make* the results of such a study our own, but this involves a feature of selection which essentially transcends that study—an element which is brought to light whenever we wonder whether or not we *should* or *ought to* make such a choice.

Behavioral science is thus precluded from directly providing normative ethical principles *per se,* differing from ethics both substantially (in terms of what is vs. what ought to be), and linguistically (resulting in indicatives instead of imperatives). In spite of this, we wish to maintain that behavioral science can have a deep significance for the pursuit of ethics. But to clarify and develop this point, we must first consider a certain methodological parallelism between science and ethics, and for this we will return, largely for convenience, to theoretical *natural* science.

Let us consider the relevant aspects of the scientific method conceived in its widest generality, in terms of the various stages of the process by which scientific knowledge is acquired and verified.[9] Initially, we encounter the level of protocol experiences, the sense data, the observations which, being incoherent and devoid of order in themselves, require 'explanations' and rationalization by supplementary concepts which are not directly given in the protocol domain. Explanation involves conceptual procedures, which function in the following way.

When analyzed logically every science begins with very general propositions called axioms. These axioms differ in the different sciences; only occasionally, when branches of inquiry attain a very high degree of development, do their bases coalesce. This happened, for example, in certain parts of physics and chemistry when quantum mechanics was discovered. Whatever the axioms of a given science (or a part of a science) at a given time might be, they give rise by formal deductive explication to less general propositions which are ordinarily called laws or theorems. From various theorems, one derives still more particular inferences. For instance, in geometry we might begin with the axioms of Euclid, which lead to the various theorems about plane figures, which in turn provide particular statements about the properties of right triangles such as the Pythagorean Theorem. These final inferences are in general still devoid of empirical content, since they refer to formal elements which have no necessary counterpart in the world of sense, that is, among protocol experiences. Indeed, the entire range of conceptual procedures from axioms to particular inferences represents a formal system, of interest to the logician and the mathematician. To convert it into an applied science one must place it into correspondence with protocol experiences, and this requires the introduction of a set of relations which permit the particular inferences to be compared with the protocol domain.

In some sciences (e.g. geometry), the propositions which result from the particular inferences speak of sides of triangles, angles, lengths of lines, which immediately suggest comparison with actual observable objects. In others the connection is very remote. For instance, a great deal of analysis and insight was required before Max Born recognized that the simple construct ψ, which appears as the solution of the Schrödinger equation, has reference to a probability distribution of observations in the protocol domain. A special set of rules stating that relation had to be discovered, a set of 'rules of correspondence.' Closer inspection reveals that every science requires rules of correspondence, although their presence has long gone undetected. This is true even in geometry; for the lines and angles of an ideal triangle, which is the object of the conceptual procedures, are not truly identical with the elements of concrete figures drawn on material blackboards. Nor is the temperature, which functions as an abstract symbol in the propositions concerning heat phenomena, propositions which flow ultimately from the axioms of thermodynamics, recognizable as in any sense identical with the indication of a material thermometer. The two are related by an operational definition, and that operational definition, like the other connecting links just mentioned, is what we have called a rule of correspondence.

It is by virtue of these rules that the conceptual procedures can be brought into contact with protocol experiences; through them, scientific verification of theories becomes possible.

Thus far, our attention has been confined to the description of the connections between various levels of a scientific theory and the protocol plane. Let us now raise the question of *entailment*. Clearly, when the axioms are given we can move without injection of further postulates to particular inferences. The conceptual procedures are more or less self-contained. But to go from these inferences to protocol experiences

B

we need the rules of correspondence, and these are not entailed by that which they connect. They are *chosen,* much as one chooses axioms, with an eye upon how the entire scheme of explanation is most likely to work successfully. The gap between such particular inferences and the protocol plane is a logical hiatus which a special postulational fiat must bridge.

It is difficult to overemphasize the point that science, in order to verify the theoretical constructs which flow more or less directly from its axioms, needs postulates which are not prescribed by the logically antecedent parts of theory. Among these we have here singled out for discussion a special set, called rules of correspondence. But there are others, such as the choices made by scientists when they accept or reject observational data falling within or without a certain arbitrary measure of dispersion, or even the very decision that their reasoning shall account for observational fact, in complete rejection of Parmenidean aims. These matters, however, can not be brought within the confines of the present discussion.

The axioms, of course, are likewise unentailed; they are subject to human choice. Again, this was not clearly understood in earlier periods of science, when axioms were regarded as ultimate, unchangeable truths. We now know that they do change as science develops, and that their flexibility imparts to science the dynamism, the self-corrective qualities which are so generally admired and which a static basis cannot provide.

We conclude our survey of the method of science by emphasizing once more the postulational character of both the axioms and the rules of correspondence. If scientists were not free to choose these important elements of their method, or if they entertained major disagreements concerning them, their enterprise could not be successful; it would probably be in the same state as current theories of value.

Having studied the methodology or, in current though perhaps perverse terminology, the fundamental language of science, we now examine the language of values with special reference to human actions. We propose to develop that language by means of an outline very similar to that traced in our analysis of the scientific method. Our basic concern shifts now from the goal of *explanation* to the goal of *suasive control of human actions,* from a descriptive analysis of what happens to a hortative language of how men ought to act. In view of this shift the grammatical form of all relevant statements must be altered. Whereas the axioms contained declarative sentences, in ethics one speaks in imperatives or commandments. To be sure, other starting points of ethics have at times been proposed by philosophers, but the testimony of history demonstrates impressively that all effective moral philosophies have begun with imperatives. The commands *imply* specific rules of conduct, propositions relating to particular human situations. Thus, the commandment 'thou shalt not kill' entails that one should preserve life; hence human *life* becomes a value. If 'thou shalt not steal' is included as a command, *property* becomes a value. In this respect, such values may be regarded as deductive consequences of the commands. However, we do not wish to regard values as a *logical* explication of the commands since we do not look upon logic as the primary determinant of ethical systems: the values follow from the commands through a process of *living*; a social group dedicated to certain commands evolves values not by speculation but by concrete actions. In further detail this living process engenders particular patterns of behavior. The ethical enterprise from its basis in commands to its vital implications in terms of specific patterns of behavior is therefore continuous, but this continuity seems to end at these patterns of behavior.

Science became an empirical, verifiable system of reasoning because the rules of correspondence permitted a confrontation of the level of particular inferences with protocol experiences. Their absence would have left science without application, like some parts of pure mathematics. In a similar way, ethics remains unverifiable, devoid of universal oughts if analysis is forced to stop at overt behavior. The behaviour itself satisfies no criterion of external validation, for it follows from certain commands and can therefore not be used to validate those commands. The passage from commands to behavior is 'vitally tautological,' that is to say, a given group of people, a culture, living in accordance with certain commands will automatically exhibit certain behavior patterns. What then, in ethics, can be said to correspond to protocol experiences in natural science? What is this ethical protocol, and what are the rules of correspondence which join it with overt behavior patterns?

Many moral philosophers, especially in occidental cultures, have tried to develop a system of ethics from postulates concerning human goals. Eudemonism, hedonism, utilitarianism are names of such attempts. The telling characteristic of all these endeavors is that by themselves they remain ineffective. A living ethical system has never come out of any proposition which merely records that man's goal is happiness. That knowledge is simply not sufficient to guide man's action in specific circumstances. But if a principle claiming that happiness is man's desirable goal were used as a *criterion of validity* for the actually occurring patterns of behavior, the ethical enterprise could be satisfactorily completed. The empirical facts of actual behavior could then be compared with the ideal protocol behavior *defined* by the principle of happiness.

For this reason we are loathe to accept eudemonism and all the other human goals which have been offered as *the* basic principles of ethics. They are principles in terms of which chosen sets of imperatives can be validated. We therefore prefer to call them principles of validation, or postulated *primary* values (in contradistinction to the values which automatically result from the commands). If this understanding is accepted, our situation in ethics takes on a remarkable similarity to our outline of the scientific method given above. The primary values function in a role comparable with the rules of correspondence and similar postulates of validation, enabling comparison between patterns of behavior and ideal ethical protocol behavior. There are differences, to be sure, but their discussion will be omitted in this concentrated account.[10]

The scientific process is successful when the particular inferences of a system agree with protocol experiences. The ethical process is successful when actual behavior agrees with ideal protocol behavior. In the former case, scientific theory is verified; in the latter, ethical norms are validated. Before verification scientific constructs form hypotheses, afterwards they become true, confirmed theories or laws which state universal (though not ultimate) truth. Before validation, ethical imperatives are tentative, reflect local patterns of behavior and make no universal normative pretensions; after validation they transcend the 'est' and take on the 'esto' character of an ought.

We now summarize and exhibit the loci of values, to be sure, values of different kinds, within the structure of ethics, a structure which parallels science without incorporating the latter's content. The ethical enterprise has at its origin a set of postulates or axioms in the form of imperatives; at the end of its range stand other postulational commitments called ethical goals or primary values. They are in essence means for validation. In the middle range we encounter the behavior patterns which adherence to the imperatives and hope for fulfillment of goals engender. These are the objects of sociological and anthropological studies. We wish to call them *est*-values, or *de facto* values, for they have no ideal, normative quantities—unless one stupidly invokes the pseudo-argument that what is generally done is right. However, the *est*-values become *esto*-values or normative values, the 'is' rises to an 'ought,' when fate or history or the wisdom of man decides that a given set of imperatives leads, through the medium of living which embodies the *est* values entailed by the commands, to the ultimate realization of the primary values or goals.

We thus encounter three kinds of values. First the *de facto* values generated by adherence to a chosen set of commandments (ten commandments, golden rule, stoic continence, etc.). These are purely empirical and lack hortative force. Then there are the primary values, which are postulational and therefore analytic as to their mode of definition. Finally we are asked to select from all systems of *de facto* values (together with their engendering imperatives) those which, in the experience of men—of all men ideally—maximally satisfy the primary values. The *de facto* values then transform themselves into *esto*-values, into validated norms of behavior to be enjoined upon ethical men.

This paper has been written as if ethics were a collective concern, not a matter of individual commitment. The methodology developed, to be sure, is applicable to personal as well as group experience. For example, if the Biblical commandments were used as imperatives and personal happiness were the primary value, validation might well occur in a single life. But somehow the chance that even a criminal might achieve happiness is not inconsiderable, and one is hardly willing to regard this as an example which falsifies the code. There is safety in numbers. One encounters here something in the way of individual instances which mathematics tends to rule out as 'events of measure zero' and refuses to regard as disconfirming episodes.

More important, however, is the observation that living ethical systems avow the 'statistical' method of validation, the only one which justifies personal sacrifice, for example. For that reason we advocate strongly the use of ethical methodology in group contexts, not as a matter of personal decision.

What then, can one say about a person's attitude toward an act which has no particular implications for the group in which he lives? Is suicide an immoral act if it relieves both the victim and his loved ones from anxiety? The only correct answer, we feel, is that this question transcends the domain of ethics. There are levels of significance[11] higher even than the ethical, circumstances where a man's acts must be judged in transmoral terms, where commitment is of such personal character that even the validated norms of approved tradition do not apply.[12] An ethical system which disregards this fact, which draws its imperatives in all too tight and embracing fashion, is a legalism which is bound to fail as a human enterprise.

APPENDIX: Are Values Measurable?

Measurability is sometimes regarded as the criterion of scientific status. Before answering the question above we wish to comment on the propriety of this criterion. As indicated elsewhere,[13] the constructs of science form many classes among which there is one, designated as the class of quantities or observables, whose members are subject to operational definition, i.e. are measurable. An atom, a field, a biological organism (entities called 'systems') are not observables in the strict sense here employed; their positions, charges, colors, however, *are* observable. Very roughly, the distinction here is that made by Aristotle between substances and their attributes. We thus find that values, even if they are not measurable, may nevertheless be useful in a scientific sense.

We now direct the question specifically to the three kinds of value encountered in our analysis. First come primary values which are postulated as the goal of the ethical process. Common among them are survival, happiness, tranquility, all of them states of mind whose presence one usually assumes to be certifiable. We believe that they are in fact 'measurable,' i.e. ascertainable, perhaps not with great precision but with sufficient assurance to make the ethical enterprise work. Note, of course, that measurement is a very general concept, not at all tied to the specific instrumental procedures useful in the physical sciences. Inquiries based on questionnaires and other statistical procedures employed in the behavioral sciences are measurements. The question of the measurability of introspective qualities is a purely scientific one and is not for the philosopher to answer. In our view it will be answered affirmatively in time, and in that case primary values become measurable.

Similar comments probably apply to the *de facto* values with which the behavioral sciences are beginning to be concerned. Again, there is at present no uniformly accepted way of quantifying honesty, chastity, respect for life, etc., the attributes which flow from adherence to common commandments; but there is no intrinsic reason for supposing that they will always remain in this 'qualitative' state.

To appraise their situation with respect to the measurability issue a scientific analogy is useful. Just as *est*-values arise in midrange between postulated imperatives and the final act of validation, scientific constructs are often generated midway between initial postulates and their ultimate verification. In the (Schrödinger) quantum theory, a fundamental differential equation determines the state of an atom, yielding a function often designated as ψ. It is related to observational experiences, to measurements, by certain statistical rules of correspondence. Hence it plays a methodological role similar to values in ethics. Is ψ measurable?

The answer given by most physicists is no. In spite of this, nobody doubts the extreme usefulness of this function or denies its important scientific status. And there is an interesting mathematical sequel to this observation. It has been shown[14] that the function of ψ can indeed be ascertained be means of a doubly infinite sequence of measurements. In principle, therefore, the answer is positive. Yet nobody would go to the trouble of measuring ψ, which remains an important station on the way from initial postulates to final observation. In our analysis, *de facto* values play precisely that role.

Finally, there are the normative values, the 'approved' *de facto* values which generate the primary ones. From the point of view of measurement, what has been said about *de facto* values applies to the normative ones as well.

Notes and References

1. A related analysis of esthetic values is given by Ervin Laszlo in *J. of Value Inquiry* I, pp. 242-253, (1967-68).

2. Cf. Everett Hall, *Modern Science and Human Values*, D. Van Nostrand, Princeton, N.J. (1956).

3. See, Henry Margenau, *The Nature of Physical Reality*, McGraw Hill, New York (1950), pp. 75–101.

4. An interesting contrast to this conclusion which is based on the project of science as a search for truth is given by Jacob Bronowski in *New Knowledge in Human Values*, ed. A. H. Maslow, Harper and Row, New York (1959), pp. 52–64.

5. Cf. G. E. Moore, *Principia Ethica*, Cambridge Press, Cambridge (1959), Preface and Chapter I.

6. Cf. Richard S. Rudner, *Philosophy of Social Science*, Prentice-Hall, Englewood Cliffs, N.J. (1966), especially pp. 1–67.

7. Also, cf. Ernest Nagel, *The Structure of Science*, Harcourt-Brace, New York (1961), pp. 473–502.

8. Moore, op. cit., pp. 20–21.

9. An extended discussion is given in H. Margenau, *The Nature of Physical Reality*, op. cit.

10. See Henry Margenau, *Ethics and Science*, D. Van Nostrand, Princeton, N.J. (1964). This view has recently been questioned by A. S. Cua in *Philosophy Today*, **12**, 215 (1968).

11. Henry Margenau, 'The Pursuit of Significance,' *Main Currents of Modern Thought*, **23**, No. 3 (1967), pp. 65–76.

12. Such a distinction between personal significance and morality is made emphatically in J-P. Sartre, *Being and Nothingness*, Philosophical Library, New York (1956). See especially p. 38.

13. H. Margenau, *The Nature of Physical Reality*, op. cit.

14. Henry Margenau, *Phil. of Sci.*, **30**, 138 (1963).

Recover Values in a New Synthesis: a Manifesto

LANCELOT LAW WHYTE

London, England

My theme is large, my space small. I shall therefore first make clear what I am not attempting, and then condense into minimal form, with little argument in support, the basis of my belief in a *possible* recovery of values in 'the age of science.' I do not suggest that this is a *probable* outcome. In our ignorance regarding historical processes that term has no useful meaning; who can know what is probable tomorrow, since history is a web of surprises? I shall present my views tersely* (without other qualification than to put some terms which can be misleading in quotation marks) and I claim for them no authority, scientific or other. They arise from two adverse sources: my personal conviction of desirable, but as yet inadequately realized potentialities of the human organism, and my observation of the mood and behavior of western mankind since 1914, a period covering the death of God, the spread of nihilism, two World Wars, Belsen, Hiroshima, Stalin's terror, Vietnam, the continuing misuse by white peoples of their transitory power and nuclear confrontation. This half-century has shown that only some unprecedented factor, realizing human potentialities in a new manner, can arrest the progressive collapse of civilization and the final corruption of those values which are still in some degree effective. It is possible, I suggest, that tomorrow holds a major surprise of this kind. Anyhow I am certain that no-one has the right to assert that he knows that this view is mistaken.

But first the negatives. I am not concerned with the moral evalua-

---

* They have been developed elsewhere, originally in *The Next Development in Man*. In the present paper I have concentrated on what I now consider to be crucial issues.

B*

tion or devaluation of history, with ethical theory in the usual sense, with the supposed values of 'scientists,' with the social control of 'science,' with issues of only a few years, or with organic evolution which, even guided by man, will require many generations. My theme is those universal human values, expressing a sense of order, beauty, and joy in living, which may be experienced and lived by ordinary young men and women, if they are given a chance as the result of a new development during the next few decades. The chance, I mean, 'to make love, not war,' to love and reconcile, rather than to hate and divide. Let me have the courage to say it: if men must have obsessive symbols the female nude is better than the crucifix.

This paper is not an intellectualist or idealist exercise, but a personal, historically oriented, manifesto, one marking a hundred years advance: coordinative, not communist. I am not considering the reformulation of ideals in words, or hierarchical systems of verbally expressed values, but something more fundamental: the rediscovery and rejoicing in the daily living into action of vital values *as the result of a changed human condition* or state of organization, individual and social, the development of which all will facilitate who are not perverted. The 'new synthesis' to which I point is not only a philosophical and scientific unification of rational knowledge. It is that and much more: a human synthesis, an organic co-adaptation, reorganization, and harmonization of human capacities in some respects equivalent to, but more profound than, the spread of a new universal and unifying 'religion,' in the traditional sense of a doctrine involving transcendental features and lacking coherence with scientific knowledge.

Such redemption from the intolerable failures of the past has long been a human dream. Strange as it may seem to some, I believe that it is now historically conceivable, for reasons more fully developed elsewhere. Such a new, better grounded organic coordination and harmonization of the expressions of human potentialities is the last hope of authentic humanity, now at the precipice, physical and moral. One type of man is preparing general suicide. Who ever denies my hope, damns the race.

My final negative is, with our Convenor's permission, to question the title of this Conference! For I consider that the terms 'science' and 'natural science' are inappropriate and misleading where basic issues are at stake. It is obvious that in certain contexts the term 'science' has a clear and useful meaning. But we have reached a stage of awareness of human characteristics and of introspective insight which enables and requires us, in dealing with fundamental matters, to look behind such cultural categories as 'science,' 'philosophy,' and 'art'—which refer to activities or to components of activities, that are not adequately separable—to the primary ordering processes of the human psyche, or organ of thought and feeling. These latter are the unconscious and conscious mental processes creating the essentially aesthetic order from which all culture springs. In my view 'Human Values and Natural Science' is a theme which can best be clarified by looking outside it to the source of all cultural and scientific activities.

This attempt to bring into consideration more general features of the psyche, or of cerebral processes conditioned by the fact that they are within the organism, is not intellectual presumption or premature speculation. It is, in my view, one of the necessary conditions for achieving understanding of the optimal manner in which values can be restored. In particular the ethical problems of what we call 'the age of science'—actually this is 'the age of partial science' for scientific knowledge is not yet fundamental, it lacks unity, balance, and completeness—will not be solved by a merely analytical, non-historical examination based on a casual and sometimes grossly unscientific misuse of the term 'science,' a misuse which begs all the basic issues wrongly.

Behind the dozen or so distinct types of 'scientific method,' behind the continuous spectrum of outlooks of 'scientists' which extends without break into other partially differentiated professional groups, and behind the damagingly isolated departments of 'science' called 'natural science,' 'psychology,' 'medical science,' 'sociological science,' and so on, there operates a single human faculty, underlying not merely 'science,' but also 'art' and 'religion.' It is to this and not to any conventional conception of 'scientific activity' that we must turn our attention if we desire to understand either 'science,' or values in an age of 'science.' To see a pattern one must stand outside it. Certainly we do not yet understand this primary formative activity of the human brain-mind. That need not restrain us. It is a useful first step to identify and name what we do not understand.

My hope, as already hinted, rests partly on the mainly unconscious formative tendency of all non-pathological brain-minds. Though still neglected by many philosophers and psychologists—accepted psychological theories do not yet grant it a basic role, and most thinkers are still coy about it, the omnipresent being hard to accept—the formative, ordering activity of the human mind is the primary and most obvious factor in the emergence and development of *homo sapiens*. It has been the indispensable agent in all the imaginative achievements, unconscious or conscious, of the species, from the development of language and of culture—a term I use for all activities displaying aesthetic, religious, philosophical, or scientific aspects—to the eve of that crowning achievement, in a historically restricted sense, which must come within a generation if——. Much to expect of the unconscious? Certainly; but less will not serve. The healthy formative unconscious must prepare the new coordination so that reason and will can realize it.

This is a hope; that is all we need or can expect. The old value which the pathological unconscious of the disillusioned older generations is now blindly destroying, the healthier unconscious *plus* conscious-with-insight of youth must now replace with new, and that means deeper ones. Weary perverts who obstruct this will be dismissed without mercy, if they do not succeed in destroying all of us first.

But how can this healthier condition be brought about and stabilized? Where is the redeeming factor which can reinforce the appropriate expression of this formative power, in time? Do not the failures of the species in the past and its, to some, hopeless condition today, impose, for human reason, hope-destroying restrictions on the possibilities of the near future? No! They do not, on one condition: provided that a genuinely unprecedented factor of sufficient psychological depth and social power can be identified which (i) *is already at work,* (ii) *is compatible with past failures,* and (iii) *can none the less offer the possibility of an authentic recovery tomorrow.* But that factor must be realistic to the disciplined human reason. It must not involve rationalistic naivety, romantic utopianism, religious *hocus-pocus,* unidentified psychic faculties, or transcendental illusions born of despair. The problem is real, stubborn, and immediate. To solve it we must remain within nature, and call biology to our aid.

Homo sapiens is a social organism, a primate with unique capacities one of which is relevant: his hereditary constitution is such that he is capable of understanding nature and himself. Here I use 'understanding' to mean not merely intellectual-analytical knowledge of isolated particulars which can be verbally formulated and communicated (in the contemporary technical sense), but also intuitive coordination of the relevant implications of such knowledge, including its relation to oneself so that, *understanding,* one joyfully accepts one's own role in the totality of things. Understanding is not a stationary condition, but an active coordinated process of the mind flowing towards action and implying a recovery of values. It is coordinated knowledge *plus* acceptance leading to implementing of its implications for living. The doctrines of Marx and of Freud both offered partial understanding; hence their power to inspire to action those who could accept them. *Balanced* understanding will be a different matter.

Homo sapiens has demonstrated its ability to exploit its material environment and has discovered, in principle, its capacity for understanding. Why then are we doubting the viability of our species? Is the only possible answer that the human story is the testing and rejection of a haphazard genetic re-arrangement that does not work? An unhappy mutation of no adaptive value, incapable of appropriate coordination?

If that were so, whence the ideals of beauty, truth, and goodness? Whence the superb aspirations of mankind, the perpetual longing for harmony, and the noble unifying achievements of high genius? It would be a strange kind of organic realm that thus teased man with the biologically impossible! The entire story a phoney strip-tease act promising the sight of something that didn't, and in principle couldn't exist: human harmony? Biological common-sense rejects this as silly.

There is a likelier answer. *Homo sapiens* may be a social organism uniquely endowed with an organ of understanding, which cannot develop the harmonious, viable, and stable mode of life appropriate to its hereditary constitution and potentialities until that organ has achieved biological maturity by the attainment of a comprehensive balanced understanding of the universe and of its own proper mode of living. This is scarcely a hypothesis. It is good biological sense. A species capable of understanding must possess balanced understanding in order to survive. Otherwise in the excitement of exploiting partial and unbalanced knowledge it will destroy itself.

Is man made to trust his reason? Or is he mad to do it? If reason has ever aided man, let it do so now. This diagnosis of the transitional condition of man may be correct. So let us use it as a *working hypothesis* and get down to work!

My suggestion is that to live properly, *homo sapiens* must learn to think properly. It is as simple as that, though no man can as yet measure its implications. But 'thinking' means more than analytical intellectual reasoning. To experience and to act in an organically appropriate manner, man must be in possession of complete aesthetic, intuitive, philosophical, and scientific understanding (our misleading terms compel this clumsy description) of the basic features of this universe, such as matter, life, and mind, or more precisely: elementary particles, organic coordination, and the structure of brain-mind processes. That includes, of course, understanding of his own potentialities. Coordinated understanding based on unified knowledge is the criterion of biological maturity and viability for man; without it any crisis may prove mortal. Religions, philosophies, idealism, and finally rationalism, have all failed to provide adequate guidance. Inevitably so; they could neither reach this definitive biological diagnosis of the human situation as that of an only partly developed thinking social organism, nor facilitate its maturing.

This is the deepest insight which man can reach about himself prior to its fulfilment in the achievement of unified scientific knowledge and comprehensive balanced understanding. It is, I suggest, an idea of a new order. It opens a re-consideration of the plight of mankind during the XXth century on a deeper level than was previously possible. It may be merely a mistaken conjecture, historically irrelevant. Or it may be a historical-scientific discovery, subsuming within a more balanced view the important but partial discoveries of Marx and of Freud, regarding the present condition of *homo sapiens,* a discovery to be proved valid soon, perhaps within the rest of this century. For this positive confirmation two severe conditions must be met within a few decades: (i) the achievement of a scientific unification of unprecedented scope, covering elementary particles and organic coordination, and (ii) parallel with this, a re-orientation of the main visible trend of the historical process, from its recent phase of disintegration *towards a human synthesis* by a recovery of values.

If this interpretation is correct, the optimal path is clear. Our task is not to rely on transcendental factors, to dream of an evolutionary Superman, or to worry about particular moral issues, but here and now to do what is possible for each of us—and that is much—to ease the way for authentic organic men and women of younger generations, and for a society in which they can prosper. This is an old ambition and task, now re-interpreted and seen more clearly, for we have begun to understand the rich human meaning of 'organic' values. Moreover it is not a hopeless task, for the unconscious and partly conscious historical process in millions has been preparing the necessary adjustment for several decades, as we shall see.

This basic theme has many aspects, only some of which can be considered here and these only in brief summary.

The Union of Contrasts

Every viable organism displays a tendency and capacity to develop, and when disturbed to restore, *the coordination of its differentiated parts.* The expression in man of this universal organic *nisus* is the process of, or impulse to achieve, the union of contrasts. This tendency is evident in heterosexual love, in marriage, in the family, in the formation of human groups and communities, and in all cultural creation. This is the characteristic human task in which, when normal, all rejoice. 'Science' is one partly differentiated expression of this human ordering tendency, so is 'religion,' and prior to these is the 'aesthetic' impulse, itself identical with this primary underlying global *nisus.* The achieved union of contrasts, and not the quantitative 'maximisation of happiness'—a strangely naive conception without any useful meaning, for who can weigh, say, a phase of happy communion between man and woman against a good week's work?—is the criterion of human self-realization as an instrument of universal factors, which every organism is. The authentic type of man which should now emerge is one whose social and self-realization is facilitated by comprehensive rational knowledge *plus* that unified recognition of, and identification with, his own historical and personal role, here called 'understanding.' In great art, in authentic religion, and in valid science, the imaginative individual expresses what is universal: this organic *nisus* in a human form relevant to all.

Ordering and Disordering

Our present knowledge of physical processes suggests that there are two major tendencies, or movements towards characteristic terminal states, in the universe: toward spatial geometrical order and toward dynamical disorder, though their relation is not yet understood. The processes displaying the first may be called 'morphic,'* and the second 'entropic.' The first class has been relatively little studied, for technical reasons connected with the conservation and flow of energy. This is unfortunate, because the morphic processes, in combination with the entropic, certainly play a basic role in the origin, evolution, growth, and functioning of all organisms, and particularly in human mental processes, both the less conscious formative and the conscious symbolic. In fact the morphic processes, under circumstances which are not yet understood, must generate and sustain all organic coordination, including the coordinative processes of the mind. Thus man is the supreme instrument of the morphic processes of nature. This is his

* See 'Organic Structural Hierarchies,' in *Unity and Diversity in Systems*. Essays in honour of L. v. Bertalanffy. Ed. Jones and Brandl. Braziller, N.Y. 1969.

pride, opportunity, and joy, and the source of all his values. Since aesthetic factors are perhaps best defined as those promoting unity in multiplicity and variety, the morphic processes are essentially aesthetic. In a strict and precise sense 'love' and 'divinity' are aesthetic conceptions, being concerned with a unifying order.

Fact and Value

The distinction between facts and values, or between factual and normative statements, is sometimes treated as fundamental. But once the existence of morphic processes is admitted this needs re-consideration. For to man, a coordinated organism with an ordering brain, order necessarily possesses value. Thus as soon as morphic processes are recognized as pervading much of this universe, in particular the organic realm, many factual statements will concern the presence or absence of order, or of ordering processes, and hence of value. Indeed in a morphological philosophy emphasizing morphic processes 'fact' and 'value' are seldom separable.

It is actually an expression of man's deepest nature, both as organism and as a member of the species *homo sapiens,* to value order, and especially the particular ordering which constitutes organic coordination and implies health. Only the possibility of organic, social, and personal order gives value to human existence.

The truth of this is not prejudiced by the fact that we do not yet understand the precise form of order, i.e. the precise class of structural arrangements, which constitutes organic coordination. Nor by the fact that mathematicians, denying at moments their ordinary humanity and following their calling to explore the furthest imaginable abstractions, may believe that, in their realm, order and disorder are merely consequences of the type of representation employed, and that these properties are therefore interchangeable at will. This is not so for the ordinary human person. For him, living in the immediacy of his experience, order and disorder are not ambiguous, any more than are 'health' and 'sickness,' the meaning of which we know all too well. When we are not deviant, we seek clarity and order. If a human community emerges from the current confusion, so also will strengthened values of beauty, truth, and goodness, as expressions of organic coordination. There is no ambiguity about this.

Unifying conceptions in ethics, philosophy, and science

In a period of convergence like the decades since 1920, it is not difficult to make useful conjectures regarding the attitudes and conceptions which may hold a central place in any unification that lies ahead. Many such guesses made before the major syntheses of the past proved to be near the mark. It is as though tens or hundreds have to prepare the ground before the decisive clarification becomes possible.

Though no individual conjecture is likely to cover the whole field correctly, and though the terms which have to be used today will change their meaning or acquire a new emphasis after the event, my guess, for what it is worth, is that many current attitudes and concepts will decline in relative importance and that their role will be taken over by a new and *more clearly coherent group of ideas*. The great scope of any future unification implies that aesthetic, ethical, philosophical, and scientific ideas will be simultaneously involved. In the following table the left column is intended to refer to the first two-thirds, and the second column to the last third, of this century, though this use of a particular hundred years is no more than a convenient device at this moment.

	Recently emphasized	Increased emphasis expected
Attitudes	'Masculine,' mechanical constructive, aggressive.	'Feminine,' organic, promoting coordination and stability.
	Self-expression of the ego.	Self-realization as an instrument of universal factors.
	'Objective truth' a high value.	Clarification of man's relation to his environment.
	Novelty as a high value.	Organic, social, and personal coordination as the supreme value.
	Traditional moral and religious attitudes on particular matters.	Aesthetics of order and coordination. Morphological understanding of the unity of nature and of the shared characteristics of all men.
	External moral constraints influencing special aspects of behavior in a preconceived direction.	Internal personal coordination, promoting behavior appropriate to condition of person.
	Human life as merely tragic, comic, or absurd.	Life also as opportunity for joy in attainment of beauty.

	Recently emphasized	Increased emphasis expected
Philosophical and Scientific conceptions	Intellectual, analytical, disparate, knowledge.	Vital coordinating understanding, using knowledge.
	Equivalence, equations, symmetry, elements of one status, statistics of random systems.	Order, non-equivalence, inequalities, asymmetry, coordinated hierarchical arrangements of ordered patterns.
	Space-time cyclic and reversible processes. Tendency towards disorder.	One-way processes leading either to ordered structures or to disorder.

God and the Unconscious

The theoretical division of the psyche with two supposedly separate, or partly separable, classes of processes, one associated with immediate awareness and the other not, is widely agreed to be only a first step towards a more adequate theory of the mind. Subject to whatever adjustments an improved theory may require, it is meaningful and valid to say that all inspiration, intimation of new possibilities, imagination, and clues to invention, reach awareness from initially less conscious or wholly unconscious processes, i.e. from cerebral activities not associated with immediate awareness or focussed attention. (This is true, for example, of the ideas expressed in this paper.) But on special and rare occasions these intimations display a quality which renders them profoundly revered by the individual who receives them from mental processes of which he was not previously aware. Such intimations appear to be touched with a more than ordinarily human perfection. Thus one of the uses of the term 'God' may arise from the giving of a quasi-personal name to the source of these highest quality experiences. This does not imply that 'God' is always present in everyone, for only when an individual is in a condition enabling him to undergo such an experience, does 'God' come to him. The experience of such a 'visitation by God' may be the culminating phase of the processes of the healthy ordering unconscious (not of course of the Freudian pathological deformed unconscious) when a state of the highest, indeed perfect, coordination is momentarily reached, which new unity comes to the attention of the person as transcendent ecstasy.

This interpretation of 'revelation' as a higher type of natural mental process is far from new. To mention three examples: one school of Gnostics in effect identified the unconscious self with the Godhead, Nietzsche saw in such highest functions of the human spirit a sublime type of organic function, and Margharita Laski in her *Ecstasy* has recently emphasized the importance of this naturalistic interpretation. Our contemporary sense of values, disturbed by a partial science and its consequences, would be strengthened by an organic philosophy granting to man's experience of the 'divine' its appropriate status in man's conception of nature. Many forms of happiness and joy, rising to transcendent ecstasy in rare cases, may be the awareness of different degrees and kinds of organic coordination, rising sometimes to a perfected inner union of all the highest coordinating functions of the person. A valid neuro-physiology of man will doubtless confirm this within a few decades. Meantime no intelligent science, fit to approach man, can neglect such experiences, for the scientific search for a unified order of nature arose as one of the expressions of the religious-mystical *nisus* towards unity. Truly scientific minds and religious persons seeking essentials rather than transient cultural stepping stones will find no difficulty in accepting the need for a unifying organic and naturalistic approach to the totality of the experienced universe. My formulation is certainly faulty and language is prejudiced by hidden assumptions, but this idea is none the less radiant with significance.

Man and Nature

The human person can only fully accept, and appreciate the consequences of the fact, that he is part of nature, if he can see a single continuity running through all realms of the universe—that means through the 'physical,' 'organic,' 'mental' and 'spiritual'* realms— which enables him to understand his relation to nature. (This is no empty abstraction: a sick man is not only comforted, but may recover quicker, if he is convinced that there is in organic nature a powerful repairing or therapeutic power, frustrated only in the worst diseases such as cancer and perhaps extreme psychosis.) This suggests a severe criterion which might be required of the most general scientific laws: it should be possible to recognize in them the logical germ and the geometrical essential of 'life' and of 'mind.' If the whole is indeed one

* The term 'spiritual' is here used, without prejudice or provocation to, cover these aspects of human experience and personality lying outside the scope of the current behaviorist interpretation of 'mental.' Unfortunately the English language possesses no equivalent to the German 'Geist.'

unity, this criterion is appropriate and in any case it can serve as a powerful heuristic instrument. We can ask that the fundamental laws should display the formative, ordering, and coordinating property which could account, in principle, for the development, within an inorganic background, first, of viable organisms, and, second, of non-pathological minds. If that condition were met in a future unification it would facilitate the emotional-intuitive understanding appropriate to harmonious living. Not until then can man fully know what it can mean to know oneself one with nature and to recover an effective sense of values.

These amplifications of my main theme are all very well, but what is their relevance to the hard facts of 1969? One of the gravest of these, for many, is the current spread of violence from traditional international wars, which seem to be socially acceptable, to the present activist protests of youth, which seem not to be. Here a radical biological interpretation, using the best recent ideas, not the mistakes of a century back, is necessary.

A recurrent process of active excitation, or stimulation into full activity of the various functional capacities, is indispensable for animal and for human health. Here 'excitation' means an extended process of rising stimulation leading to culmination and release, not a stationary condition which, if persisting without increase and release, tends to distort other cycles of function. (Here Freud made an elementary error, being influenced by Fechner and conditioned by the physiology of 1880; the organism seeks excitation as well as relaxation.) The animal organism does not 'seek,' or benefit from, the supposed tendency towards quasi-equilibrium, in partial isolation from the environment, called 'homeostasis.' This strange, entirely unbiological mistake has long persisted, and now must be rejected. Is it not obvious, at any level of analysis, that random fluctuations, repeated pulsations, and even sudden shocks, arising from the environment are necessary to animal *life in an environment*? Animal vitality does not 'seek' equilibrium, but its own enhancement. The animal only grows, matures, reproduces, and perhaps enjoys itself, when stimulated, provoked, and challenged. (Does not woman do all three to man?) There is no 'death-wish' in the organism, except when sick or dying. But there is always present, in every healthy man and woman, even if it is sometimes suppressed from awareness, a desire to be excited.

Thus there is no ground for fundamental alarm, still less for moralistic homilies, when the younger generations in the West, bored with the separatist follies of a declining civilization, set out to explore human capacities for experience to the very limit in all directions. This is an expression of healthy vitality, and *it is vitality from which everything valuable springs. All values spring from vitality.* Without vitality nothing, with frustrated vitality violence, with adequate vitality a new order may be achieved.

The naive unconscious (?) hypocrisy of those over 50, or 60, or 70, who have happily promoted two World Wars, and are still keeping the pot boiling in the name of 'Christianity,' 'democracy,' and so on, is scarcely credible. The difficulties are obvious, but so is one major step, which, sitting in their chairs of authority, they have not yet troubled to take. They have not yet even begun to formulate, or to develop by inviting world-wide cooperation:

*A Universal Human Programme for 2000 A.D.**

a political and social Programme which by its authentic universally human organic quality must necessarily appeal to all non-pathological individuals, not only in China and Russia, but everywhere. Such a Programme alone can give pause to the accelerating tendency in China, and amongst coloured peoples, to dedicate themselves to a moral and military crusade against the West. The stupid omission even to announce the first steps towards such a Programme—an omission which springs from lack of vitality and moral vacuum—renders futile, *as far as world peace is concerned,* all the paper routines and committee activities of UNO, UNESCO, etc. Does the West accept such rulers? It has so far. This is not surprising, as long-established communities and institutions have often shown this blindness both to their own interests, and to those of larger sections of mankind. In 1969 there is a streak of hope: many western Establishments may have really been rattled by the recent protests of youth.

But I must leave the politicians and come to the scholars, and first the philosophers. It is not surprising, and is partly an expression of longer-term trends, that, just when the major human issues become as stubborn as they have since 1914 (though this was foreseen earlier), the academic philosophers in many centres of learning in the West should desert what A.N. Whitehead said was the purpose of philo-

---

* This proposal is easily misunderstood, and would require a long explanation. It must satisfy severe criteria, involve step-by-step procedures, correlate ideals and long-term aims with what is immediately practical, transcend regional interests, and so on. No scheme yet proposed, as far as known to me, comes near to what is necessary. Has any U.S. Foundation yet supported the first steps towards this aim?

sophy: 'to rationalize mysticism' and 'to maintain an active novelty of fundamental ideas illuminating the social system.' Instead of this there has been a retreat either into linguistic, logical, and mathematical analysis—all valuable techniques which should not be prejudiced by treating them as the only valid philosophy—or into doctrines over-emphasizing the paradoxical or absurd aspects of human life.

And what about the scientists? 'Science' has unique prestige, unique achievements, and unique responsibilities. The first, I suppose, is that scientists should be scientific. Assertions should be clear and precise, and their field of relevance made explicit.

How then is one to interpret the following clichés now widely current?

'The science of man.' There is none as yet. Scientists do not yet understand organisms, let alone *homo sapiens*. In what precise sense does the 'science of man' remain a 'science'?

'Scientific humanism.' This cannot exist, or pretend to offer guidance, in advance of scientific understanding of man.

'Evolutionary humanism.' Those who claim to offer guidance in the name of biology should be scrupulously careful not to misuse terms like 'evolution' which most biologists consider should be restricted to the 'evolution of species by natural selection.' The term 'evolution' has become an omnibus trap for pseudo-scientists. 'Social development' is a different matter, relevant to this century.

Finally, 'science.' Under what restrictive conditions does this rag-bag term acquire scientific precision? I defy anyone to define it appropriately. The social movement we loosely call 'science' changes its methods, purposes, personalities, and responsibilities every 25/50 years. No-one knows any longer what 'science' means, except in restricted contexts.

This criticism has a purpose. It is to draw attention to the following suggestion:

From now on no generalization is to be regarded as scientific, without an associated TAG reminding the reader that the generalization is only valid under certain restrictive conditions (already known, suspected, or still entirely unknown). The TAG, in effect, clarifies the meaning of the terms used in the generalization, or warns the reader that their meanings and scope are not yet fully clear. For all rules and laws contain hidden assumptions, though the existence of these is often forgotten. But our heightened awareness of the content of our own thinking has now reached the point when the use of TAGS can facilitate the further advance of knowledge. From the point of view of the late XXth Century to neglect the TAG is to be pre-scientific. *Scientific validity is always conditional.*

This is a saddening recognition, as most of the best minds of the past fail by this standard. Advance is usually painful. Remarkably few scientists have tried to remain aware of the fact that their own achievements were conditional, and to utter warnings. I leave to you the instructive exercise of discovering where precisely the great names of the past in their classic vista-creating publications have left out the TAG.

And why should this care not also be expected of logical philosophers? Even Russell offered absolute assertions, and for example never explained to his readers, on what precise assumptions the method of 'logical atomism' was, and was not, justified.

Most of the failures of the last fifty years are obvious. But there is one which has long disturbed me though it has been little discussed. Relatively to the dangers facing mankind in the period, and relatively to their privileged situation, the educated of the West have not provided the quality of leadership that is urgently required and might have been expected. A military crisis finds its Winston Churchill, but the general moral crisis since 1914? It is true that a few men, now over 70, have endeavoured to outline a possible future for mankind: Julian Huxley, Karl Jaspers, Teilhard du Chardin, Arnold Toynbee, and others. But the unmistakeably authentic quality of a new vision ahead of the common awareness and combining discipline, clarity, and timeliness is lacking in these men born before 1900, and the younger generations, surprisingly, have not dared to follow them!

Why this current failure of the intelligence of the West? A definitive decline? I think not. It may be due to the fact that we are near the mid-point of a significant historical transition: those humanists who have not received a scientific training are paralysed by a sense of their own inadequacy in a technical age, while the younger generations of scientists have (apparently) still to accept the fact that they are human beings and citizens of the world before they are scientists. They have opportunities and can experience duties as men and women which are more fundamental than, and prior to, those which may follow from their specialized training. The world awaits the voices of a new generation of scientists who are persons first. Perhaps John R. Platt is one.

If failures of past leadership filled the picture, there could be no hope. But the following favourable or promising factors, all partly the expression of unconscious influences in recent history, signal the gradual, progressive emergence of new values.

1. The years since the second World War have been marked by *several favourable developments of the first order*: a spreading sexual emancipation from hideous moral pathologies (this may have consequences that cannot be foreseen); medical and psychological prophylaxis and therapy for increasing numbers; some steps towards the elimination of the harshest contrasts between rich and poor; and the recent moral revolution of youth, particularly in the U.S.A. Taken together these represent a momentous historical movement, doing much to balance the grim features of this period cited at the opening of this paper. God is dead, but he is being replaced. This movement will surely continue unless even harsher conflicts frustrate it.

2. Throughout this century sensitive observers, religious thinkers, philosophers, and recently scientists, have become increasingly aware that this is, for reasons which are not only technological, a period of *exceptionally rapid and profound social transformation* and therefore of unprecedented possibilities. Today this needs no argument. Though it may be impossible fully to understand one's own time, it appears to many as if two sharply contrasted paths lay ahead: one leading straight to species disaster, the other towards a world community of a new order, rich with promise. This schizoid interpretation may be mistaken, but the threat and the promise are both unmistakeable.

3. In several respects the years since 1900 appear to constitute a period of *convergence*. There are signs of a convergence in various realms: towards universal human attitudes and norms, common social institutions, and technological procedures. There is also the vigorous search for a unified physics, biophysics, biochemistry, and biology. This apparently convergent characteristic of a period cannot be objectively established until after decisive steps have been achieved. But to those sensitive to such factors the simultaneity of similar ideas and actions, and the apparent presence of collective factors guiding many individuals towards similar, or at least coherent, conclusions, are in a special degree characteristic of our time. Yet *this convergent trend provokes a healthy and inevitable resistance and reaction*. There is a widespread sense that differences must be preserved. The key to this complex and tantalizing situation lies in one crucial fact: the authentic form of unity in variety appropriate to the human situation in the second half of this century, the form of unity which will not provoke successful resistance, has not yet been discovered and formulated in any realm, or at any level of the various social hierarchies. *Those who can identify and make effective the various historically appropriate modes of unity*

in variety will be the universal heroes of the late XXth century, the creators of new values.

4. The further development of this convergence and its expression in a spreading and ultimately *universal consensus* of judgment, does not, fortunately, depend on the privileged and established, but on the general conscience of mankind. The social achievements of the recent period have been due to an awareness, in smaller or larger groups outside the major institutions, of what is necessary, and this awareness has been effective against the resistance of the leading western Churches, and of most of the influential senior scholars in the major centres of learning, in spite of noble exceptions. Popes and University Presidents are rarely moral leaders. Maverick thinkers, supported by audiences which they have themselves created, have led the way in the past, and surely will do so in the future. The consensus, if it is to come into being, may be expected to be at first most evident and active outside the great institutions inherited from the past.

5. It is scarcely open to doubt that an *organic philosophy of man* is one of the emerging factors behind the already evident convergence and the coming genesis of a consensus. Today there exists no explicit organic philosophy and no valid fundamental biological theory (both require a theory of organic coordination). The deepest yearning of men and women everywhere is to be allowed to live, and aided to live, in accordance with their own natures as human organisms. This means for each to achieve the union of contrasts, of all the relevant forms.

6. If a favourable result is to come, it will not be by individuals passively waiting for the deepened understanding which a scientific unification will facilitate. Vital individuals, if not pathological, cannot so wait. Every person of good-will has today his own glimpse, hope, or conviction of the possibility of an historically appropriate human synthesis—aesthetic, social, ethical, and scientific—and his actions will be guided by it. Such imaginative judgment on the part of individuals always precedes rational clarity, intellectual justification, and collective social action. The adventure is to act in advance of the unmistakeable signals which always mark the opening of a new phase in social history. Tomorrow's values will be forged by personal example. If one is not appropriately active, it is difficult to avoid occupying himself with the 'probability' of a favourable outcome. But this matters not a whit. The soldier does not expect to know in advance if the action will be successful.

In some sense it may already be too late, but that we cannot know.

Only if we are ready to go down with flags flying, understanding what we want and working for it to the final moment of doom, are we equal to our rôle in the general task.

We want the achievement of full human lives in an organic human community. But if we fear the 'restriction on freedom' which this may seem to imply, something is wrong. The choice is between the authentic human order which we have to discover and to create, and either social collapse or a totalitarian order.

'One must have chaos within one to give birth to a star.' (Nietzsche) This may be true also of the community. I quote the opening and closing sentences of *The Next Development in Man* (written in 1942/3): 'Thought is born of failure.' 'The failure of past methods will force man to accept a new conviction lest the old Adam destroy him.'

The Mind, the Brain, and Education

ALBERT SZENT-GYÖRGYI

Marine Biological Laboratory,
Woods Hole, Massachusetts

I am a biologist and will approach my problem as a biologist. As a biologist I know that whatever man does he has to do it first in his mind. I also know that there is no function without an underlying mechanism, and a mechanism can do only what its structure allows it to do. The mechanism underlying the mind is the brain and so my first question has to be: what sort of mechanism is this brain?

The brain is often compared to a computer. There are certainly many analogies between the brain and a computer but I will limit myself to one. What a computer does depends on its programming. The same is true also for the brain. Most animals are born with a fully programmed brain and know exactly what to do under various conditions, even if not allowed to learn from their fellow animals. Man differs from all other species by being born with a completely unprogrammed brain. The programming has to be done after birth and is what we call 'education.' What the individual will do during his life depends largely on this programming, which makes education into the most important human occupation. As we teach today, so the morrow will be.

Education was always the most important human problem, but is doubly important today because the rapid development of modern science has changed the face of human life. It changed all important factors, all parameters of human existence, changed all human relations, while our social structures, relations and institutions and thinking remained unchanged and have to be rebuilt from the bottom up if mankind wants to stay alive. This rebuilding will have to be done by the next generation which we are educating today.

But how can we educate for this rebuilding if we do not know, ourselves, how this new world should be? It would be wrong to try to program for this rebuilding, because when doing so we would transmit all our prejudices, fears and hatreds which make us unable to build a better world. How then, can we prepare our youth for this great work of rebuilding?

We can teach two things: firstly we can teach an attitude, a love of truth and intellectual honesty, we can teach them to challenge all ideas before accepting them. In old Persia, youth was taught two things: to ride a horse and to speak the truth. The love of truth is today still half of education. The other thing we can give our youngsters is material for their thinking, material from which they can draw conclusions and with which they can build their scale of values. This material can be nothing else than the past experience, the history of mankind, which makes history the most important subject in school.

By history I mean the real history of man. The real history of man is the story of how man rose slowly from his animal status to his present level. The rate at which man rose depended on the balance of the two trends in his mind: on his trend to create and his trend to destroy; to create knowledge, beauty, new intellectual and moral values, and destroy what other men have built and kill or dominate his fellow man.

Accordingly there are two kinds of history: a positive and a negative; the positive—the history of creation, and the negative—the history of destruction. What I myself was taught in school (and this is still true for most teaching today) is the negative history which measures the greatness of the historic figures by the number of people they have killed. The central events of this negative history are wars, battles and the meaningless shift of temporary political boundaries. This negative history is a deceitful and false history because most wars were not decided by kings and generals but by rats and lice which have spread diseases. There is no need to falsify history because history has a trend to falsify itself in that it is always only the alive who return from wars to tell their stories and talk about the 'glorious dead.' If only once these dead ones could return to tell us about their ignominious deaths, then history could take a different course. A real impartial world history has never been written. I was taught in school Hungarian world history, and there is also French, English or American world history. The heroes of one play the role of the villains in the other. This history teaching inculcates in early youth a partisan spirit and falsehood.

The positive history, the history of creation, the laborious process of widening man's intellectual horizon, is not taught. The story of how man worked himself up from squalor, misery and disease to a more dignified existence. The great heroes of this history are not the kings and generals but the great minds, searchers of truth, who created knowledge, beauty, moral and ethical values. To my mind Galileo, Kepler, Newton and Pasteur are among the greatest figures of human history, but you will not find their names in textbooks of history— although you may find them in textbooks of science. Such a positive history would teach to our youngsters human solidarity instead of partisanship, would teach them to appreciate our values, and inculcate vocation, the desire to contribute to the creative process however small this contribution may be.

The main factor which dominated human life was always man's relation to nature, the question how far man understood nature and could use its forces for his advantage. The first great strides along this line were the discovery of fire, the needle, the wheel and the like. These discoveries belong to the prehistoric era. In the historical period man's relation to nature is represented by what is called 'science.' Since it is the rapid development of science which has brought us into our present critical situation I would like to discuss, briefly, where we actually are, how we got here, and what the trouble is.

One can distinguish three periods in the history of science. The oldest one is the science of antiquity. This is characterized by a boundless confidence in the power of the human mind. Why make crude measurements or observations when the mind reigns supreme and can answer all questions? Characteristic of this attitude is Aristotle's statement that a big stone falls faster than a small one, and that women have fewer teeth than men. The remarkable thing about these statements is not that they are wrong, but that it never occurred to Aristotle to count the teeth or try the stones. He might have felt insulted by such a suggestion.

The second classical period of science has its origins in the awakening of the human mind called the 'renaissance' which brought a new attitude with it, which is characterized by a greater modesty: If we want to understand nature we must observe and measure. This period begins sharply with a boisterous young man's climbing a leaning tower and carrying two stones, a big one and a small one. These the young man, Galileo by name, dropped simultaneously after having bidden his companions to observe which of the two hit the pavement first. In this period not only the teeth were counted but the whole body was studied in the greatest detail. Galileo was followed by a crowd of people measuring and calculating, and building classical science which reached its peak with Newton and Darwin. The science of antiquity with its speculative nature left no imprint on the face of human life. Classical science led to the 'industrial revolution' of the last century which improved human life immensely.

Modern science begins sharply at the turn of this century with the discovery of X-rays, radioactivity, the electron and the quantum. It disclosed to man the existence of an entirely new world of which man had no inkling before, a world which is, in a way, more real than the world he knew before. Man did not know about this invisible world because our senses are not only unable to reveal it, but are made positively so as not to reveal it. If I would see quanta instead of buses I would be knocked over in no time, and if my ancestors had seen atoms instead of bears they would have been eaten. This new science changed all the parameters of human life. It abolished distance, made our globe shrink most tragically, replaced the speed of the horse with that of light, replaced the few hundred degrees of our flimsy terrestrial fires with the millions of degrees of atomic reactions, enabled man to move mountains or dig harbors in seconds. Classical science dealt with the world man always knew and did not bring new forces into human life. It dealt with forces of human dimension. Modern science made man the master of cosmic forces, which shaped the universe. The new insight and new powers enabled man to build a world of undreamt wealth, beauty and happiness, a world free of hunger, cold and disease. The trouble is that instruments can equally be used for construction and destruction, and construction is mostly slow, while destruction is fast. So modern science enabled man not only to build a better world, but enabled him also to eliminate himself with a stroke.

This new world opened up by science cannot be run without mortal danger by the old sentimental political methods, greed, lust for power and domination. It can be run only by the spirit which has built science itself, and if we want to stay alive we must rebuild our political and social thinking and institutions from the ground up in the spirit of science which is that of human solidarity and mutual respect.

We often hear it said that science has no moral content. This is wrong and if the world is in trouble today this is just because it has run away with the results of science, leaving its spirit and morals behind. Morals are the simple rules of human behavior, what to do and what not to do, and science has one very definite advice to give: if you have a problem, meet it as such, *as* a problem, knowing that problems are like equations which cannot be solved with blows or bombs, not even by atomic bombs. Bombs only create problems, not solve them.

To solve a problem meet it with a cool head, with uncompromising intellectual honesty, unbiassed by greed, fear or hatred, collect data and try to find the best solution. If you have an adversary, look upon him with respect as your associate with whom, together, you have to find the best solution. If this spirit would prevail at the peace talks in Paris, peace in Vietnam could rapidly be achieved.

Modern science has changed not only the face of human life, it has changed the face of science itself.

Classical science left our knowledge of nature cut up in single principles, like chemistry, physics, biology, etc. Modern science has given a deeper insight into nature and made these various principles fuse into one single mass of knowledge and understanding. We understand the stars since we understand the atom and we can start teaching medicine today by teaching the structure of matter. While science consisted of more or less isolated observations, now it teaches the deeper interrelations. Modern science unified knowledge. It not only looked deeper into the atom, it looked deeper into the human mind itself.

This deeper understanding of interrelations is what feeds the mind. With this deeper insight many problems which belonged earlier to the realm of philosophy have become problems of science, which has hereby become a humanistic subject. The knowledge of nature has become a part of humanism. A man who has no idea of where he is, what his place in nature is and what his relation is to others, is not a humanist. On the other hand it is difficult to imagine a real scientist without a sense of beauty, without esthetic and ethical values. This makes the whole of human knowledge fusc into a new single magnificent culture, making ideas about 'two cultures' outdated. Culture by its very essence can be but one, embracing all the values man has created, giving meaning and context to life.

PART II

Values Beyond Science

RAYMOND POLIN

Sorbonne, University of Paris

Traditionally, two groups of philosophies have been in opposition over the problem of the scientific knowledge of values. To be clear and short, it would be preferable to draw a very simple outline.

For the first group, values are concrete realities, and like any other reality, they are the possible object of a strictly scientific knowledge. But, even inside of this group, this common position can be held by people proceeding from very different postulates. For some of them the reality of values is identical with their very being; the degree of their perfection is proportional to the degree of their being. As Plato once said, what absolutely is, can be absolutely known: they believe in a scientific ontology of values. For some others the reality of values is the adequate object of an empirical inquiry: the choice of values is grounded upon experience like any other science of reality. For the last members of this group, the reality of values is incomparable. Since it is a specific and original reality, it has to be the object of a specific experience, *whether* that experience is *ein Erlebnis,* a fact experienced originally in one's own life, from which it is possible to build a comprehensive science, *or a sui generis* intuition of a phenomenological type which can be elaborated into *eine strenge Wissenschaft,* into a rigorous science.

For the second group, on the contrary, values escape any possible scientific knowledge, that is, any knowledge which in applying to the values a system of determinations, would pretend to describe and to explain them, according to their causes and to their laws. In this second group, we have to set apart the sceptics, because they do not deal specifically with values as such, neither in their systematic critique of every form of knowledge, nor when they conclude by rejecting any kind of scientific and positive knowledge. To this second group belong also those who affirm that values as such are not knowable at all, are not even comprehensible (in the meaning of *die verstehende Philosophie*), because they are merely affective reactions, and because they have no meaning of their own, one can not say if they are true or false. The validity of an affective *preference* is always indeed a gratuitous affirmation and, at the limit, this affirmation is undetermined and deprived of any reflection and intrinsic sense. There is no possible science of such a unique, incomparable and ineffable object. Close to the French and German existentialists, one could place Anglo-Saxon moralists, whose empiricism has built the so called emotive theory of values. However, for some of them, if not a science, at least a noncognitive theory of values would permit a description and clarification of human values and actions and the establishment of a theory of the information they afford.

For a science of values	—scientific ontology of values. —scientific empiricism of values. —*sui generis* specific scientific understanding of values (phenomenology).
Againt any science of values	—scepticism. —neither science nor theory of values, values being identified with affective or existential reactions. —values being reduced to the illusory consciousness of underlying hidden conditions, there is a science but of their conditions. no science, but understanding of evaluations, i.e., of the practice of freedom.

Other members of this same group affirm that values are just secondary phenomena, just reflections or appearances, which do not, as such, constitute objects of science. For them, values are just illusions, delusions, a delusive and specious consciousness, the epiphenomena of underlying realities, psychic pulses for some, social structures for others. There is no science of values for them, but there is a science of their causes and of their conditions, as the only concrete and meaningful realities able to be analyzed and deciphered. Such a science can sometimes be reduced to a scientific hermeneutic, to a science of interpretation.

As far as I am concerned personally, from my study of the *creation of values,* I have resolutely adopted the metaphysical point of view that values are just evaluations; that is to say, the direct or indirect expressions and actions of our freedom to exist. I have learnt from Kant that there is science only of the data determined by empirical intuition within the frame of its *a priori* structure and of the development of these structures. Of freedom, to which there is no corresponding intuition, of its actions, of its works as such, there is no science.

I shall try to demonstrate this position from a phenomenological point of view, and to bring back the knowledge of values to their right level, which is, at least so I believe, the level of a comprehensive re-invention.

May I evoke a personal memory? I had, when I was a young man, a very close friend with whom I had very few convictions, very few values in common. As long as he lived, we discussed our position, our actions, as the cirumstances of our lives presented them to us. Never was one of us able to convince the other that his values were well founded in spite of the fact that we were able to understand each other perfectly well. We lived in perfectly good faith, in a clear agreement about our differences, and each of us remained capable of acknowledging, in a permanent state of reciprocity, the intentions and values of the other. I wonder whether this experience has not been decisive in my radical refusal of any knowledge of values which presents itself as a rigorous science.

I

Values as such are not ontological realities; they are not objective. They belong to the order of action: that is to say to the order of freedom, and not to the order of being, or the objective determinations of reality. We could say then that there are no values, only evaluations; I mean, schemes of possible actions, with their meanings and their practical intentions. To evaluate is to begin to act, if we take the word *action* in a very strong sense, in order to distinguish the *actions* from the *operations* which develop mechanically the determinations of our biological and social trend of life. To act is to manifest one's own freedom, to let it be literally manifest. To act is to be grasped in the three dimensional world of society and history. To act is to try to achieve something new, to add something new to the given situation and to oneself. To act is to go beyond oneself, to pass over oneself, so that in such an activity of transcendence, one expresses one's freedom, one's power of discontinuity and indetermination, by which I mean, one's power of freedom, of perfecting, of producing oneself as one's own which is the properly human power to make oneself, to make oneself a man. 'Let us make man': that is the motto of human freedom. To be a man, is to make oneself a man. Put in another way, it is to produce oneself in one's own action which, in its new way, in its originality, in its history, constitutes a human existence and the fragment of a history.

The evaluation constitutes the initial *moment,* a purely imaginary one, through which the given situation is criticized, and surpassed in the perspective of a possible action. Progressively, by such successive movements of transcendence, by such successive renewals, this evaluation takes the form of a project to be experimented with and desired as an end, and it may possibly be, according to the circumstances, that other people will join in such action. Progressively, this initial evaluation transforms itself into an end, and that end into a norm of action for oneself and for others, until at last this practical cycle of successive efforts of transcendence accomplishes its end. Whether it is a success or a failure, the movement of creative transcendence, which is the source of evaluation, exhausts its potential of creation, its charge of freedom and transforms the given situation into a new one, the result of which becomes a new given and static reality. This new given reality by itself is now completely deprived of any intrinsic sense or value. The work and the situation as such, is once more neutral, just as the initial situation had been before it had been criticized and surpassed by the creative evaluation.

This creative evaluation is an act of freedom, an act of transcendence. As such, the activity of evaluation escapes any theoretical knowledge: the activity of transcendence, which constitutes its possibility, is incompatible with the activity of knowledge, which is an activity of immanence. Or, to speak in Kantian terms, acts of freedom escape the determination of the sensitive intuition *a priori*; for lack of determinable data, they cannot constitute adequate objects of knowledge. For Kant they can form a theory, but this theory is not a scientific one; it proceeds, not from intuition, but from the postulates of practical reason.

According to the same principle, it is not possible to speak of the truth of values, and the science of values would be, if it could exist, a science without truth. The truth of values ought to be adequate to their reality; it should reveal this reality. But a value, which is nothing other than evaluation, a liberation, an activity of transcendence, does not imply any reality to be revealed. In its essence, a value is imaginary, illusory, it is just the way of thinking, of appreciating, of intending a reality. It reveals neither the situation it criticizes, nor the work it projects. The value that an evaluation attributes to a given object passes by the object on every side.

How could it be possible to apply to the transcendence which is a becoming, an act, constituting a value, the immanence which reveals a true knowledge? There is no possible equivalence between an act of transcendence, which is a way of becoming different and going beyond, and the operation of a true knowledge which is an operation of identification. To affirm the truth of a value means indeed that you are proclaiming your faith, your certitude in this value; it is an affective belief, a voluntary decision which is added to the evaluation. It is the affirmation of that conviction which is unduly presented as a true or false proposition, and through which one pretends to transfer an act of freedom into the realm of truth. The existence of an act of freedom does not belong to the order of truth. One cannot rightly speak of the truth of a transcendence, nor acknowledge the truth of a value.

Reciprocally, it follows from the same principles that truths are not values, since they are not evaluations. Traditionally, truths were considered as logical values and the unity of all species of values was affirmed. But this conclusion depended in fact on the principle of the ontological reality of values. It was valid for Plato, but as soon as this principle is abandoned, the heterogeneity of different species of values, and even of each value in contrast to any other, becomes evident.

Rickert did try, at the beginning of the century, to maintain truths in the rank of values. But to justify this statement, he would explain that the modus of existence of truths were 'validity,' *die Geltung.* Truths are but evaluations. A theoretical judgment is but a judgment of value. In the last analysis, all values would be reciprocally identified with truths and in this way the 'open' system of values Rickert was proposing would have found a new unity.

Following the indications of Husserl, we have tried, on the contrary, to demonstrate the irreducible specificity of each axiological region. But whereas Husserl considered that all values were participating in one and the same essentiality (*Wesenheit*), we think that, not only is each region of values specific and to be taken separately, but each evaluation, each invention of value is original, unique and incomparable with any other, because each one is, in its own principle, an irreducible and incomparable manifestation of our freedom. All the axiological classifications are outside of values; they only describe the level of development of their inventions, and also the modalities or the regions of their application. The realm of values is the realm of the infinite diversity and of the irreducible difference achieved in the creation of newness. In the realm of values, there are no scientists, because there is no science of what is essentially different, essentially new and irreducible to anything already known, because there is no science of freedom in itself or in its achievements.

II

The reader should not draw from such a radical conclusion the idea that the world of values is the world of absolute disorder, every instant appearing and disappearing, like an indefinite multitude of fulgurations vanishing away without continuity, without leaving any trace.

An evaluation is indeed, for each man considered in his freedom, the way of discovering himself, in his difference, in his incomparable originality. But he succeeds only if he becomes able to manifest his freedom to others, so that to exist for others, his evaluation his actions, have to leave traces, which can be, if not known, at least interpreted as signs of a human presence in the neutral reality of a given situation. Through his activities, through the traces his action imprints on the surface of reality, each man exists for others, not only as a spatio-temporal object, but as an activity creative of senses and values. Such activity is not a value, but it is the sign of a value which can be imagined and interpreted. Through the evaluations and their consequences, indirect means of communication can be established between freedoms essentially distinct and separate.

The axiological is the proper way to exist as a human being for others. Another man in his freedom, in his power of creation, escapes any definition or determination in terms of science; he remains unpredictable. He cannot be directly known, but he can be indirectly *understood,* through the hypothetical interpretation of his works. In such a way the creator can be imagined and revealed in his uniqueness, in his creation. Most certainly, to understand an evaluation and its accomplishment consists in re-inventing, in reproducing the process of creation, to imagine and repeat the attitude of the creator. It is impossible to repeat the creative evaluation which is unique, but an evaluation can be invented in correspondence, in harmony with the initial one. The understanding of evaluation is never knowledge but always a hypothetical interpretation. To interpret, we have to try, with the help of the original work, to re-invent, to re-create.

This hypothetical re-evaluation is never equivalent to the original one. A value cannot be invented twice, not even by the original creator. Each effort to re-invent, which is a new evaluation of the first one, i.e. another evaluation, implies in its turn irreducible original elements. The interpretative re-evaluation aims only at harmony, at coherence with the initial axiological intentions. The axiological hermeneutic cannot have any other hope, nor any other ambition. It is sufficient to appreciate the unfaithfulness of an interpretation; it is insufficient to reduce all the possible coherent interpretations to a single one. I mean that an interpretation can be false, if it is not in harmony with the axiological, but no interpretation can be exclusively true. Which means, as I have already said, that there is no possible truth of our evaluations.

But all the end results of an axiological process of creation belong to the realm of reality. They have exhausted and lost their potentiality of value, their intentional charge of transcendence. We have said that they are quite neutral. That is why they are just hypothetical signs, the marks of creative labor, which can play the part of catalysts in the interpretative re-invention.

We could find a striking illustration of our thesis in the present trends of literary critics. Several types of scientific research are possible; they produce interesting information about the surroundings of the works of art; they are fruitful, as long as they do not claim to deduce a certain evaluation of works from their scientific study. The evaluation of works, which aims at their beauty, at what properly makes their value, is of another order. It depends on a hermeneutic, which is subjective and historical. The interpreter is also a creator. His evaluation contributes to the value of the work. At the limit, his contemplation produces, by a sort of resonance, a work of art in harmony with the original one which orients its evaluation and its meaning.

That is the reason why the interpretation of works of art varies from interpreter to interpreter. The interpretation of a work of art implies by itself a history, but can never, even when it appears to be the most faithful one, pretend to be the unique and definitive interpretation. As a work of art itself, it constitutes an evaluation which can become the object of ulterior re-interpretation. At least, that is what we can learn from the history of taste. It is no less true of other creations. They are the first support of the changing values attributed to them in the course of history.

C*

Along with the hermeneutic which deals specifically with the creation of values and their interpretation, that is to say with evaluations, human creations can also be the object of scientific investigations. But science can only consider their material reality and spatio-temporal forms, as free from any axiological meaning, as historical facts inasmuch as they belong to the realm and to the laws of nature. Science catches only the external manifestations of evaluations and actions, of the practice of freedom, their results imprinted in the given neutral *data*.

A work is achieved only when the whole cycle of the axiological creation is accomplished. But the development of this cycle, from imaginings to evaluations, from evaluations to ends, from ends to norms, from norms to acts and to beginnings of works, and very often back and forth, is seldom completed; it is a failure more often than a success; its accomplishment is neither necessary nor inevitable. But this process always interacts with the real situation, leaving traces of the existence of the author and of the situation around him. We shall mention here two varieties of such traces: the transformation of evaluations into 'goods' with their charge of activity, and their transformation into 'social norms.'

We have tried to show that an evaluation sets one free from the pulses and pressures of affectivity, that it is, in its essence, independent of passions, because it is of another essence, it belongs to another world. But axiological productions become the objects of desire and of need, and as such they are progressively transformed, degraded, and corrupted into 'goods,' which constitute the points of reference and, so to speak, the knots of the affective tissue and of the affective existence. Evaluations liberate, goods enslave. If an evaluation is a process of activity, each affective attachment to a good is in itself passive. It expresses an abandonment, a renunciation, a refusal to transcend oneself through action. One does not attach to an evaluation, but attachment to a good, involves a reality overcharged with affectivity and already absorbed by overwhelming desires and passions. A passion for a good, a love for a person is in reality independent from the value attributed to that good or that person. Love can be conscious of the mediocrity of its object and remain, however, irresistible. *Meliora video protoque, deteriora sequor.*

Through their degradation into reality, goods and affective relations are not only products of creation, but also objects of science. Now, as it happens these values degraded into goods, these evaluations absorbed by passions define the situation from which new axiological creations can free themselves through the movement of transcendence, and the scientific study of them permanently interferes with the hermeneutics of evaluation and claims to build a positivistic science of values.

Our phenomenological analysis allows us to set aside, each on its own terms, the two classical doctrines which claimed to build sciences of values: the one because goods depended on the orientation of desires and the other because desires depended on the nature of goods, for the actualization of values depends on the dialectic of creation and attachment, of free action and passion, of transcendence and immanence, beyond any possible science.

A similar analysis could be applied to the next step of the axiological cycle when the integration of the evaluation into a personal existence at the level of affectivity is followed by its integration into collective existence at the level of normativity.

All evaluations do not develop into ends and all ends do not develop into norms. Only those in a given situation which are the objects of a decision of action are transformed into obligations towards oneself and towards others. Born from an activity of transcendence, the axiological consciousness becomes a normative consciousness by finding itself the movement and the energy to transform a hypothetical evaluation into an obligation. Through this obligation, the evaluation becomes a practice, an action with which others can join and which engages in the transformation of the given reality. In this way norms acquire permanence, stability, and external characteristics. They become means of communication, projects, orders and they are understood, acknowledged, and obeyed. They are also means of collaboration. They affirm themselves as projects or works and of action. Further, they permit relations of communications which are more and more theoretical and less and less axiological. Even the obligations they carry become more and more a pressure and a restraint upon the existing material and social situation. They tend to establish in a special area universal intelligibility and the principles of a rational order. They reach their full efficiency when to the power of obligation already acquired is added the political obligations, and even the physical restraints, by which the existing social forces are transmitted.

The reader will understand that we designate social values under the name of norms. As such, they manifest an objectivity, at least an extra-subjectivity; they are fixed, hardened, susceptible of being determined theoretically and of serving natural causes. At the extremes, they are social realities and no longer values. There is no value in a strict sense; there are only norms, only social facts.

These norms, amalgamated and integrated into tradition, into manners, into the whole *Sittlichkeit,* are emenable to the social sciences, just as goods are amenable to a science of psychology.

There is no need for a longer conclusion. It is clear that, insofar as we understand under the name of values only goods and their affective contents, norms and works, can be objects of science. They belong then to a realm of reality which is, in fact, radically neutral, *wertfrei.*

But, insofar as values are evaluations, movements of transcendence, acts of freedom, creations in being, they escape any scientific determination. They are the genuine object of a hermeneutic. But that hermeneutic is a phenomenological research and, by itself, another effort of evalution, another invention, another freedom in being, aiming at an harmonious understanding as coherent as may be achieved.

The goal of the philosophical approach is not truth; it does not intend to teach dogmas. It tries to establish a comprehensive agreement between freedoms, between free human beings and not to deduce from a pretended scientific truth the necessity of certain behavior and of certain policies. We know too much of those often naïve and sometimes less naïve scientists, who transform themselves so easily into sorcerers, justifying the historical changes they try to impose by any natural, even by violent means, by the invocation of pretended sciences of values and of human deeds, of human history. Nothing is more specious and fallacious than this possible dogmatism fostered by the modern myth of science. Nothing is more dangerous for human freedom, for the capacity of man and of each man to create himself new and different, to act according to values he is indeed able to invent freely by himself. It could be forecast that any science of values would radically suppress values along with freedom.

The phenomenological analysis we propose tries to safeguard the irreducible role of philosophy as a theory of values, but not as a scientific one, in order to give sense and value to the action of man and to the world he is creating around himself. In the final analysis only philospohy would be able to reintegrate into a meaningful and valuable world the scientific descriptions and explanations of human behaviour.

And this is man's chance. Simply because this is man himself.

What Criteria
for Scientific Choice?

RUBIN GOTESKY

Northern Illinois University

I

Within the last ten years, as government support of scientific research throughout the advanced nations has grown almost exponentially, a new question has come to the fore: To what extent shall society support such research, or to quote Dr. Alvin Weinberg: 'What criteria can society use in deciding how much it can allocate to science as a whole rather than to competing activities such as education, social security, foreign aid and the like.'[1]

To answer this question, Dr. Weinberg wrote two papers, which he entitled 'Criteria for Scientific Choice, I and II.'[2] He felt that the very asking of the question is in itself remarkable, since it was hardly ever asked before or during World War II. Yet *not* asking this question prior to World War II seems to us perfectly reasonable, since science received little or no support from government. During World War II, this question was not asked, because support of science was almost entirely related to the war and after the war, for some time, to 'war and the fear of war.'[3] During or immediately after the war, anything was supported which was closely related to the war. However, with the thermonuclear stalemate, says Weinberg, support of science became separated from support of the military. At this point, support of science became simply one more demand among many for a share of the public purse; and at this point the question, 'What proportion of public funds does science deserve?' began widely to be asked. It must be remarked that this question never involved the question how much support of science for the military; such support has usually been provided by Congress without demur or question. This question primarily concerns the support of science for peace time and purely scientific purposes.

As head science administrator of the Oak Ridge National Laboratory, Dr. Weinberg admits this question cannot casually be pushed aside. Certain conditions of our material life, he maintains, prevent it being taken casually: First, public funds are not inexhaustible.[4] Second, the public frequently considers such needs as public housing, slum clearance, good roads, poverty, education as having higher 'social' priorities. Third, scientists are not necessarily better qualified than non-scientists for making right choices among 'social' priorities. Moreover, because of their occupational perspective, scientists are likely to be biased in their assessment of social priorities. Consequently Weinberg believes that workable objective criteria need to be established to determine the 'relative validity and worthwhileness of the various fields of science supported by society.'[5] He does not intend this to mean that criteria are needed to judge the worthwhileness of science, as a whole; for science as a whole, has already proved its worth.

According to Dr. Weinberg, such criteria already exist and are widely used, but they have not been made explicit. Making them explicit is the task which he sets for himself. Of such criteria, he says, there are 'two kinds: internal and external. Internal criteria are generated within the scientific field itself and answer the question, How well is the science done? External criteria are generated outside the scientific field and answer the question, Why pursue this particular science?'[6] Weinberg believes the second question more important, since it is a particular science and not science as such which requires the large-scale support of the public. Of internal criteria there are also, he says, basically two: (1) the state of development of a science at a given time (which he calls 'ripeness'), and (2) the level of competence of scientists in that given science (which he simply calls 'competence'). However, of external criteria, there are three: technological merit, scientific merit and social merit.[7] Technological merit seems to involve one prime consideration: the technological end or aim. Granted that the technological end is approved, then the scientific research as well as all other means required to attain it must be provided. Nevertheless, the important question is whether the technological end should be approved; and such approval he insists cannot be rationally justified without criteria of approval. The criteria he suggests are, all over again, the internal and external ones he has already recommended. The important questions, then, are: (1) Are the social outcomes worthwhile which the technology would make possible? (This is the external question.) (2) Are the technologists 'any good i.e., 'competent,' and the technologies or sciences involved ripe?' (These are the internal questions.) It should be noted that the first question involves social criteria of worthwhileness, which are nowhere directly provided. Weinberg's reason for not providing them is that a consensus on such criteria is not easily come by.[8] The second question on the other hand, states the criteria involved: competence and ripeness.

'Scientific merit' according to Weinberg, is a terribly troublesome concept largely because it has been given so little consideration. Nevertheless he is convinced that scientists within a given field are not competent to make rational judgment about it. The scientific merit of a given science or research project is determinable solely by the extent to which it contributes to 'neighboring scientific disciplines.'[9] And this is all Weinberg has to say about 'scientific merit.'

'Social merit' is determined by the extent to which the sciences or a science is relevant to 'human welfare and the values of man.'[10] Nevertheless, this relevance is handicapped by two difficulties: (1) Who defines such values? and (2) Even if such values can be 'identified,' which sciences are most relevant?"[11]

Dr. Weinberg does not explain what he means by these questions. The first one 'Who defines these values?' opens a Pandora box of ambiguities. Does he mean by 'who,' some being like God? Is he misusing the word, 'who' to mean 'What logical or other grounds determine the validity of any value or set of values?' This last question still raises the question of 'who?' Who, for example, is or are to decide what grounds are to be accepted? and who is or are equipped, intellectually and morally, to apply these grounds to given cases? Undoubtedly such questions will produce endless controversy. But if he is asking the question: Who, among men, has or have the authority to make such determinations and applications of value?, there should be no difficulty in arriving at an answer: obviously men in official positions of power. It is they who determine whether it is 'right' to make war, provide money for slum clearance or weapons research. Weinberg ought to understand this, since he prepares budgets and submits them for approval to men in official seats of power.

The second question also raises no serious difficulties, even though differences of opinion may occasionally arise among experts and laymen. Experts usually agree as to the sciences required to explore the means by which an 'identified value' can be achieved. And even if disagreements at first exist, the success or failure of researchers in

given fields to find appropriate means, either theoretical or technological, ultimately opens the door to sciences previously excluded. In
short, there are no really sound reasons for asking either of these
questions.

The above states Weinberg's essential contribution to the establishment of criteria for determining the extent to which any science
should be supported by society. These criteria may be vague and even
in some cases useless, but Weinberg must be given credit for facing
an unavoidable problem and trying to find a solution. Admittedly his
contribution is modest, but nevertheless it is a beginning.

II

Dr. Weinberg appreciates the problem of criteria of scientific choice
because, as an administrator, he has had to submit at specified periods
a budget and justify it to the federal budget director. This budget is
in itself not insignificant, but it is insignificant when compared with
the total budget requested by all institutions involved directly or indirectly in scientific research and development. This total sum adds up
to about 18 billion dollars for the year, 1968. To request such a sum
and have it granted by Congress requires considerable explanation and
justification. Even if Congress felt towards science as a father does
toward a son, they would be compelled to ask as a father would: 'Why
so much money?' 'Why should we give it to you?' 'What will we get
in return?'

Before such huge demands were made on any public or nation, it
was always easy for scientists to say scientific work, in seeking truth, is
its own justification or above criticism or 'value-judgment.' Such statements were not usually queried, because scientists in the main, supported their own work. However, by the thirties of this century, the
era of scientific self-support came to an end. Scientists had to turn
more and more to outside supporters such as industrial corporations
and the state. Consequently, they were no longer able to assert—except
in isolated cases—'Support us, for we seek the truth; and seeking the
truth is its own justification; or above criticism or 'value-judgment.'
Now they invariably had to answer the question, 'What good would
this truth—presuming you could discover it—do us?' Later, as given
sciences became increasingly useful, states and corporations began
dictating to them what kinds of truths to look for.[12] Scientists were

offered high salaries and privileges or they were compelled on the basis of patriotism and national need to seek, find or produce these truths. In some cases, states and corporations went so far as to tell scientists, not merely what truths to seek but also what they were to regard as truths.

However, even if we assume that science is its own justification, given the huge amounts asked in support of science-research, it is no longer possible to accept it as a sufficient reason. Scientists must answer such questions as: Why should the state support you and your work? And again, why should it support one rather than another kind of research? The traditional answer that such questions cannot be answered, because one cannot tell in advance how valuable such research will turn out to be, is entirely unsatisfactory. When such huge sums of money are being asked for, a state or a corporation wants to know, in advance—as far as possible—what benefits it will derive from supporting this or that research? and who else may also benefit? A State, for example, will want to know if it were to support this or that scientific research whether it will become more powerful than other states or more acceptable to its subjects or citizens. If scientists say only science will benefit, what is wrong with the state replying: 'I grant this, but why should I support you? You benefit; I don't.' If scientists offer plausible reasons to show that such research will benefit some state other than itself, why should not the state reply: 'I admit its value to another state, but that is just the reason for my not supporting it?' For instance, if it is valuable to the Soviet Union, why should I (the United States) support it?' Again, if scientists should offer plausible reasons to show that such research benefits mankind, what is wrong with saying: 'Very nice, indeed! I'm happy to know this; but, supporting it will not bring any benefits to myself.' In short, the criteria of 'valuable' or of 'worthwhile' are ambiguous without specification of the 'for what' and the 'to whom'; and when such specifications are made, those who can provide support may not want for good reason to provide it.

What we have so far said in criticism is incidental. We wish now to begin our basic criticism of Dr. Weinberg's attempt at providing criteria of scientific choice. Our criticism, for lack of space, will be reduced to pointing out the consequences of using certain terms like 'society,' 'aim' and 'criterion' without appropriate specification of meaning. At another time, we hope to be able to elaborate and sharpen Weinberg's criteria and supplement them with new criteria.

III

Criticism of the Looseness of Certain Terms

Our basic criticisms ultimately reduce to two: (1) the looseness with which Weinberg uses certain key terms such as 'society,' 'aim' and 'criterion' permits him to arrive at conclusions which cannot be justified. Thus he often talks as if *mankind* rather than the United States government, were satisfying his own budget requests; and as if there were values common to all mankind which were being used by governments to determine whether proposed scientific research is to be supported. Neither way of talking is legitimate. (2) The same loose use of key terms leads him to assert as criteria of scientific choice what are not criteria and cannot function as criteria. For example, 'technological aim,' as he uses this expression, is not a criterion at all. It becomes one only when it is *approved of*. But one cannot approve 'technological aim,' one can only approve a *specified* 'technological aim.' Thus the technological aim must first be specified before it can be approved of. Second, it must be approved of before it can be used as a criterion for accepting or rejecting a research project. If a 'technological aim' is disapproved of, it cannot possibly serve as a criterion. Third, an approved technological aim—if it can be used as a criterion —is never specific enough; it always permits a number greater than one of scientific projects to fall under its umbrella. Thus it is never adequate to serve as a criterion for selecting the ones finally accepted. To make such final selection, other criteria are needed such as those used for approving a given technological aim, and those necessary for judging between projects that satisfy the approved technological aim. It should be emphasized that neither of these sets of final selection criteria is technological. The former set—those used to approve a 'technological aim'—belong to what Weinberg loosely calls the 'social'; the latter belong to those which include more than what he loosely calls the 'scientific.' We shall now attempt to justify these basic criticisms.

IV

There are three terms which Dr. Weinberg persistently uses without specifically defined meanings: (1) 'Society' with its grammatical variants: 'social,' 'human,' 'mankind'; (2) 'aim' with its variants, 'end,' 'purpose'; and (3) 'criterion' with its variants: 'standard,' 'norm.'

1. There seems to be a special magic about the word, 'society,' as if like the word, 'god,' it embodies, in some unexceptional fashion, all the highest values of mankind. Yet just a little analysis will show that it incorporates the most varied and conflicting values. The society which is Russia or Nigeria supports values which are certainly not American. Weinberg recognizes this at times by pointing to the difficulty of determining what are these highest 'social' values.[13] Plainly there are, even today, a number of societies which differ in their 'values' and in the status they give to those values which they may be said to hold in common. Even within a society, different groups and individuals have different and special sets of values. Consequently, it is impossible to talk of *the* value of science to *society*. One can intelligently speak only of the value of science to a *particular* society—a feudal, capitalist, corporative or communist society.

However, even this way of limiting the value of science is unsatisfactory—particularly if one is concerned, as Weinberg is, with getting a state financially to support the work of science-institutions owned or controlled by that state. Plainly, 'society' does not provide this support; states do. No director of a government laboratory or institute ever asks society or—to use another favorite word of Weinberg's—'mankind' to provide money, equipment and personnel. This sort of appeal makes no sense, since mankind is as yet in no legal position to provide them. To obtain support, he must appeal through appropriate channels to a state; and he must make his appeal according to the rules and regulations laid down by that state or its agent institutions. Furthermore, he must appeal to the specific state which has created and which legally controls his laboratory or institute. It makes no sense for him to appeal to *any* state. A director of an American state laboratory would lose his job and be accused of treason, if he appealed to the Russian government for support and vice versa! Consequently, in terms of the concrete, legally established modes of support of science today, it makes no sense to speak of the 'social' value of science. In the concrete, there is only the value of science to a state; and states differ widely in their evaluation of science as an official instrument of state policy.

Of course, that science has primarily a national or governmental value does not exclude the possibility that states all over the world may agree to co-operate in the support of medical research into epidemical diseases or some other area of science and even lend to each other their laboratories and personnel for such a purpose. But this possibility depends upon governments, not on mankind as such.[14] The important point is that confining the 'social' value of science to states does serve to explain why states do not usually co-operate in supporting, for example, common military research. Extending the concept of the value of science so that it incorporates the values of mankind makes this kind of failure to co-operate inexplicable.

It may be that, at some future time, mankind will have progressed to that hoped-for stage when the primary and only purpose for supporting science will be the benefit of mankind. It is only then that one will be able effectively and meaningfully to speak of the 'social' values of science. At that time, directors of science institutions and scientists will be able effectively to use this ground for appealing for support of research to some sort of world state or world union of states. Unfortunately, that time is not yet. At present, science directors and scientists must make their appeal for support to their respective governments. At present, the 'social' value of science is simply a projection of values beyond their national base, values which some men expect and hope will effectively and universally become institutionalized.

However, it must be emphasized that there is today only one effective criterion which determines whether science will or will not be supported: *the state 'interest.'* However much some directors of science institutions and some scientists may wish to forget this, it is nonetheless so. Most science directors and scientists these days are so embued with national patriotism and status ambition that they take this criterion of state interest to be a natural law of society, not to be disputed by anybody.

2. Weinberg frequently speaks of the 'aim' of science as something apparently simple. As he uses the word, he often means 'value,' 'merit,' or 'worth,' of science.[15] However, he also uses the word 'aim,' in the sense of an 'objective,' a 'goal,' or an 'end-to-be attained.' For example, science is often described as having as its 'aim,' *truth*. Now to speak in this sense of the 'aim' of science as truth is to admit that the truth has not as yet been attained. Some truth may have been attained, but not *all* truth. In the case of science, it is usual to admit that only a small part of the total truth is known and that we are aeons, perhaps forever, removed from attaining the whole truth. Attaining it is a Sisyphean task, and even to believe that we shall at some remote time attain the greater part of it seems to be an illusion.

However, admitting this is not enough, for it has far reaching implications. The *aim* of any complex activity like science is usually not simple and undifferentiable; in practice, it is inevitably conceived of as an aggregate of specific aims, each at any given time, hierarchized into some order of importance. Truth, in other words, is not just some simple, undifferentiated aim; it is an aggregation, a complex, or a system of aims, depending upon how one views the way in which truths are related to each other. In short, scientists do not at any given time seek *the Truth*; they seek and can only seek *certain* truths; and they seek them because, in given circumstances and under given conditions, the finding of certain truths, if possible, are considered more *important* than others. Thus many physicists today consider the truths of solid state physics more important than those of theoretical physics; and many biologists, the truths of molecular biology more important than those of other areas of biology. Basically, the coming into existence of a 'body' of science, the splitting up of a 'body' of science into distinct 'bodies' of science and the disappearance of certain 'bodies' of science are sufficient evidence that the search for certain truths or 'bodies' of truth rather than others is determined by the importance men, in given social orders, attach to attaining them.

Why the search for certain truths is considered more important than the search for other truths is not the issue we need consider here; nor need we consider the conflict between scientists or between scientists and non-scientists as to what truths are important. Men may consider the 'truths' concerning cancer or death more important that the truths concerning hatons or mesons. Men may consider the truths concerning political society more important than the truths concerning the stars; and vice versa. What is important is that a contest over which truths are to be sought proves *that men do not and cannot seek truth as such*.[16] They seek and can only seek certain truths or 'bodies' of truth. And this fact means that considerations other than truth itself are involved, considerations such as cost, labor, the advantages and disadvantages of seeking such truths to a state, a class, an elite. We are, of course, assuming that those who make such decisions *want to know the truth*.

At this point we feel we ought to reiterate something that may have been forgotten.

We are concerned here with Big Science—to use Weinberg's term. We are concerned with setting-up criteria acceptable to the United States government for supporting the research activities of Big Science. Such criteria cannot be general, such as the usefulness of science to society; they must be specific enough to be able to justify the selection of one kind of scientific research over another, of the research of one science over another. We are not concerned with 'little science,'[17] or 'personal' science, i.e. science which an individual or a small group of individuals is capable of supporting. It does not essentially matter what reasons or rationalizations such scientists offer for working at science: whether it be the search for truth, to help mankind or to please oneself. But it does essentially matter what criteria are used to justify Big Science, since Big Science needs the support of the state and cannot exist, if such support is denied it in adequate amounts. The directors and scientists of Big Science cannot offer 'truth,' or the benefit of mankind or self-pleasure as reasons for being supported. They must not only specify the truths they seek, but inescapably, they must offer other specific considerations, such as, getting to the moon first, winning a war, preventing and curing given diseases, increasing industrial or human efficiency, or making men politically and socially compliant and docile.

In short, with Big Science, truth, i.e. given truths, as the root value of science, is inextricably commingled with other values. These other values determine whether certain truths are important enough to be searched after and whether a state should provide the moneys, personnel, and equipment to attempt such research. These values—whatever they are and however they are come by—are fundamental, for by means of them, rulers can perpetuate the state and keep themselves in power. All other values—however encompassing they must be, even those called 'cosmic' or 'divine'—are usually considered of negligible importance. No believers in Fate or the Judeo-Christian God have refused to make war, if, as rulers, they felt the oil-resources of their country were threatened by a competitor, or if they had a good opportunity to get such essential oil-resources. Yet oil, however valuable as an energy source to a state, hardly deserves the status of a cosmic value.

What, then, are these fundamental values which perform the function of determining the extent to which Big Science and its recommended researches will be supported? These fundamental values cannot be mouthfilling abstractions such as Democracy, the Dignity of the Individual;[18] nor can they be the sort which talk abstractly about national survival, national interest. Weinberg is concerned with the United States, not with any other state; and it is from the United States that support of Big Science must come. Consequently, it is the specific values of the United States—insofar as these can be realistically determined—that one needs to know, for they determine the extent of federal support and the areas of Big Science which will be provided support.

3. In speaking of 'technological aim' as a *criterion,* we said it must possess two characteristics, at least. 'Technological aim' must always be on the one hand a specific aim like reaching the moon; and on the other, it must be approved of. No 'aim,' in short, can be used as a criterion unless it is specific and approved of. But this does not as yet tell us what a 'criterion' is, i.e., how it should be defined. Here we do not mean to define 'criterion,' as a general term. In this general sense, it is easily defined as a *rule* for measuring, distinguishing, separating or grading entities, processes, or characteristics of given kinds. We mean to define 'criterion' in a sense in which it will be useful in evaluating *criteria* of scientific choice.

In attempting to state the differentia of such a *criterion,* we shall touch the heart of Weinberg's paper. For given such differentia, we shall be able to say whether he has or has not fulfilled his intention of providing *criteria* of scientific choice.

Let us begin our attempt to set up such differentia by first describing some of the institutional conditions within which this attempt must be made. We describe these conditions because we believe that the differentia of such a criterion cannot be set up abstractly, independently of circumstances.

There are science-institutions—some owned and controlled by the United States government, others, public or corporate, owned by universities or corporations—which need money, buildings, hardware and personnel in certain specified amounts or numbers in order to continue operating on a sustained and even expanding basis. In these days, most of their support comes directly or indirectly from the United States government. Consequently, these institutions must recommend the sort of research and development projects which will result in adequate support. In large part, of course, the requests for such research and development originate with non-scientific institutions like the DOD, business and agriculture, but often enough the scientists employed by these institutions are the ones who recommend the projects that ought to be supported. Thus it is essential that such a criterion should be able to formulate the objectives or goals which must be satisfied. However, formulating these objectives or goals is not enough. Such a criterion must also contain rules for judging whether certain other designated objectives or goals are appropriate or feasible. Thus it must be able to show that such and such objectives are politically or militarily indefensible—as, for example, controlling the nation's economy and government—or again, that such objectives, no matter how desirable, are, for a long time to come, impossible to satisfy or satisfiable only at inacceptable costs to life and property—as, for example, space ships capable of travelling between the stars or a world nuclear war. Further, such a criterion must be able to distinguish objectives or goals essential to the survival of these institutions from those which are not. For example, physics institutions serving the DOD could not survive if they repudiated the basic goals of the DOD. On the other hand, they might reject, for good reasons, a military goal such as the search for some force which could so completely immobilize an area that motion of any kind in that area would be impossible. The scientific objection would be that no such force is discoverable.

However, these characteristics are not sufficient. The directors of science institutions would still be unable to order their projects in terms of preferability. By these characteristics, they could rule out certain projects as opposed to the inevitable goals set for their institutions, and, even if these projects could satisfy such goals, as impossible of attainment, but they would still be unable to answer the questions: In what order of necessity shall such projects be arranged? Must this project be defended to the end? Can that one be sacrificed? Consequently, such a criterion to be adequate must also contain *rules of* preferability capable of distinguishing proposed projects in an order of descending importance or inevitability. In short, such a criterion must be able (a) to formulate the specific, approved-of-goals of such institutions; (b) determine which of these goals are inevitable; (c) distinguish between projects which support such goals and those which do not; (d) distinguish between projects capable of completion and those which cannot be completed or are extremely risky; and (e) order such projects in terms of an order of descending importance or inevitability.

We are now in a position to ask whether Weinberg's criteria of scientific choice satisfy these characteristics of an adequate criterion. Plainly, they do not. 'Social merit,' for example, does not designate specific 'social' goals, nor does it, in spite of the use of the word, 'merit,' designate a specific rule for ordering scientific projects in terms of importance or inevitability. We need not emphasize the ambiguity of the word 'social,' since we have already dealt with it, but it is necessary to emphasize that without specifying such 'social' goals, it is impossible to know whether they are really approved of. Similar criticisms apply to 'technological merit.' No specific goals are given and no rule or rules of preferability for ordering such projects is proposed. Only respecting 'scientific merit' are criteria proposed: 'ripeness' of a science and 'competence' of scientific personnel. Unfortunately,

Weinberg neither makes clear the rules by which 'ripeness' of a science or the 'competence' of personnel is determinable. He assumes further that these 'criteria' are approved of; but no one, except himself, has approved of them, and even if those in power were willing to approve of them, they would be logically and experientially handicapped by not knowing what these criteria specifically mean and consequently how and in terms of what objectives they are to be employed. Weinberg reduces further the significance of these concepts by saying that no scientist belonging to a given discipline is capable of using such 'criteria' to judge projects within his discipline.[19] While Weinberg asserts that 'social merit' is preferable to 'technological merit' which is preferable to 'scientific merit,' he provides no concrete rules for making such judgments respecting proposed research projects.

V

It is sad to note that what seemed to offer so much should end in offering so little. It is a Herculean task which Weinberg attempted; and it is obvious that Weinberg is no Hercules. Even so, this should not be taken as criticism. It is of greater importance to point out the reasons why he failed and why inevitably he had to fail. (1) He did not study in detail the actual modes by which he, his committees and others made evaluations of proposed research projects; how they, in the light of their experience, assessed what had been done and what needed to be done; and how they related all such evaluations and assessments to the problems of keeping their scientific institutions going. (2) He made no attempt to extract the large number of explicit or implicit rules which were used in making such evaluations and assessments. (3) Finally, he made no attempt to determine the extent to which these rules are compatible with each other. To set up such criteria is extremely difficult; that it is a job that needs to be done is obvious; that it will never be done by science administrators as it needs to be done is equally obvious. Science administrators, who have enough difficulties as is in retaining their posts, cannot question the inevitable goals of the state and corporate institutions which support them and their science institutions.

Notes and References

1. Alvin M. Weinberg. *Reflections on Big Science*, Cambridge M.I.T. Press, 1967, p. 85.

Rubin Gotesky

2. Both were originally published in *Minerva* I and III, I, 159–171 (winter, 1963) and III, 3–14 (autumn, 1964); they are now republished in *Reflections on Big Science*. See footnote 1.

3. p. 85, *Reflections on Big Science*.

4. p. 68. *Ibid*.

5. p. 71. *Ibid*.

6. p. 71. *Ibid*.

7. p. 72. *Ibid*.

8. p. 73. *Ibid*.

9. p. 75. *Ibid*.

10. p. 76. *Ibid*.

11. *Ibid*.

12. See Schilling, 'Science, Foreign Policy and Politics.' *The Politics of Science*, Oxford, 1968, pp. 361-2.

13. p. 76. A. Weinberg, *Reflections on Big Science*.

14. The same point is made from a different point of view by Professor W. R. Shilling in his paper, 'Scientists, Foreign Policy and Politics,' published in *The Politics of Science*, edited by William R. Nelson (New York: Oxford University Press, 1968). Scientists have suddenly begun to realize, since World War II, that their sciences no longer serve, as they formerly believed, 'mankind.' They have suddenly begun to realize they serve their states, the national policy of a given state. ' . . . the governments of the major Powers have endeavored to find ways to make themselves . . . more active in determining the course of science and technology.' (p. 361). Further, Professor Shilling coins several expressive phrases to express the concern of some scientists over this change in the traditional aim or ideal of science. Scientists, he says, have a 'Sense of Paradise Lost,' i.e., of being controlled in their activities by the state (p. 372), and of the failure of their original ideal, 'Science Serves Mankind.' (p. 373). Even though Professor Shilling admits that science and technology are now primarily instruments of the national policies of different states, he still likes to talk as if it could be significantly otherwise, as if the *human ideal* can actually influence and direct science and technology. He concludes his article with the following mouth-filling but hardly significant assertion. 'The contributions that science and technology will bring to international politics will largely turn . . . on the purposes of statesmen and the theories they have about the political world in which they live.' (p. 383) This is just a pompous and obscure way of saying that science is an instrument of national policy and largely controlled by the politicians (here called 'statesmen') who run the national states.

15. See pp. 72, ff. *Reflections on Big Science*.

16. That the selection of *what truth to search for* involves other considerations than simply the search for truth is stated in another way by Robert Gilpin in 'The Intra-Scientific Conflict over a Nuclear Test Ban: The Problem of Conflicting Expertise.' (p. 328, in *Politics of Science*). He says that social responsibility, the intertwining of public policy issues with scientific issues is inevitable and inseparable parts of the 'scientist's advice.' Gilpin is here concerned not with the search for truth, but with the *use* of truths already discovered. Nevertheless, this essentially makes no difference to the point being made. The point seems more obvious when truths are already known

than when they are being sought. In the former case, the interpretation structuring the truths can often be seen more easily as a *tour de force*! Gilpin particularly has in mind the difference between Bethe and Teller concerning the technical feasibility of developing devices for the detection of nuclear explosions.

17. A. Weinberg, *Reflections on Big Science*, 'The Problems of Big Science: Scientific Communication,' p. 39.

18. A rather dreary example of such mouth-filling useless abstraction is found in the last chapter of Russell L. Ackoff's book, *Scientific Method: Optimizing Applied Research Decisions*. Chapter 15, 'The Ideals of Science and Society: An Epilogue.' New York: John Wiley & Sons, Inc., 1962.

19. *Reflections on Big Science*. pp. 73–4.

A Value-Oriented Framework
for Education and the
Behavioral Sciences

W. RAY RUCKER

United States International University

Who has not heard it said, 'Young people have no values,' or that ours is a 'valueless' society? Disagreements with behaviors failing to conform to conventional norms of taste or morality lie behind such assertions. When people restrict the meaning of value and confuse value with norm in this fashion they contribute to the mounting ambiguity of communication in our interpersonal and institutional relations. Educators and other behavioral scientists add to the confusion by using overlapping and vague definitions of drive, need, motive, aim, objective, and purpose, as well as value. Is it possible that the term value can integrate the meanings behind all of such terms referring to human motivation? Increasingly, behavioral scientists are turning to this age-old term as a semantic bedrock for classifying the meanings and for describing the core of man's nature as well as the substance of what is communicated in human relations.[1]

Toward a More Comprehensive Value Theory

Is there anything universal about values? Are values peculiar to an individual personality? Are values facts? Are values something that 'ought' to happen in the human situation? Are values a medium of exchange in human communication? It is time educators and behavioral scientists realized the answer may be *yes* to all of these questions. Abraham Maslow[2] affirms that basic needs and basic values are one and the same. He considers such basic values species-wide. Fulfillment of such value-needs depends upon the richness or poverty of the physical and social environment. The development of the individual, however, illumines value patterns that are unique. These patterns are related to the potentials of the person but also reflect uniqueness in everybody's environment.

Axtelle[3] and others have affirmed that values can be both *facts* and *oughts*. To the individual undergoing an experience the values imbedded within it cannot be disputed save as matters of fact. Not until it is asked whether such value facts are worthy of being valued do we raise the *ought* or axiological question so often associated in the mind of the layman with the term 'value.'

From his rich experience in encouraging persons to discover their inner processes of valuing, Carl Rogers[4] postulates fundamentally generic or organismic bases for value directions in human behavior. Freed from coercive influences of other persons and institutions, self-directing, full functioning persons tend to value common objects, experiences, and goals. Such organismic commonality refers not to norms but to categories of things which people desire or need because they are human. These categories are not limited to questions of morality or taste, but cover the full gamut of human needs and aspirations from the most mundane to the loftiest, from the most immediate to the most distant.

The cross-cultural and socio-political studies of values and valuing by Harold Lasswell[5] complement the Rogerian approach and affirm the species-wide value-needs suggested by Maslow. He discovered that while valuing techniques and strategies differ over long stretches of geography and time, men everywhere and in all ages tend to direct their behavior toward certain categories of needs and wants. Behind the specifics which seem at first glance to present gross difference and relativity from culture to culture, are the sometimes heavily camouflaged but nonetheless universal value goals of men. These are *affection, respect, skill, enlightenment, power, wealth, well being,* and *rectitude*.

Theodore Brameld[6] suggests that a peaceful international order depends upon the development of a world education which first takes into account the common needs and purposes shared by all men. His list closely approximates Lasswell's list of basic value categories.

These great thinkers link 'social-self realization' and 'realization of human dignity' with significant access to and enhancement in each of these fundamentally human categories of striving. Thus social scientists, philosophers, and psychologists join in identifying the bedrock of humanistic studies. The basic categories become clear whether one is searching within man's organismic nature or within the social contexts he creates out of his behavior. Valuing becomes the most fundamental human function.

Man is Man, and not only animal, then, because his thinking-feeling behavior (his valuing process) distinguishes *homo sapiens* as a species in evolution from all others. Yet, because men become different persons due to varied genetic endowments and different environments, *ways* of trying to achieve values differ. Difference in personal strategies to achieve basic values is what one is led to believe Maslow had in mind when he postulated that some values are peculiarly individual in the self-actualization process.

The Lasswell classification model is not a set of norms but a framework of open-ended, continuum categories based on comprehensive cross-cultural, psychological, and historical data as well as on wide ranging empirical studies, including the Vicos Community Project in Peru under the sponsorship of Cornell University,[7] the Power Sharing Project at the Yale Psychiatric Institute,[8] and other studies reported in his and his associate's writings. His list of general categories is, by no means, the only useful scheme for classification.[9] It is preferred for its contextuality, economy of terms, and precision in isolating fundamentally human goals. Other schemes tend to emphasize 'religious,' 'political,' 'intellectual,' or 'social' values which obviously overlap and become relatively ambiguous in scientific studies of man. The framework presented by Lasswell is a factual synthesis emerging out of and facilitating studies that look with increasing objectivity at the valuing events going on in human behavior.

The general categories, developed by Lasswell originally for political science, are redefined here for education and the behavioral sciences.

Value Category	*Principal Value Goals*
1. Affection	Provide a climate supporting acceptance, trust, emotional security, love, congeniality, friendship and intimacy.
2. Respect	Provide an atmosphere in which each individual may achieve identity, a recognized social role, and self-esteem without fear of undeserved deprivation or penalties from others.
3. Skill	Provide opportunities for each student to develop his talents to the limits of his potential.

D

Value Category	*Principal Value Goals*
4. Enlightenment ..	Provide experiences for awareness and openness and encourage students to find their own truth in every issue without losing sight of social norms and the significant events of human achievement.
5. Power	Provide situations in which the student will have opportunities to participate in making important decisions and to exert informal influence according to his talents and responsibilities.
6. Wealth	Provide facilities, materials, and services to promote excellent learning while guiding the student to produce wealth in the form of materials and services himself.
7. Well-being	Provide resources and interpersonal relationships which nurture the physical and mental health of each student.
8. Rectitude	Provide experiences enabling the student to develop a sense of responsibility for his own behavior, consideration for others, and a high sense of integrity.

These operational definitions of categories of valuing, while specific for education and child development, point to the use of similar definitions for identifying and classifying valuing events in other contexts. These include those ranging from the deepest personal to the most complex societal concerns. No hierarchy is claimed in the value list. Events, however, appear to give primacy to a particular value or values. That is, discrete situations and behaviors may bear the stamp of value priority, but in the continuum of the personality or the society over time, the categories interact and condition one another with relative equality.

If valuing is the most basic human function, how else can we understand man except through better understanding of value dynamics? If we assume the value categories advanced by Lasswell form the framework for synthesizing modern humanistic science, our next task is to point up how the new context harmonizes and enhances the best we know about the actualization processes of therapy, education, child rearing, and institutional development.

The Dynamics of Value Shaping and Sharing

Personality is not a meaningful entity apart from the social process.[10]

Both concepts emerge as bipolar aspects of the human situation. What unites them and makes them one configuration is value transaction. To transform one is to transform the other. The societal and the personal worlds are viewed holistically and with special reference to the value dynamics operating in the flow of experience in the particular field under observation. There is a continuous inflow and outflow of experience and a transaction of one pattern of values for another either among participants or within the self.

The most basic criterion for facilitating the procedures of cooperation (or socialization) is *value sharing*. Too often democracy has been defined only as power sharing. Its ultimate appeal to men everywhere will come when it is understood that wide sharing of values in all categories is the basis for a society oriented to maximum realization of human dignity for all men. The dams against cultural exchange and people to people assistance will then be removed. While democracy cannot be imposed from without, the vision and the techniques of value sharing can be transported and can be learned if exemplified and demonstrated in the personal behavior of those attempting to do the transporting. Acceptance of institutional models of democracy await rich person-to-person exemplification of value sharing.

Value analysis becomes the central process of diagnosis in personal and social problems; patterns of value deprivation, enhancement, or overindulgence reveal the antecedents of present behavior. Value maximizing on a relatively broad front is the clue to health and actualization of human potential. The valuing process encompasses and focuses learning no matter whether the learner is concerned with data or procedures. Value analysis becomes an objective tool in the consideration of content in both the curriculum and in counseling. The framework becomes a filter for data passing to and from the counselor or the client. It protects the counselee from interjecting the values of the counselor or of others; it promotes a self-directed process of value clarification.

Education, research, and therapy are each viewed, then, as specialized practices for clarifying, analyzing, and modifying the valuing process in both conscious and unconscious experience. The observations and analyses focus upon valuing (the process) as much as on values (the goals, outcomes, or products). Value dynamics in human events can be defined very much as John Dewey or Herbert Mead did the transactional process in the social context and within the self. An individual seeks and selects values in the environment. The environment seeks and selects values in the individual. Choosing to diminish one's own access to a value or values in order to gain access to others is typical of self behavior. For example, physical well-being may be given up temporarily while 'burning the midnight oil' to gain enlightenment and skill through study. Such gain may, in turn, lead to increments in purchasing power (wealth) which may be used to 'buy' physical comforts. Although value profiles (or value systems) of individuals and institutions are of interest, particularly for purposes of diagnosis, it is critical for the behavioral scientist and educator to gain and facilitate insight into the probable *value consequences* of the transactional process to all those concerned in the events under study.

Any teacher who consciously applies the value-oriented framework to the school situation will become immediately aware of a simple and fundamental fact: *Any act of a teacher is an act either of sharing with or of withholding values from children.* The teacher should become more and more aware of his every influence, subtle and direct, on the learning process. He should evaluate the long-term consequences of his own behavior in the personality development of the children under his influence and control. In turn, the effects of student sharing or withholding of values on his behavior and on the behavior of other children should be viewed with more objective concern.

One of the early perceptions of a teacher who consciously value-analyzes children is that each one has a different value profile; that is, each child has achieved a unique status in each value category. The teacher perceives a pattern of past value deprivations and indulgences. He knows that value statuses emerge from many cultural forces acting on the child either to withhold or accord values in the milieu of experiences through time. Whether the teacher decided to view child development this way or not, value dynamics inevitably will be operating in the lives of the children, and in his own life, affecting for good or ill the relationships of participants in the socio-educational process and thus the personal destinies of all. Learning to look at children through the value framework is a first step in gaining facility in the use of the framework in teaching.

Value sharing does not just happen. Value *shaping* must produce opportunities and channels and contexts within which sharing may flourish. Institutions are examples of such contexts, and the types and varieties of institutional practices determine the opportunities available. The familiar institutions are family, school, church, and government. These institutions specialize not only in shaping but also in sharing values. It is in these institutions that intensive efforts should be made by adults to invent and foster practices and behaviors of

Valuing in Personal Experience
Value Deprivation—Enhancement Continuum

Movement Toward Pathology		←Low Value Status→	Movement Toward Full Potential		Value Category
Alienation Hatred	Fear Suspicion	Indifference Withdrawal	Caring Acceptance	Trust Intimacy	AFFECTION
Degradation Disintegration	Discrimination Segregation	Isolation Inferiority	Self-esteem Identity	Esteem of others Integration	RESPECT
Incompetency Failure	Non-achievement Inadequacy	Under-achievement Awkwardness	Achievement Adequacy	Competency Success	SKILL
Distortion Deception	Confusion Misunderstanding	Uncertainty Ambiguity	Awareness Openness	Empathy Sharing	ENLIGHTENMENT
Resistance Aggression	Submission Coercion	Conformity Dependence	Self-direction Influence	Cooperation Participation	POWER
Indigence Destitution	Non-productivity Marginal	Maintenance Subsistence	Productivity Creativity	Abundance Affluence	WEALTH
Anxiety Illness	Irritation Frustration	Existence Unhappiness	Hope Joy	Contentment Health	WELL-BEING
Malice Depravity	Irresponsibility Unscrupulousness	Apathy Negligence	Responsibility Consideration	Integrity Altruism	RECTITUDE

value sharing. To 'invent and foster practices' is, again, to shape values. For instance, governments through both legislative acts and executive actions tend to produce and limit the arena within which values of all citizens are shaped. At the same time, government is shaping the contexts for facilitating and sharing of, or the witholding of, values among the people. There is, then, an intimate relationship between shaping and sharing. Often shaping becomes the vehicle for the sharing where human learning is concerned.

The value shaping process is of particular interest to those in schools who are responsible for curriculum process and materials. The processes of the curriculum consist of the strategies, methods, climates and other planned contextual activities of teachers and learners which control the type and degree of interactions in the classroom. Curriculum materials such as course outlines, books, audio-visual aids, etc., determine to a large degree the access learners have to the content areas of human enlightenment. Curriculum process and materials, then, shape values by producing them, by setting the stage for learning events, and by providing the ground rules for action in the learning arena. Both the quality and the quantity of value sharing experiences are determined to a large degree by the planned provision of a curriculum context for learners which shapes—but which also may selectively deny—values. Curriculum planning, then, is a particular case of deliberate value shaping in terms of the goals of education. Federal aid to education obviously is aimed at shaping values on a wide scale and providing opportunities for richer experiences of value sharing.

General Implications for Method

A general method for education and the behavioral sciences emerges from the comprehensive value theory outlined above.

First, a general method assists in discovering who has access to values through institutional or personal strategies.

Leaders of any group activity facilitate through forms of social organization, emotional climates, and personal strategies the degree to which individuals have opportunities to realize their valuing potentials. Daily practices in the classroom, for instance, often can prevent learners from having access to the values they seek. Classroom tasks may be assigned only to those members of the class who are most able to perform them. In this situation some children are selectively denied access to the skill activities necessary to the development of their latent talents. Some students may be denied opportunities to achieve status in respect and affection by personal strategies employed not only by the teacher but also by other students in the classroom. Thus, the prescribed institutional practices of the school as well as the variable personal strategies in the teaching-learning situation can determine the degree to which the classroom moves toward a configuration of wider value sharing.

Second, a general method may permit the observer to gather data on comparative value profiles which would suggest or predict differentiated behaviors. Is there a value profile of democracy? Of communism? Of Shintoism? Of Black Power? Of traditional or progressive schooling?

Comparative analysis of the distinctive value profiles of democracy as against, for example, those of autocracy, indicates the probability that the former is developing on a grand scale when human values are being *widely* shared. In despotic societies, where many values tend to be withheld from the people by a ruling clique, a high indulgence in all value categories is reserved only for a privileged few while relative indignity is assured for the many. Human dignity and self-actualization are seen as descriptive of democratic man—a man nurtured by a climate of wide value sharing.

American democracy has had difficulty in exemplifying itself before the world not merely in demonstrating how to share power, the more obvious departure of democracy from despotism, but also in emphasizing that such a society distributes all human values on a much wider scale than other systems. The implication is that each of us should better exemplify democracy in our own thoughts and actions and that we test same constantly against the criterion of whether we are sharing or withholding values so as to test whether human dignity—or human indignity—is being served by our behavior. This is a simple but highly effective short-cut to a constant awareness of man's personal responsibility to be his 'brother's keeper.' Moreover, it is astonishing to realize how much freedom each of us has to act in either direction, and how salutary or destructive our individual influence can be in the human situation.

Third, a general method can indicate when a personality is self-actualizing in and congenial to a context of democracy. The self-actualizing individual can be described as one who consciously tries to share values with all human beings in *all categories*—not witholding emphasis from any category, but maintaining a relative and flexible balance. His behavior is characterized by such qualities as congeniality, openness, trust, and integrity. He has a multi-valued personality. He is what some have referred to as a 'democratic person.' A person who is less mature may give lopsided emphasis to only a few of the value categories. Such a person can be characterized as biased, prejudiced, inflexible or even mentally ill. He tends to be autocratic and authoritarian.

Fourth, a general method involves setting in motion a systematic technique of thinking with values (problem solving). Such inquiry is guided by the component operations of problem solving expressed as five basic ways of thinking. Value consequences are considered in every phase of the process. The following chart, 'Schema for Systematic Thinking with Values,' is suggested as a *map* to leaders for keeping participants aware of the total process of inquiry and to assist leaders of deliberating groups in keeping a record of progress and matters needing further attention before the deliberating bodies. Problems are seldom solved in neat, sequential steps. Such systematic thinking with the aid of a 'map' eliminates the need for slavish sequence; any part or step can be kept open throughout the deliberations. The innovation consists in unifying value analysis with the reflective process. Emphasis should be placed on setting free the participants in a system which tends to guarantee the fluidity, the open-endedness, and the comprehensive coverage of the value dynamics in the whole problem.

Fifth, a general method focuses on the individual's self-esteem, which can be appraised by systematic analyses of his value deprivations and indulgences, as a key factor in the realization of his potential as a human being. Each individual has achieved at any given time a unique 'status' in each value category. This status can be estimated by gathering data on the pattern of past value deprivations and indulgences. Knowledge of such data will aid in the creation of an environment most compatible with the value goals of the person striving to achieve his inherent potentials as a human being. Young people form self-concepts by relating to people and objects. An individual estimates himself from the reactions of his parents, peers, teachers, and other adults to his behavior. He tends to learn those things that are value enhancements to the self.

Sixth, a general method provides maximum opportunity for unlike learners to realize potential in a social context where creative and responsible use of difference makes a richer world. Relative uniqueness for the individual is both a fact of biology and a requisite of democracy. The preference for uniqueness, however, could be carried too far if the degree of uniqueness results in the 'lop-sided' value profile.

Schema for Systematic Thinking with Values

Component Steps in Problem Solving	Goals	Past Trends	Present Conditions	Future Projections	Alternatives
Values					
Affection	In	In	In	In	In
Respect	Terms	Terms	Terms	Terms	Terms
Enlightenment	of	of	of	of	of
Skill	Values	Values	Values	Values	Values
Power	Involved	Involved	Involved	Involved	Involved
Wealth					
Well Being					
Rectitude					

NOTE: Trend, condition, projective, and alternative data should be analyzed and appraised in terms of their relevance to the goal. One singular advantage of this chart is that it enables investigators to maintain orientation to the total process involved when moving in either direction from one intellectual task to another.

D*

Over-indulgence in any value category at the expense of a relative balance in the personality leads to an unrealistic and even absurd uniqueness. A democratic context requires an open-ended concept of potential and an infinity of possible patterns of personality or uniqueness. In the healthy human interaction characteristic of democracy, both extreme statism and individualism are held in check inherently within the transactional functions of the system.

Summary

The valuing process characterizes man's conscious or unconscious striving in both personal and institutional contexts. Education helps learners to clarify, analyze, and modify their valuing processes. Therapy unifies value thinking with expressions of feeling in the therapist-client relationship.

A more comprehensive value theory is provided by the converging perceptions of several leading thinkers. Both valuing (the process) and values (the goals, outcomes, or products) emerge as the bedrock of humanistic studies. A list of categories in which to classify human valuing events aids the researcher or practitioner by providing a common framework and vocabulary which can bring more comprehensive coverage yet precision of analysis.

A general methodology for unifying the behavioral sciences, including education, is indicated in the following generalizations:

1) A general method assists in discovering who has access to values through institutional or personal strategies.

2) A general method may permit the observer to gather data on comparative values profiles which would suggest or predict differentiated behaviors.

3) A general method can indicate when a personality is self-actualizing in and congenial to a context of democracy.

4) A general method involves setting in motion a systematic technique of thinking with values (problem-solving).

5) A general method focuses on the individual's self esteem, which can be appraised by systematic analysis of his value deprivations and indulgences, as a key factor in the realization of his potential as a human being.

6) A general method would provide maximum opportunity for unlike learners to realize potential in a social context where creative and responsible use of difference makes a richer world.

The challenge to education and to the behavioral sciences is to innovate techniques within this configuration as a test of its power to unify, to promote keener communication, and to open the floodgates of creativity in an age of catastrophic crises produced by man's inhumanity to man.

Notes and References

1. W. Ray Rucker, V. Clyde Arnspiger and Arthur J. Brodbeck, *Human Values in Education* (Dubuque, Iowa: William C. Brown Book Co., 1969), Chapter 4, 'A Descriptive Science of Values.'

2. Abraham Maslow, *Toward a Psychology of Being*, Second Edition (Princeton, N.J.: D. Van Nostrand Co., Inc., 1968), pp. 34, 152.

3. George E. Axtelle, 'The Humanizing of Knowledge and the Education of Values,' *Educational Theory*, **XVI** (April, 1966), **No. 2**, pp. 106–07.

4. Carl Rogers, 'Toward a Modern Approach to Values: The Valuing Process in the Mature Person,' *The Journal of Abnormal and Social Psychology*, **Vol. 68, No. 2,** 1964, pp. 165–66.

5. Harold D. Lasswell, *The Communication of Ideas* (New York; Harper and Brothers, 1948); *Power and Personality* (New York: W. W. Norton & Co., Inc., 1948); 'Universality in Perspective' from *Proceedings of the American Society of International Law*, 1959.

6. Theodore Brameld, *Education for the Emerging Age*, New York: Harper and Row, 1965, pp. 92–93.

7. Allen R. Holmberg, 'The Changing Values and Institutions of Vicos in the Context of National Development,' *The American Behavioral Scientist* **VIII, No. 7,** (March, 1965).

8. Robert Rubenstein and Harold Lasswell, *The Sharing of Power in a Psychiatric Hospital* (New Haven: Yale University Press, 1966).

9. Such schemes have been developed by Charles Morris, Henry Murray, and Gordon Allport, among others.

10. V. Clyde Arnspiger, W. Ray Rucker, and Mary Preas, *Personality in Social Process* (Dubuque, Iowa: William C. Brown Book Co., 1969), pp. 1–9.

Reason in Science and Conduct

ERROL E. HARRIS

Northwestern University

I

The salient characteristic of our times is the conspicuous contrast between the achievements of the human intellect in science and technics and its abysmal failures in the spheres of morals and politics. Yet both these spheres of activity have traditionally been regarded as the products of reason, in some sense of that word. So to regard them is, I believe, no mistake, and I shall try to show that there is a sense of the word 'reason' in which both theoretical science and social order are its products. If this is so we are faced with the paradox that the same human intellectual capacity has produced, in one sphere, the most spectacular results, and, in the other, only the most dismal failures.

Consequently, we are capable today of changing the face of the earth, flying, not only in the air, but out into space, increasing the life-span of human beings, manipulating the hereditary mechanism of living things, and harnessing the elements in the service of our own purposes beyond limits that have ever in the past been contemplated. Yet at the same time our most 'civilized' and advanced societies are plagued by acts of violence and barbarism, increasing crime rates and rebellious youth. War and conflict between societies is a continuing reality. We have failed as completely in distributing wealth as we have succeeded in increasing its production. Social inequality and oppression excite rancour and resentment, which exacerbate the violence of conflicts, and the very achievements of science, because of the irresponsibility and irrationality of governments, threaten the human race with annihilation, at the same time that they offer it the opportunity of unprecedented progress.

The two spheres of reason have not always seemed to be in such marked contrast. The discrepancy between the progress of science and the regress of morals has become noticeable only in relatively recent times. From the 17th to the 19th centuries the two spheres of human activity seemed to be advancing hand in hand. As modern science emerged from mediaeval obscurantism, so freedom of conscience won out over authoritarian dogmatism. As Newtonian science advanced, so the Enlightenment liberated men's minds and the political movements of America and Europe won liberty for subject people. As technology and industrialization progressed, so did social reform and the relief of poverty. Slavery was abolished and human rights were recognized and promulgated, and organized labor became a physical force. By the end of the nineteenth century T. H. Green was able to demonstrate in some detail in his *Prolegomena to Ethics,* how far modern morality had progressed even beyond the admired standards of the ancient Greeks. Even in the twentieth century, after one of the most bloody and costly wars in history, man still believed in continuing progress and Woodrow Wilson was able to excite imaginations with the idea of a coming age of permanent peace administered by the League of Nations. It was only when this aspiration failed, after the advent of Hitler and the Second World War that the idea of progress became thoroughly discredited and the predicaments in which we find ourselves today became apparent. Now we see reason in conduct utterly defeated, while reason in sciences is resplendently triumphant.

How has this paradoxical situation come about? If I can give a plausible answer to that question I shall be content and shall leave the further question, How can it be remedied? for consideration on some other occasion, possibly by some abler thinker.

II

The traditional conception of reason, as it was exercised both in science and in conduct, was difficult to define and often left vague. Different philosophers gave different accounts of it, so far as they gave any at all. For Plato it was the dialectical discovery of universal forms, for Aristotle and Descartes an intuitive grasp of self-evident first principles and necessary nexus between clearly and distinctly perceived concepts; for Hume it was the slave of the passions, and for Kant the faculty of transcendental knowledge.

Kant made the distinction between understanding, as constitutive of scientific objectivity, and reason as merely regulative through its conception of noumenal ideals. Hegel protested against this merely abstract normative notion, and demoted the understanding to a lower level of knowledge than that which he claimed for reason. The understanding, he taught, was that lower phase of the dialectic in which reason makes sharp distinctions between concepts and keeps them fixed by rigid definition, in abstraction from others to which they are related, and by their relations to which they are determined. Understanding is thus the faculty of analysis and of reductionism. It reduces things to their least parts, seeks to grasp their nature by tracing them back to their elements. It is the science that murders to dissect, and by dissecting loses *das geistige Band* which gave its object individuality and life. The understanding is typified by mechanical science which reduces all activity to the notion of atoms propelled by forces measured in terms of their masses and distance. In practical life it is the capacity to analyse situations, discriminate means from ends and relate them externally each to the other. So it serves an instrumental purpose, performing no constitutive function. It finds but does not create its data and then proceeds to analyse them. Practical aims are given to it and it discovers means to their achievement by elaborating the causal relationships of events.

On the other hand, reason comes into its own, for Hegel, when it transcends the range of the understanding, recognizes its object as its own construct and itself as its own object—in short, becomes aware of itself as self-creative.

In Hegelian terms, our modern situation is marked by the ascendency of the understanding, as represented by science, and the eclipse of reason proper. Indeed, in our day the function of ratiocination has become wholly instrumental and does correspond, by and large, to what Hegel would have identified as understanding. In science it is commonly restricted to mathematics and symbolic logic, the construction of deductive systems, whose primitive terms are indefinable, whose postulates and transformation rules are arbitrarily chosen, and in which logical truth is the same thing as tautology. This type of reasoning is in no way constitutive of knowledge and is purely instrumental. It comprises the construction of calculi, by means of which to derive results from facts otherwise known. Its work is increasingly assigned to the computer, which processes information but creates none.

The other form of reasoning currently recognized by philosophers of science is induction, and this too is uncreative. Its conclusions are generalizations from particular facts that have been ascertained by observation. Induction, however, is the perpetual bug-bear of logicians and its procedures have never been conclusively validated. At best the conclusions it reaches claim only probably truth, and reliance upon them depends on the calculus of probabilities—another branch of deductive mathematics which is purely analytic, formal and instrumental. The substantive knowledge from which these precarious generalizations are made is all directly acquired by immediate observation.

It follows that the sole source of factual knowledge in the natural sciences is observation, and this is reputed to be the basis of their exceptional success. Whether or not it is so is a question to which I shall return. At this point, we may note that the current view of reason in science, as shared by large numbers of scientists with a considerable body of influential philosophers, is that it is purely instrumental and mainly analytic.

III

The reduction of reason to a purely formal instrument and the belief that substantive knowledge can be derived only from sensuous observation produces a complete revolution in attitudes to morality and political ideals. For pure intellectual analysis is indifferent to good or bad, right or wrong, and provides no motives for action. Even Aristotle, who venerated reason, declared that pure intellect moves nothing. Moreover, *qua* purely analytic, it cannot be the source of any constructive conception of human nature.

The older philosophers held that men through their self-awareness could reflect upon their own conduct and upon the impulses and desires which moved them to action. In so becoming aware of themselves, those philosophers taught, men were able to make themselves their own objects, both in knowledge and in action. Hence the exhortation, 'Know thyself,' as a propaedeutic to right conduct. In making oneself one's own object in practice, one formed an ideal of self-hood, a conception of the sort of person one aimed at becoming; and success or failure in that endeavour became the source of one's self-respect. Thus both the conception of human nature and the aim of human endeavor were held to derive from man's capacity for rational self-knowledge.

But if the doctrine is espoused that reason is purely analytic and only sensuous observation can give us factual knowledge, the knowledge of human nature and the motivation of action will be no exceptions, and we are referred for the understanding of these matters to the empirical psychologist and the sociologist. So, in our day, the old traditional doctrines, that philosophical reflection could reveal to us the nature of man and the kind of life he ought to live, and that the good life was the life of reason, have gone by the board. In the first place, if reason is purely analytic it can pronounce no substantive judgments of value. Secondly, human conduct has come to be interpreted in large measure in terms of behavioristic psychology, which abstracts from consciousness and ratiocination. That again, so far as it is held to operate in human behavior at all, is reduced to a mechanical process analogous to (if not identical with) the operation of an electronic computer.

Or alternatively, human conduct is viewed as the product of emotional, and ultimately physiological drives, explicable in terms of endocrinology, and the practice of 'rationalization' as merely an activity of subconscious window-dressing to make the repressed motives seem palatable to the behaving subject. Consequently, the whole concept of human action has changed from what it was in the days when moralists spoke of rationality as the source of human freedom and moral responsibility. Moral objectives today are held to be determined by sentiment and feeling, which are largely, if not wholly, physiologically determined, and reason is simply the computerized instrument for discovering means to emotively determined ends, or the contrived exterior trappings, masking hidden and conventionally disreputable motives. Moral judgments, and in fact all judgments of value, are then seen to be subjective, and moral codes to be purely relative. No rational *justification* can ever be given on this view for the ends that men pursue, because their attractiveness results from purely emotional or temperamental causes.

This type of outlook has been strongly supported by the findings of anthropologists who have investigated the cultures of different and widely separated peoples and found the rules of conduct of one culture not only different from those of another but often in mutual conflict. Yet in the culture to which they belong the behaviors that the rules sanction is held to be right and obligatory. Once again, moral relativism holds the field and subjectivism of moral judgments seems obvious.

In this setting politics become a matter purely of rival interests, unregulated by objective principles of right and wrong. Such regulation as occurs is regarded as the outcome simply of custom or convention, itself the ultimate result of coercion by a ruling group or individual. When in sophisticated societies it is recognized as such, alleged political principles are seen to be illusory and the gross conflict of interests is accepted as the basic motivation of political action. The Marxist type of doctrine fits in very aptly with a view of this kind. It maintains that these interests are organized as class interests determined by economic factors, and that so-called political ideals are mere ideologies hypocritically used to disguise exploitation of one class by another. Reason once more is a form of bogus rationalization and material forces are now the ultimate determinants of political action.

The depreciation of reason in all these various ways stems originally from its reduction to a merely formal instrument, and the resulting view that theories of human conduct are all, in one way or another, products of empirical science gathered inductively from observation.

It is not surprising that the practical consequence of such theories is a loss of respect by the rising generation for moral standards, the rejection of all authority pretending to represent such standards, and an upsurge of moral and political anarchy. It is true that some of the doctrines I have sketched are made to support totalitarian systems, but the distance between anarchy and tyranny is only one step. Where there are no rules, the strongest and most ruthless calls the tune; and where each follows his own inclination the interests of the stronger prevail.

The explanation of the contemporary confusion in morals and politics and the failure of mankind to solve its practical problems is therefore not far to seek. It is the degradation of reason first to a mere formal instrument in empirical science and then in conduct, to a bogus and hypocritical stalking horse for the pursuit of self-interest. Practical issues are then left for decision by the conflict and interplay of irrational forces, economic, ideological and violent.

IV

But if this explains the failure of morals and politics does it equally explain the enormous success of natural science? I am inclined to believe otherwise. The view of reasoning in science that I have sketched above and the theory of scientific method that goes along with it are, I believe, totally misguided. I should not deny that the use of mathematical calculi is of the utmost importance and value in science, but I gravely doubt that it can be reduced to a merely analytic process, as many of the currently most influential logicians contend. On the other hand, I should certainly support Karl Popper in denying that inductive reasoning, as it is usually conceived, is ever indulged in by reputable scientists, even in spite of some appearences to the contrary.

The belief that observation ever is or ever could be theoretically neutral, and that scientific laws are drawn from theoretically neutral observed facts by inductive generalization is altogether false. All observation is theory-laden and all scientific experiment is devised, conducted and interpreted in the light of a theoretical (or conceptual) scheme which is prior to observation. I am not arguing for any innate ideas, but I would argue very strongly for an innate activity of organization which constructs from the elements of sensory experience the objects of perception. Contemporary physiological and psychological research on perception has amassed a wealth of evidence supporting the view that perception is an activity of structuring, and that the perceived object is the product not simply of passively received impulses but of an active response determined by past experience, by contextual relations, by the mental set of the perceiver and by a very complex and elaborate activity of interpretation of sensory cues. If this is true of ordinary unreflective perception, it is much more true of informed scientific observation, the whole value of which depends upon the skill, scientific knowledge and insight of the observer.

A layman presented with the photograph of vapor trails in a Wilson chamber, or the electrical record of a neural impulse is unlikely to make much of either. The mere sensory appearance of such objects is not the datum from which science proceeds. To make scientific use of observed material, it has to be read in the light of scientific theory. The structure and significance of the apparatus by means of which it was obtained has to be known and understood. The objects it presents must not simply be seen, but must be *seen as* the tracks of elementary particles, variations in electrical potential, or whatever it is that already elaborated theory dictates. Science is throughout, from its first beginnings to its most abstract and mathematical formulations, an amalgam of observation and theory, neither of which could be what it is without the other.

Our knowledge of the world is not, and could not be, a picture constructed piece-meal out of isolated sense-data. It is at all stages a structured totality in which sensory elements are organized, and so rendered intelligible, by conceptual principles. Scientific observation and experiment are part of the process of development of this conceptual system, the articulation of which gives rise to new questions, and their investigations lead to progressive modification (sometimes radical) of the total system.

The progress of theoretical science, in consequence, is a process of continual organization and reorganization, in detail, in depth and in increasing comprehensiveness, of our experience of the world. Apart from such organization, and the conceptual principles which make it possible, no significant observation is possible.

For the sake of brevity, I have had to state my position dogmatically, but I base it upon direct examination of the actual procedures of major scientists in the history of science, and I can call as witnesses to support my case theorists such as N. R. Hanson, Thomas Khun and P. K. Feyerabend, as well as a host of psychologists who have investigated the psychological character of perception.

Reason in science, therefore, I should define as the activity of organizing which gives rise to systematic theories of special departments as well as of the whole of experience. In fact, the special theories are rooted in the more comprehensive world-view because the latter supplies the currently accepted conceptions of the ultimate elements in nature and the fundamental laws of their interaction. Thus the entire scientific scheme is a rational structure of inter-related sciences, the constant tendency of which is towards greater and more embracing unification on the one side, and finer elaboration of detail on the other. In short, the activity of the scientific intellect is, throughout, one of organizing and articulating in systematic form the manifold details of our experience of the world.

It is this organizing activity of reason that accounts for the success of the sciences—the ultimate and continuous interplay between observations and theory. And the kind of science that it produces is essentially theoretical science. It is the science of Newton, Clark-Maxwell and Einstein, of Lavoisier, Pasteur and Mendlejeff, of Harvey, Cuvier and Charles Darwin. But man is not content with theory; he promptly seeks to turn it to his own advantage, and theoretical science enables man to harness the forces of nature for his own purposes by discovering the laws of their operation. So he builds engines and machines, derives the power to move them from the sun, the air, rivers and the sea. He leans to fly and to plumb the depths of the ocean; and he finds new ways of producing food and the commodities of living in abundance.

The utilization of scientific knowledge for practical purposes is technology. It involves the employment of theory for the development of techniques or skills. Once the techniques have been mastered, the theory need not be remembered, for the technique can be repeated without recourse to theory. The good mechanic does not need to be a physicist, nor the successful veterinarian a theoretical biologist. Nevertheless, the technician is always ultimately dependent upon the theoretician for the progress of his technology, and without theory technology would neither come into existence nor develop.

From the technological point of view, however, theory is a mere means to a practical end. It's role is reduced to that of an instrument. It dictates the relations between the stages of the practical activity and the quantitative ratios of the forces which it harnesses. Thus the contribution of theory can be set down as a program which can be formalized and a machine can be constructed into which it can be built and which can carry it out automatically. If theoretical science is identified as reason, then in technology it becomes a mere instrument and its contribution can be progressively computerized in the automation of technical operations. What the computer does is to process supplied information according to formalized procedures. But such procedures are never creative, because the process of creative thinking is never wholly, if at all formalizable. Technology, therefore, while it is dependent upon theoretical science, can never produce theoretical science. Computers may guide rockets and space-craft and perform all sorts of wonders of automation; but it is highly doubtful if they will ever produce a new scientific theory.

Nevertheless, although technology is the child of theoretical science, theoretical science also owes much to technology. As experimentation becomes more complicated it depends more and more upon technical skills and appliances for its apparatus. The connection between science and technology is therefore intimate and inseparable. But technology cannot be substituted for scientific theory and so far as there is danger of a take-over in that direction, so far science, and technology itself, are likely to decline. The degradation of reason to a purely analytic and instrumental role holds, for science, this grave danger of substituting technology for theoretical science. In actual fact, the former is parasitic upon the latter, and if all science were to degenerate into technology, technology itself would gradually decay.

V

This degradation of reason, as we have seen, has already occurred in the sphere of morals and, if the analogy holds, we may take it as a warning light for the future of science. For reason in conduct, in the proper sense of 'reason,' is precisely what it has been and should be, in science—the self-conscious activity of organization, both in the regulation of personal conduct and in that of social relations. It is indeed man's capacity to think systematically and to reflect upon his own experiences that enables him to resolve the conflicts in himself of appetite and impulse. He does so by self-discipline and self-control, an act which he acquires by long practice and in the course of a somewhat arduous educational process. Even what the psychologist calls 'conditioning' has been found, at least in part, to be a reflective process which correlates stimuli according to their relation to satisfaction. But that is not the essential point here. Abandonment to the impulse of the moment may be characteristic of the lower animals but, for man, who looks before and after, it leads only to frustration. The extent to which the agent is aware of this is the measure of his ability to adjust his desires to one another and organize his activities according to a plan. He has the capacity to choose, which marks the transition from merely instinctive behavior to responsible action.

Moreover, human beings can survive only in society. They depend upon one another for the realization of their wishes. The unfettered pursuit of personal interests would lead to internecine strife, which would completely destroy this possibility. But because they are intelligent enough to realize that unrestrained conduct is destructive of all desirable ends, they accommodate their activities to one another's aims and subject their conduct to rules which take other people's welfare into account. If they did not, co-operation would be impossible and the common purposes that mutual interdependence generates could not be pursued. But this subjection to rule of social relationships, and the consequent mutual accommodation of cooperative activities, have as their counterpart the self-discipline of the individual in his own private life—for no human life is ever so private as never to involve mutuality of any kind. Quite the contrary.

Accordingly, it is indeed reason that, by reducing the conflicts of appetite and passion to order and subjecting them to rule, is the mainspring of morality. And it is reason which, by adjusting to one another the interests of social groups and subjecting them to law and order, makes possible in society the pursuit of common ends.

Moreover, if these common ends are to be successfully attained, the capacities of the cooperating members of the society must be used to the full, and the society ought to be so ordered that it provides for each and all the greatest possible opportunities for the development of these capacities. Such opportunity is what we call liberty, and its provision without special favor or discrimination we know as social equality. A social order governed by any other agency than one which is intelligent, self-critical and self-reflective is unlikely to encompass any of these goals.

Reason, therefore, is also the foundation of social justice and political freedom. These and most other desirable ends are frustrated if political business is carried on by methods of violence, conspiracy, or chicanery. They are most likely to be realized through the settlement of differences by discussion and negotiation, by the mutual accomodation of demands, through common recognition that civic interdependence underlies the need for common objectives and the realization that these can be achieved only by cooperation and mutual respect. Such are the methods of reason—the methods as well as the results of its self-conscious organizing activity, and they imply personal self-discipline and self-control which is the effect of that same self-conscious ordering activity at work in the regulation of individual conduct. Without this sort of reason there is no real morality and can be no lasting social order. Without it, likewise, there would be no science and no technology.

Our contemporary ills are surely the result of the decline of reason, in this sense, in the modern age. Our failure in the sphere of conduct is too obvious to need demonstration. Is it possible that our success in the sciences is only a legacy of the reasonableness of the past, which we are rapidly forgetting? And could it be that our future may be overshadowed by the usurpation of the place of true science by technology, with disastrous results for both?

Survival Value

STEPHEN C. PEPPER

University of California

I am raising the subject of survival value in this paper because it is a source of value most commonly neglected in contemporary discussions. In the nineteenth century when the biological theory of evolution was fresh in men's minds, there was a lot of emphasis on survival value stimulated particularly by Darwin's pregnant phrase 'the survival of the fittest.' The term 'fittest' clearly had the form of value significance. Darwin himself led in calling attention to its bearing on human affairs in ways which I find still deserving of serious consideration.

Conceptions of value based on biological evolution later fell into neglect partly on account of a shift of interest among philosophers to other phases of value, but mainly, I think, on account of errors of interpretation that gained currency during the subsequent decades. I will mention a few of the principal ones.

The most serious was an interpretation draining the term 'fittest' completely of value significance. It was affirmed that the term was simply a technical biological term to distinguish the organisms that survive in the course of evolution from those that perish. One could as well speak of the 'survival of the survivers.' That some organisms survived was just an observed fact and calling them 'fittest' was logically a tautology having no value significance and certainly having nothing to do with the concept of 'ethically best.' It was like distinguishing the snow that fell on mountain tops and settled in deep packs from that which fell in the valleys and melted with the first sun. This interpretation seemed utterly convincing to almost a whole generation of men in the period of reaction to Darwinism. Of course, what is left out is the description of the selective process and the nature of the material selected. It just happens to be living organisms that are being selected in respect to their capacities of adaptation.

A second erroneous interpretation is not quite so drastic, and is almost acceptible. It is the commonest way today, I think, by which writers dismiss survival in their development of value theory. They admit that biological survival in its stress on adaptation to one's environment is relevant to human values, but only as a *condition* for values, not as itself a value. Again what is neglected is the dynamic process of natural selection which actively brings into being some value activities and blocks off others in ways hardly consonant with its being regarded as a valueless condition of human valuing.

A third erroneous interpretation comes from accepting as representative of survival value certain theories which place it in distorted or exaggerated prominence and so are easily refuted. Bertrand Russell in his *Authority and the Individual* (Simon and Schuster, Inc., Boston 1949, p. 74) conveniently telescopes several such theories in the following passage:

> What might be called the biological theory is derived from a contemplation of evolution. The struggle for existence is supposed to have gradually led to more and more complex organisms culminating (so far) in Man. In this view survival is the supreme end, or rather survival of one's own species. Whatever increases the human population of the globe, if this theory is right, is to count as good and whatever diminishes the population is to count as bad.

Russell here mixes up three exaggerated and oversimplified views of survival value: (1) the view of a progressive complexity of biological structure culminating in man as the value ideal; (2) the view that mere survival itself is the supreme end; and (3) that life (at least within one's own species) is 'good,' so that the more life (that is, the greater the population) the better.

The first view has indeed been seriously developed. Its best known proponent is Julian Huxley. With certain modifications it can, I think, be partially justified. Its weakness is that some of the simplest organisms are still surviving beautifully and bid fair to outsurvive man. But Russell drops this view and concentrates on the last two which are caricatures of any biological value theories within my reading. His refutation is: "It would be easy to find a simple acre containing more ants than there are human beings in the whole world, but we do not on that account acknowledge the superior excellence of ants. And what humane person would prefer a large population living in poverty and squalor to a smaller population living happily with a sufficiency of comfort?"

After realizing the inconclusiveness of such supposed refutations of the value of survival value, one may become more receptive to the idea that it may well be an effective source of value. If so, it would seemingly be most sympathetically developed in the framework of an empirical value theory. I shall now undertake to show how it may be not only consistent with such an approach but even required for its completeness of treatment.

The most detailed and thorough empirical treatment of value in recent times I find in R. B. Perry's writings and Dewey's, and, may I add, my own *The Sources of Value.* These all agree in finding the locus of value in certain activities of the organism in relation to its environment. Rollo Handy in his recent book summarizing such theories (*Value Theory and the Behavioral Sciences,* Springfield, Illinois, 1969) calls these activities 'transactions.' Ervin Laszlo in a new book (*System, Structure, and Experience,* New York, 1969) calls them 'feedback circuits.' My name for them is 'selective systems.'

Purposive behavior furnishes an excellent example of a selective system. Here a dynamic agency (call it a need, a drive, a desire, or an interest arising either from changes within the organism like hunger or thirst, or from external stimulation like a sudden down-pour of rain, or a nail in your shoe) presents a pattern of tensions with accompanying conditions of satisfaction. In appetitions these acts lead to instrumental and terminal goals and often a consummatory act yielding pleasure. In aversions there are acts of avoidance of objects of apprehension and actual pain terminating when there is relief from these tensions.

Here is a dynamic structure of activities. The structure institutes a norm on the basis of the conditions of satisfaction intrinsic to the specific need or drive or desire. Acts and objects are selected as correct or incorrect in proportion as they serve towards the attainment of the conditions of satisfaction for the dynamics of the purposive structure. It is a selective system. And values of various kinds spread out along the route of these transactions. There are positive and negative conative values, and as goal objects are anticipated these are potential objects of value, and there are also objects of potential value instituted in the environment. There are frustrations and achievements, and pains and pleasures all closely bound up with the intensification or relaxation of tensions of the patterns of the purposive transactions. And in the process of achievement the purposive dynamics selects towards the shortest path.

There is no question that such a selective system institutes values and sets up norms for the good and the bad and the better and the

worse within its range of application. Questions arise only when different purposes all at the same time converge with different ends, and
particularly when these purposes and their divers ends are held by
different persons. My view is that such convergence of purposive activities among a number of persons gives rise to a social situation which
constitutes another selective system which supervenes over the various
individual purposive activities that enter into it. I find Dewey's writings most illuminating about the dynamics of social situations. In
principle I believe the normative selective action of a social situation
is no different in form from individual purposive achievement. The
dynamic agent now is the resultant action of all the persons involved
in a social situation, and, as Dewey makes plain, the dynamic structure of the situation itself in relation to its environmental setting gives
implicitly the conditions of satisfaction and so the norm for the selective actions of the group in resolving any problematic tensions.

There are also selective systems for social institutions and cultural
patterns which have their influence on social situation. They constitute, in fact, also part of the environment which any personal or social
situation must often take account of. In all these levels of selective
systems, as I have described them so far, their dynamics goes back to
and comes out of the needs and drives and interests of individual organisms and their combinations in social groups.

And now I guess you can already foresee what is to be the trend of
my argument arising from biological natural selection. It will be that
this latter is also a selective system instituting norms out of its dynamics bearing on human life and behavior and so yielding human values
just as the other selective systems described earlier do.

But one very important difference is to be noted, that is the difference between the basic dynamics and the aims of the purposive selective systems and that of biological natural selections. The dynamics of
the purposive systems is based on individual needs, drives and impulses and the overall aim is towards individual and social satisfaction.
The dynamics of biological selection is based on the reproductive activity of interbreeding populations (that is, of biological species) and the
overall aim is towards adaptive survival of the species. Ultimately
the biological dynamics lies in the genes and chromosomes which control the patterns of growth and behavior of a species of interbreeding
organisms. The science of genetics studies the mechanisms of heredity
which determine the general pattern of the species and the variations
of organisms within the general pattern. The science of taxonomy

studies the diversity of species, and classifies the various species, and describes the ways in which the diversification comes about.

Biological selection develops from the competition of the diverse individuals of a species for the most advantageous conditions of survival and propagation within the environment where they are placed. Those more adapted to their life zone survive and propagate, or at least survive longer and propagate more prolifically than the less adapted. Thus the pattern of the interbreeding population becomes progressively more securely and fully adapted to its living conditions. And when diverse species are competing for a particular life zone, biological selection operates upon the patterns of the species themselves, and a species unable to adapt to this sort of environmental confrontation may become extinct—or alternatively it may through genetic variations develop into a new species capable of maintaining itself competitively in its life zone.

Now, man is a biological species and has been and still is subject to biological natural selection. But the way in which biological selection operates upon man is somewhat unique. As a biological species man inherits two traits that have given him extraordinary survival capacity. One of these is the trait of docility or learning capacity which produces purposive behavior. The superiority of purposive behavior over pure reflex or instinctive behavior is that a docile animal can learn to adapt to a great variety of environmental conditions even to the invention of tools to serve his needs, while other animals are bound to their single instinctive mode of adaptation. The other trait is his social capacity. Except for man all the other highly developed social species, like the ants and the bees inherit their social structures bodily as instinctive patterns embedded in their organisms. Man is the only highly socialized docile animal. This combination of intense social needs with extraordinary powers of learning and invention, including language, has rendered man almost immune to serious competition with any other biological species.

It has, however, introduced another kind of biological competition almost entirely novel to evolutionary history. This is the competition between diverse social groups within the same species. It is the competition of tribe with tribe and nation with nation for dominance over certain areas or certain social patterns. Such human groups differ from one another (sometimes widely) in their cultural patterns. Thus in the human life zone, cultural competition has taken the place of strictly biological competition among biological species. But it should not be thought that the competition is any less severe. As more powerful forms of cultural organization develop, the less powerful forms unadapted to the ensuing competition are either extinguished or put at great disadvantage. This is clearly visible today in the fate awaiting all barely surviving primitive societies in the surge of modern scientific-industrial forms of organization.

As we hear constantly repeated nowadays, man has only man to fear, and there is now unfortunately plenty of cause for fear. Through man's own superiority of biological traits for the survival of his species he has invented the means that may well lead to the total annihilation of his species and a lot of other living species besides. It can easily happen if one of the present competing cultural groups should seek to dominate another one by employing this destructive instrument and precipitating a general atomic war.

Man is thus also caught up in biological natural selection. A cultural pattern of social organization is just another biological species emerging on a higher plane. But this higher plane rests on the lower plane of the dynamics of the species through inheritance from the genes. For the genetic pattern of the human species with its characteristic traits of socialization and learning capacity underlies the varieties of cultural patterns which constitute the biological cultural species that compete on the cultural level.

Incidentally, the cultural species through the agency of social tradition gained also the extraordinary power of transmitting acquired characteristics not available to species on the lower biological level. Through the process of transmission by tradition a cultural pattern can endure a very long time, as long, in fact, as it continues to be adapted to its life zone in competition with other human societies and other forms of life within the physical conditions of its environment.

Biological survival through cultural organization is the human mode of natural selection. And the various species of cultural patterns spread their values throughout the populations acculturated to them. Once this outcome is fully realized, the significance of survival value will hardly be in question any longer. Indeed, most anthropologists equate values with the system of values exhibited in a cultural pattern. What I have been pointing out is simply that such systems of values embedded in a population acculturated to them constitute a biological species on the cultural level—'an interthinking population' George Simpson calls them in distinction from 'an interbreeding population' which would be the whole human species. But note also that a cultural species interbreeds propagating its specific cultural pattern.

Thus, though being on the cultural level, the competing cultural value systems do not escape from the process of biological natural selection. The survival of the fittest still applies to them in full force. They are subject to the demands of adaptation in the human life zone. The better adapted cultural patterns displace the less adapted. And if ever the principle of cultural adaptation should fail in the human environment, the human species would inevitably perish and join the company of such other extinct species as the mammoth and the dinosaur. Adaptive selection is definitely an evaluative selection bearing on human actions, as intimately and pervasively as purposive selections. Moreover, adaptive selection is just what survival value means.

One most important point for our theory still remains to be made in the relation of survival value to purposive values. For their aims are quite different and often opposed. As we have said, the overall aim of survival value is adaptation, while that of the purposive values is satisfaction. Now adaptation in the human life zone entails socialization to a cultural pattern and often drastic sacrifice of satisfactions. It leads into the domain of duties that may completely overshadow satisfactions. I know only two philosophers who seem to me to have fully grasped this point. They are Kant and C. I. Lewis. Lewis makes the point most clearly because he is very sympathetic towards an empirical treatment of value as regards satisfactions. These are not to be disparaged as Kant tends to do. Yet Lewis senses that satisfactions will never yield by their own dynamics the ultimate demands which man as a social species makes for overindividual security and harmony. In his perplexity Lewis plunges for an *a priori* to clinch the realm of moral obligation and social duties. But what a weak sanction is the logical *a priori* (or even Kant's 'good will') to offset the threat of human annihilation which the dynamics of biological survival value hold over the human species!

As I read the evidence for an empirical theory of value, there are two opposite dynamic poles for the generation of value—the pole for the maximization of individual satisfactions through prudence and intelligent social cooperation, and the pole for the continuous necessity of biological adaptation whatever it may cost in periods of emergency in the sacrifice of satisfactions. Through social intelligence men may keep the impact of the sanctions for survival at a distance and so allow satisfactions a wide range of freedom to expand. But if this social intelligence lags and fails, the penalties of biological maladaptation to the life zone man himself has largely brought into being will inexorably take their toll.

And the most dangerous way by which our social intelligence could fail today would be a persistent blindness to, and denial of, the existence and sanctioning power of survival value and its polar opposition in periods of emergency to the values of satisfaction.

I must stop here with the bare stressing of this point. For the ramifications of this bipolar interaction of human values would lead us out very far.

My main points in this paper are, first, that values are generated from the transactions of selective systems in the manner earlier described, and, second, that there are two distinct main dynamic sources for human values, that of the purposive selective system and its derivatives generated from human needs, drives, etc., and that of the adaptive selective system generated from the patterning processes of the genes through inheritance and its human derivative, acculturation. The characteristic values of the first are individual satisfactions, of the second the overindividual imperatives of social security and survival. They have a sort of polar opposition to each other. But both are essential to the existence of human values at all, and have a share in the dynamics of all intervening selective systems between the immediate purposive consummatory aesthetic satisfaction of pleasure for its own sake and the ultimate biological selective system of the adaptive preservation of the species. In short, survival value is essential to the complete adequacy of an empirical value theory.*

* An expansion of the views expressed in this paper may be found in the author's *The Sources of Value*, University of California Press, 1958, chapters 20 and 21, and *Ethics*, Appleton-Century-Crofts, New York, 1960, chapters 10 and 13.

Recommended Reading—
Parts I and II

Ackoff, Russell L. *Scientific Method: Optimizing Applied Research Designs.* New York: John Wiley & Sons, Inc., 1962.

Arnspiger, Clyde, Rucker, W. Ray, and Preas, Mary. *Personality in Social Process.* Dubuque, Iowa: William C. Brown Book Co., 1969.

Axtelle, George E. 'The Humanizing of Knowledge and the Education of Values,' *Educational Theory*, **XVI,** 1966. **No. 2.**

Barber, Bernard. *Science and the Social Order.* Glencoe: Free Press, 1952.

Brameld, Theodore. *Education for the Emerging Age.* New York: Harper and Row, 1965.

Daedalus, Holton, G. (ed.). *Science and Culture.* Boston: Houghton, Mifflin, 1965.

Darwin, Charles. *Origin of the Species.* New York: Modern Library.

DeGeorge, R. T. *Science and Ideology in Soviet Society.* New York: Atherton, 1967.

Dubos, René. *So Human an Animal.* New York: Charles Scribner's Sons, 1968.

Dupré, S. S., and Kakoff, S. A. *Science and the Nation.* Englewood Cliffs: Prentice Hall, 1964.

Glass, H. B. *Science and Ethical Values.* Chapel Hill: University of North Carolina Press, 1965.

Gregg, J. R. (ed.). *Form and Strategy in Science.* Dordrecht, Holland: D. Reidel, 1964.

Hall, E. W. *Modern Science and Human Values.* New York: Van Nostrand, 1956.

Holmberg, Allen R. 'The Changing Values and Institutions of Vicos in the Context of National Development,' *The American Behavioral Scientist*, **VIII,** No. 7, 1965.

Jonas, Hans. *The Phenomenon of Life.* New York: Harper and Row, 1966.

Kaplan, Norman. *Science and Society.* Chicago: Rand, McNally, 1965.

Knox, T. M. *Action.* London: G. Allen and Unwin, 1968.

Lasswell, Harold. *The Communication of Ideas.* New York: Harper and Bros., 1948.

Lasswell, Harold. *Power and Personality.* New York: W. W. Norton and Co., 1948.

Lasswell, Harold. *Psychopathology and Politics.* New York: The Viking Press, 1960.

Lasswell, Harold. 'Universality in Perspective,' *Proceedings of the American Society of International Law*, 1959.

E

Laszlo, Ervin. *System, Structure and Experience.* New York: Gordon & Breach, 1969.

Lundbert, G. A. *Can Science Save Us?* New York: Longmans, Green, 1961.

Margenau, H. *Ethics and Science.* New York: Van Nostrand, 1964.

Maslow, Abraham (ed.). *New Knowledge of Human Values.* New York: Harpers, 1959.

Maslow, Abraham. *Toward a Psychology of Being.* Second Edition. Princeton: D. Van Nostrand Co., 1968.

Nelson, William R. (ed.). *The Politics of Science.* New York: Oxford University Press, 1968.

Pepper, S. C. *Concept and Quality.* La Salle, Ill.: Open Court, 1967.

Pepper, S. C. *Ethics.* New York: Appleton-Century-Crofts, 1960.

Pepper, S. C. *The Sources of Value.* Berkeley and Los Angeles: University of California Press, 1958.

Polanyi, Michael. *Science, Faith and Society.* Chicago: University of Chicago Press, 1966.

Rogers, Carl. 'Toward a Modern Approach to Values: The Valuing Process in the Mature Person,' *The Journal of Abnormal and Social Psychology.* **68**, No. 2, 1964.

Rubenstein, Robert, and Lasswell, Harold. *The Sharing of Power in a Psychiatric Hospital.* New Haven, Yale University Press, 1966.

Rucker, W. Ray, Arnspiger, Clyde, and Brodbeck, A. J. *Human Values in Education.* Dubuque, Iowa: Wm. C. Brown, 1969.

Shapley, Harlow. *Beyond the Observatory.* New York: Charles Scribner's Sons, 1966.

Simpson, G. G. *The Meaning of Evolution.* New Haven, Connecticut: Yale University Press, 1949.

Simpson, George Gaylord. *This View of Life.* New York: Harcourt, Brace and World, 1964.

Snow, C. P. *Science and Government.* Cambridge: Harvard University Press, 1961.

Szent-Györgyi, Albert. *Science, Ethics and Politics.* New York: Vantage Press, 1963.

Thorpe, W. H. *Science, Man and Morals.* Ithaca: Cornell University Press, 1967.

Weinberg, Albin W. *Reflections on Big Science.* Cambridge: M.I.T. Press, 1967.

Whyte, Lancelot Law. *The Next Development in Man.* London: Cresset Press, 1944.

Wolfe, D. L. *Science and Public Policy.* Lincoln: University of Nebraska Press, 1957.

Naturalistic Facts and Human Values

The Rationality of Facts
and Values

EDWARD F. WALTER

University of Missouri, Kansas City

I

The contemporary English-American view is that fact statements and value statements are separated by a logical gulf. It is argued that value statements function in a unique way that is not reducible to the way in which fact statements function. According to this view, value judgments present a logic of their own and can be validated by the application of their own criteria.

The source of the separation of fact statements and value statements is David Hume's famous logical rule which asserted that since both types of statements belong in different categories, the latter cannot be deduced from the former. It is important for my purpose to note that it appears at the end of the first part of the third book of *A Treatise of Human Nature,* for I will argue that the basis for the rule is what is said in the earlier parts of this section. I contend that Hume seriously misconceives the reasoning and the evaluative processes, and that his rule rests on these misconceptions. The contemporary philosopher no longer accepts Hume's conception of reasoning and evaluating, yet retains the rule without offering a new justification for it. He merely presupposes that there is an essential difference between the two types of statements. Furthermore, I will argue that there is good reason to believe that this rule cannot be justified in light of the contemporary view of the reasoning process. I will try to show that both scientific and value problems require rational processes. However, since there are different subjects, each will contain unique features. Furthermore, the obstructions to rational resolutions of ethical disputes encumber scientific advances as well.

Hume begins his discussion of the role of reason in moralizing by noting that moral judgments are intended to influence passions and emotions which requires an active process. Reason, he argues, cannot account for this activity, for it is a passive process of receiving impressions.

Hume's argument is based on the truth of the Lockian notion that when we reason, we passively receive impressions, and that through this process, we obtain facts. Since morality is concerned with passions and actions, an active principle is required to direct behavior. Reason, being passive in all its forms, cannot causally influence our emotions or passions. Consequently, emotions and passions are distinct responses which are separated from other emotions and passions in that one emotional or passionate response cannot affect or be affected by another. This being so, they cannot be said to be true or false. The moral judgment, according to Hume, is the expression of emotion or passion.[1]

It certainly follows that if the Humian description of reasoning and moralizing is correct, then one cannot deduce a value statement from a fact statement. Since he argued that a moral judgment is an expression of emotion or passion that cannot be influenced by reason, it adds very little to say that we cannot deduce one from the other.

I think that most contemporary thinkers recognize that the Humian conceptions of reasoning and moralizing are untenable in light of our present evidence. There is good reason to believe that neither process is purely active or passive, that the gathering of facts is not a value-free process, and that our emotions and evaluations are causally affected by the knowledge of facts. The problem for the contemporary philosopher of ethics is to decide to what extent reasoning influences valuations. It is my impression that the contemporary philosopher who follows either the C. L. Stevenson version of the emotive theory or the present 'autonomy of ethics' approach either reverts to the untenable Humian separation of facts and values or merely assumes that they are separate.

In short, I contend that the separation of facts and values has become in our times an unquestioned assumption. In light of our present knowledge, its present status is one of a prejudice. If it is to be retained, new grounds must be offered to support it. Again, in light of our present knowledge, I believe that there is little hope for a new support for this dichotomy.

II

If Hume were right about how we reason, morality would not be the only casualty. Science, as has often been noted, would be impossible. If reason be passive in all its forms, as Hume argued, then the scientifically-essential conceptions of causality and inductive inference become denuded. The reduction of the former to a regularity of appearances and the latter to probability cannot produce the necessary connection among the relations we observe in experience without which the scientist cannot control and predict. The reliance on emotively acceptable terms like 'probability' cannot disguise the fact that scientific expectation is being reduced to psychological expectation. If regularity of appearance cannot establish a necessary connection among relations (and I agree that it cannot), then it cannot establish probability either. Regularity of appearance refers to the past, and not to the future. About this, at least, Hume was right.

However, since my paper is not primarily concerned with the effect of the Humian conception of reasoning on science, I will not develop this point further.

In ethics, his theory reduces the moral judgment to a response that is uncaused by training and conditioning, cannot be causally affected by knowledge of facts that may be acquired, and finally cannot be causally influenced by previous emotional states. Each evaluation is a separate and distinct emotional response which is unrelated to any other.

III

In the first place, the claim that the reasoning process is passive is false. The contemporary view holds that from the moment of birth perception is an active process. The newborn infant does not passively receive impressions from the world, but actively interacts with it. It is a well-attested to fact that the environment at least to a significant, although not complete, extent determines how we perceive the world. This active process involves the attempt by the organism to satiate biological needs. In the early days of life, they are satisfied by the parent or guardian. His or her method of satisfying needs influences later reactions to stimuli. It influences the way we perceive the world. We are not surprised to find that the embryonic patrician perceives the world somewhat differently from the way it is perceived by an indi-

vidual raised in a Nazi concentration camp. The very uncertainty of
life in a concentration camp may cause an individual to observe more
closely so that he can be prepared to deal with any threat to his existence. He may also respond more passionately and fearfully to changes
in the environmental conditions.

Of course, there are similarities between the experiences of two such
individuals. This is attested to by the well-developed state of communication among people. Similarities occur because we not only act
upon our environment, our environment acts upon us. If we were entirely free of outside influences, we would live in a completely subjective world which would make communication impossible. Despite
similarities, however, there are unique aspects to each individual's perception of the world which results from the particular way in which
he has been exposed to the world; the particular way he has learned to
respond to it; and the particular condition of his organism.

Modern science, I believe, supports me in this contention. J. Z.
Young, for example, investigated the visual learning ability of people
who were able to see for the first time in adult life.[2] His study surprisingly found that visual acuity had to be taught; that his subjects
did not make the visual distinctions that ordinary people make.
Furthermore, most of his subjects, even after considerable training,
found vision to be disappointing, difficult to master, and an inferior
discriminator in comparison to the other senses. Lastly, he found that
only a few learned to read and to use vision as a primary source of
experience. These final steps were only achieved when the subjects
were convinced of the value of the enterprise.

Just as our reception of the world is not value-free, our emotional
life does not develop independently of our past conditioning and our
growth of knowledge. It may be interesting to remind the reader that
according to Hume, the emotional life does not grow at all. Since every
emotional response is a complete whole in itself and unrelated to any
other, there can be only capricious, haphazard responses. There obviously would be no continuity in our emotional lives. If an individual
responds angrily to a particular stimulus at one moment, we have no
reason to expect him to react in the same manner if the stimulus is
repeated.

It is certainly recognizable, today, that the human being does not
evince two separate processes—one for reasoning and another for emo-
ting, with this latter process, according to Hume, leading to the moral
judgment. The fact is that emotions develop as a result of the training
—the knowledge and the habits of responding to stimuli—that is de-

veloped throughout a lifetime. The bearing that the emotions have on moralizing is also the result of the training one has undergone. In some instances, moral judgments are as Hume described—the expressions of emotional states. But it is important to realize that these uses of emotion result from training, and are alterable in light of future training. In other instances, people put aside feelings and emotions in moralizing. And so Major Picquart defended Captain Dreyfus' claim of innocence despite the fact that he, personally, did not like the man and that his own career was threatened by telling the truth.[3] According to his own report, he did so because he believed it to be the right thing to do. (Although he might not have been able to give a rational justification for his belief, others can.)

It is important to realize that emotions have the same effect on science—where reason is supposed to have full sway. When Copernicus disagreed with the Ptolemaic tradition concerning the relationship of celestial bodies and the earth, there were those who argued against his hypothesis on the grounds that it conflicted with the authority of the Bible. Those who defended this position fell into two groups: one, those who argued through reason that the Bible could be trusted as an authority; and two, those who expressed their emotional preference for accepting the Bible as an authority in spite of the evidence. The former individual could be convinced that his claim was false. The latter could not. In subsequent centuries, the weight of the evidence so strongly supported the Copernican theory that even the latter type of theologian had to give way. But the point is that he did so only under the threat of being discounted as a serious force in the world. In more recent times, the theory of evolution was rejected by some fundamentalist Christians on non-rational grounds because it upset their emotional security. They, too, had to give way. Again, they did so not because of the force of reason, but in order to maintain their place of eminence in the modern world.

Emotions interfere with reasoning both in moral evaluations and science. What the emotional states of an individual are and how they are used depend upon the training, which includes knowledge, which one has undergone. The importance of this for ethical theory is that we have not learned to deal with emotion in a moral problem while we have in science.

IV

The writings of contemporary followers of Hume are vague about the

E*

nature of emotions. They (Ayer, Stevenson, Hare, *et al.*) hold that attitudes ultimately determine moral beliefs. Although reasoning may occur in moralizing, an assumption will be found that contains an attitude. (Supposedly, attitudes are not found in science.) It is important for their theories that the terms 'attitude' and 'emotion' receive more explication than they give them.

Hume treated 'emotions' and 'attitudes' as immediate bodily reactions to stimuli which are independent of knowledge. In some way, the contemporary emotivist wants to retain the reduction of 'attitudes' to non-cognitive bodily processes. However, I do not believe that his wish can be fulfilled.

It must be granted that each human being has a unique physical structure that reacts uniquely to stimuli. Pain, physical exercise, etc. are individually and uniquely experienced. The amount of food required varies according to the composition of the organism. Some individuals, because of their physical structure, require more activity than others; some individuals, because of auditory acuity, are more sensitive to music. But these physical characteristics are not synonymous with or the sole determinants of attitudes. Attitudes are developed as a result of exposure (the social environment), training, reflection, and to give Hume his due, base physical endowments. A tone-deaf person will not love music despite his conditioning, but an individual whose hearing is highly sensitive will reap the advantages of a musical environment more readily and happily than his less-endowed brothers and sisters.

Attitudes, then, are dispositions to react favorably or unfavorably to stimuli. Furthermore, modern psychology and sociology credit training as an essential condition of this development. Music lovers are made, not born. Even more, sociologists tell us that the kind of music that is loved is determined by the cultural bias. Philosophy might add that reflection permits one to adjust the influences acting upon us.

If an individual is repulsed by a black (feeling), predisposed to find fault with him (attitudinal), beliefs about the constitutional inferiority of the black race and/or fears of the consequences of granting equality to them will be found. It is also certain that new information and training can modify the attitude of the white.

According to Hume, we would expect to find that the emotions and attitudes would be independent of the beliefs that the individual has. This is not the case. Neither bigotry nor tolerance, occurs apart from a social context in which certain beliefs are held and a certain training has taken place. Similarly, the ability of the individual to modify and alter feelings and attitudes depends upon beliefs that are held about them. In an environment which elevates emotion and deprecates science and rationality, the impact of new information about race will be lessened.

Attitudes, even if they are considered to be the source of moral judgments, are not as Hume conceived them to be—necessarily independent of knowledge and reason. They are developed through training and knowledge and can be altered if new information is found, old information is re-interpreted, new conditions arise, etc.

V

This being the case, that reasoning can alter attitudes, I would now like to argue that we can give good reasons for preferring this method as a guideline for behavior rather than non-rational conditioning. I have been arguing that our attitudes and evaluations are the product of our knowledge and our conditioning. In some cases, the conditioning we have been exposed to is the development of a rational process. In other cases, we learn to respond irrationally to stimuli. So, we meet people who argue that prayer cures disease in spite of any contrary evidence. We also meet people who capriciously dislike Negroes, foreigners, and communists. As children, they have been taught that certain beliefs, emotions, and values were justified without reason. In such cases we do not say that rational processes are impotent, as Hume did, we say that an individual who has been conditioned in this way has not developed, although he could have, a rational approach to his environment.

The assertion that prayer cures cancer is rejected because we have evidence that other methods may work, while there is no evidence that prayer works. The continuation of this belief in spite of the evidence is dismissed as irrational because we know only rational processes can, if anything can, guarantee man's end in developing science. The end of science is to control the physical environment so that man can develop his own interests which requires that he makes the environment serve him.

Similarly, in the case for values, if I do not learn to rationally develop and direct my feelings, I cannot master my environment.

The moral philosopher shifted from ethical absolutism to ethical relativism when he discovered that moral rules are man-made means of achieving man's ends. But man's interests are not served by permitting him to continue seeking ill-planned, thoughtless ends. Man's interests are derived from an understanding of the whole man, i.e. an understanding of his psycho-physical nature, and the social and physical conditions in which he operates. Emotions cannot lead to this understanding. Attitudes, more often than not, have been developed ignorantly. Only rational processes can lead to an understanding of the individual and his environment which produces interests which satisfy. Non-rational interests satisfy only accidently and capriciously.

While it is true that since each individual's interests, even if rationally derived, are unique because of the distinct nature of his organism and his environment, it does not follow that moral agreements among people cannot be reached. All human beings must interact with the physical and social environment. It is this fact which necessitates the development of a value system.

If no conflicts arise either among a person's own desires (smoking has no consequences other than giving pleasure) or his desires and the desires of other people (my desire for an active night-life coincides with my wife's, we have no children, we can afford it, our physical constitutions are such that we can function adequately living this way, etc.), then there is no problem of valuation. Problems of valuation arise only when we have conflicts in which the consequences of the acts are brought into question.

The possibility of developing a rational system of ethics does not hinge on the possibility of all people finding out through the employment of the rational method that they have the same desires and interests. It hinges on the fact that the best possibility of maintaining one's interests is in rationally resolving disputes with others, since our interests and desires have ramifications for others as well as for ourselves. If we are concerned with our own interests, as the opposition will suggest, and I will not deny, then we cannot avoid considering the environmental conditions in which we live, which requires that we, at times, must modify our desires and interests here and now for future interests.

VI

At the beginning of the paper, I said that I would try to prove that the contemporary philosophers who hold to the belief that there is a logical gulf between fact statements and value judgments eventually base their belief on an inadequate Humian conception of the reasoning and valuing processes or an uncritical, unjustified acceptance of the logical rule.

Many of those who hold the Humian rule might admit that the rational process may be used in *all* cases in order to determine what a person's value system is, but they would argue that this cannot guarantee that *all* moral disagreements among people can be resolved because people have different value systems. They would say that a moral agreement can only be logically attained, if both people to a dispute employ the same moral system. I think that this argument would be made by those who follow either the C. L. Stevenson version of the emotive theory or the 'autonomy of ethics' approach espoused by R. M. Hare.

Stevenson talks about 'attitudes' eventually separating disputants and Hare about 'decisions in principle' separating them. The point is the same in both cases; the acceptance of the 'attitude' or 'way of life' upon which the decision in principle is made is non-factual.

In order to illustrate my point, I would like to refer to an example used by C. L. Stevenson in his book *Ethics and Language*. He considers a dispute about whether or not it is moral to engage in pre-marital intercourse. One disputant argues in favor of it on the grounds that the reason for the inception of the rule—the possibility of becoming pregnant—has disappeared as the result of the development of birth control methods. The second disputant argues that this does not change his evaluation, for despite the rule's origin, its continuance can be justified on the grounds that the possibility of pregnancy still exists, psychological harm can be done to people if the rule is changed, etc. At this point, Stevenson asserts that the problem becomes too complicated for a rational resolution.

> As our discussion proceeds, it becomes more and more apparent, particularly since many of the methods can appear in the same argument, and repeatedly, how very complicated ethical questions can become. It is partly for that reason, no doubt, that many people consider certain matters 'too sacred' to be freely discussed. The factors that determine what our attitudes are to be are so multitudinous and bewildering that most of us are afraid to face them.[4]

He goes on to say that some people cannot continue to reason about the problem, and that the problem is resolved by a resort to appeals to authority, consensus of opinion, etc.

But to leave the argument at this point is not to prove that rational methods cannot resolve the disagreement, only that, as a matter of fact, they do not in many cases. The fact that people desert rational means of resolving disagreements does not mean that rational methods are impotent at that point. The fact that a man does not accept the scientific evidence that he has cancer does not mean that the scientific evidence is not relevant to the problem of whether or not he has cancer, it only means that the individual has deserted the rational method.

In the problem of pre-marital sex, if the person A, who favored it, went on to point out that the second person B, cannot seriously maintain his position for his argument that the possibility of pregnancy still exists is specious in that the probability of pregnancy is negligible, and that if this standard were accepted, we would not even leave our apartments, and while at home, we would not take the risk of bathing, etc. If B argued that the gravity of the problem determines the risk we will take, it can be pointed out to him that he takes greater risks with less chance of success than is afforded by this fact for less serious ends.

At this point, the disputants may digress into a discussion of the criteria of 'gravity.' Assuming that both disputants continue to use the rational method, this problem can be solved. It can be pointed out, for example, that speeding on a highway to arrive on time at a dinner party is assuming a great risk for an insignificant end. It can be shown that the gravity of a problem is determined by the consequences that accrue to a course of action, not to the feelings one has about it. An unpleasant feeling about being late for a party is not worth risking life. The consequences of the unpleasant feelings are insignificant. It will be forgotten in a day or two. If it is not, we have a subject for a psychiatrist.

Returning to the original dispute, I believe that it can be shown that B is applying a criteria of gravity that is not consonant with the facts, i.e. the consequences of an accidental pregnancy, although great, are not so great that risks are always inadvisable.

If B maintains that he still favors the rule against pre-marital sex, we would ask for another justification for his claim. If he answers that his attitude determines his decision, then he has deserted the rational method. He can be reminded of the fact that the rule was devised in the first place as a means to an end, and that he, himself, had defended it in the second place as a means to another end. He might be asked why rational arguments were relevant then, but aren't now that these reasons are no longer tenable. If B argued that the reasons did not actually give rise to the evaluations—they were rationalizations—it can be shown that this is not the case. Moral injunctions against premarital sex, and other similar rules, were developed as means to resolving problems that arose in different societies. When the rule is retained without a rational justification, we have a reliance on attitude, but one that did not have to occur. If it maintained that some people like B are incapable of using rational methods either because of lack of training or a constitutional deficiency, he may be reminded that the same fact applies to scientific methods—not everyone is capable of being an adequate scientist. This is not a reason for using an alternate method.

A comparison of some scientific disputes—those which broke new ground or upset long-established theories—with ethical disputes would turn up the same bewildering, complicated arguments. Since disputants were uncertain as to what assumptions could or could not be relied upon or what direction the investigation would take, only the talented maintained emotional equilibrium throughout the controversy. But science has emerged from its youthful search for a method which deludes observers into misconceiving its past. Ethics, as John Dewey pointed out, has not yet achieved a method since it only recently divorced itself from the platonic absolutism of its past.

Again, to return to the dispute, if B asserted that the injunction was justifiable simply because of the feelings or attitude that he has about it, this, itself, is a moral claim that calls for reasoned support. C. L. Stevenson has supplied the intellectual support in a recent paper.

> 'In this realm (of creating values) we are kings, and we debase our kingship if we bow down to nature.' . . . When we no longer have to fear that our judgments are unfaithful to something 'out there,' it may be urged, why should we evince anything more than a half-hearted willingness to revise them? Or alternatively (and the alternative is equally distressing) why should we not revise them capriciously, changing our judgments with each passing whim.[5]

We should 'bow down to nature' because we *are* part of nature and cannot avoid natural consequences; we should not revise our attitudes capriciously because we *are* concerned with consequences. Self-autonomy *is* desired as a means of attaining and setting ends. Once this is admitted, we acquire responsibility for achieving these enterprises, which requires the intelligent development of ends and the intelligent discernment of means to these ends.

VII

There are a number of misconceptions that have grown around the distinction between facts and values which obscure the real nature for the distinction. I have argued through this paper that the ground for the distinction was the mistaken notion that the rational method cannot be used, at least in some cases, to arrive at an evaluation. I have argued that it can be used in principle in all cases, although it may not, as a matter of fact, resolve every problem. It may not because of any of the following reasons: the unwillingness of the participants to use reason, their inability to use it, lack of information, etc. But these factors impede scientific studies as well.

The psychological factors which led philosophers such as Hume to doubt that rational methods can lead to 'moral facts' was that the beliefs in a God-given law and an intuited ideal good were coming under intellectual fire. The other alternative—that moral rules were man-made—was unacceptable because of the platonic prejudice against emotions and appetites. These were considered anti-rational. Consequently, any judgment considering them must be capricious, relative to the individual, and irrational. I have tried to show that this is not necessarily the case.

What the traditional empiricist who separates facts and values often does is to distinguish the unique characteristics of values from the unique characteristics of physical objects. It is obvious that I do not 'see' goodness, while I do 'see' stones and water. But perception through sense experience has never been the sole ground for asserting that something is a fact. I do not 'see' psychological states, but no one would deny that assertions about them are factual.

Nor can we base the distinction on the grounds that values are personal and alterable, while facts are impersonal and inalterable. This distinction leads to the conclusion that values are subjective and relative, and facts are objective and universal.

To say that values are personal does not distinguish them from other things about persons that are considered to be factual. Similarly, to say that facts about stones have features that other facts do not have is to identify that subject matter and no more. To say that values are alterable is to point out that they depend on the conditions in which value problems arise. Similarly, to state 'facts' about physical objects is to characterize the thing being described under certain conditions. The facts about physical objects are alterable according to the conditions as well as in the case of values. The alterability of a value that would make it nonfactual would be that it is capriciously arrived at and capriciously changed. This would be true if values could only be the expression of the desires of individuals. Then, they would be, as well, subjective and relative. But I have tried to show that while we consider desires in evaluating, we do not reduce one to the other. This follows because we realize that desires are not independent of knowledge and training. They arise because of beliefs and training, and can be changed by altering beliefs and re-training.

The relevant argument for the claim that moral judgments are not factual is to show that rationality is impotent in this regard. Hume tried to do this and failed. Too many contemporary philosophers merely assume that rationality is either impotent or limited in this regard without proving it. To point out that the rational method is not usually used does not prove that it cannot be used. To point out that moral problems, because of their multiple consequences, are not easy to resolve rationally does not prove that they cannot be. Both of these points can be made about scientific problems as well. The scientist does not desert his method because he realizes that it is the only method available to him for learning about his physical environment. Similarly, the moralist should not desert the rational method in his area because of the complexity of the problems with which he deals.

Finally, when R. M. Hare asserts that every ethical argument contains, at least, a suppressed moral premise, he merely assumes that it is non-factual. His argument only proves that each argument contains assumptions which are undefended in specific contexts. But if this be a defect, science is equally faulted. To conclude that these assumptions are non-factual requires proof. Hare does not give it; Hume tried and failed.

Notes and References

1. David Hume, *A Treatise of the Human Understanding*, Book III, Part 1, Oxford at the Clarendon Press, Great Britain, 1958, pp. 456–68.
2. J. Z. Young, *Doubt and Certainty in Science*, New York: Oxford University Press, 1960.
3. For maintaining that the truth must be told, Picquart was eventually tried and jailed. Eventually, of course, he was freed and reinstated in the army at the rank of general. Sometimes, the truth pays.
4. C. L. Stevenson, *Ethics and Language*, New Haven and London: Yale University Press, 1962, pp. 124–5.
5. Charles L. Stevenson, 'Ethical Fallibility,' Richard T. DeGeorge (ed.), *Ethics and Society: Original Essays on Contemporary Moral Problems*, Anchor Books: Doubleday & Co., Inc., Garden City, New York, 1966, p. 212.

On Bridging the Gap Between Fact and Value

MAY LEAVENWORTH

Lehman College

I

In his article 'The Relation of Fact and Value: A Reassessment,'[1] Prof. Abraham Edel has presented the hypothesis that the differences between the various positions taken in the fact-value inquiry rest upon different presuppositions concerning the nature of the self. He points out that the tradition which sharply separates fact and value, the 'ought' and the 'is,' and claims that one cannot derive 'ought' from 'is' (thereby making science irrelevant to value inquiry) presupposes the conception of a self outside of, and apart from, the casually determined natural universe. He exemplifies this theory of the self by reference to 'the free man in Russell's early essay, 'A Free Man's Worship,' brandishing his fist at matter rolling on its relentless way.'

I think that there is indeed a connection between this theory of a self separated from the universe described and presupposed by natural science, and the sharp bifurcation of fact and value. My objective in this section of my paper will be to show this connection between what I am calling the 'theory of the alienated self' and the fact-value bifurcation, as exemplified by the writings of both intuitionist and prescriptivist non-naturalists.

In neither the intuitionist nor the prescriptivist tradition do we find an analysis of the act of evaluating as being itself a natural process worthy of scientific, factual scrutiny. There is no discussion of a person's reasons for choosing his values, where these reasons express facts about both himself and his environment as he performs the evaluative act. Instead, we have, in the case of Moore, an implicit pre-supposition of a non-natural self that merely intuits intrinsic good, a non-natural property. No reason can be given for calling a thing 'good.' And in the case of the prescriptivists we have an implicit non-natural self performing a purely verbal act of commending. Again, no analysis is given of possible reasons for commending. Any discussion of the act of commending as a psychological act, rather than a purely verbal, or logical one, is avoided.

Why do we have this shunning of the use of science in ethics? The answer usually given is the open-question argument, which shows the permanent possibility of evaluating any set of purely factual premises. We may ask of any such set, 'But is that good?' Even if we include in the set of facts the needs and desires of the person evaluating, he may still ask of those psychological facts about himself, 'Are they good?' The non-naturalists then conclude that one cannot derive values from facts alone. One cannot define 'good' in factual terms, for that destroys it's evaluative meaning. Therefore, they claim that no amount of scientific study, which can only provide us with facts, can be of use in the determining of values. Value can only be determined in some mysterious, or random way, by the alienated self asking of matter as it 'rolls on it's relentless way,' 'Is that good?' Values are non-natural and non-factual, while the subject matter of the sciences is natural and factual.

On the factual side of the fact-value bifurcation, we find the natural self with needs and desires as described by the social sciences. But according to the presuppositions of the non-naturalists, that natural self cannot be identified with the other alienated self that intuits intrinsic goods or performs verbal acts of commending, for, so the argument goes, this would involve a loss of the evaluative meaning of good, since the desires and needs of the natural self may themselves be evaluated. The non-naturalists claim that, in order to have evaluation, a sharp bifurcation must be maintained between fact and value, and this requirement is based on the assumption of the alienated self whose function is to evaluate. In the second section of this paper, I shall show that not only is such a bifurcation not required, but that it is, in fact, impossible. It is only thought to be necessary because of the theory of the alienated self upon which the bifurcation rests. I shall argue that, if we replace the alienated self with the natural self of the social sciences, values become the institutions of society, and as such they are both facts and values.

But first, I want to document, in the theories and writings of prominent non-naturalists, the claims I have made concerning their presupposition of the theory of the alienated self. I also want to show that, in spite of the fact that they never did leave the alienated presupposition behind, there has nevertheless been a gradual trend toward recognizing the evaluating human being as a natural entity performing a natural function within the universe described and presupposed by natural science. In this essay I hope to take the final step in that trend by recognizing the act of evaluating as a natural function of the natural self.

To show the trend in this direction, I must start by mentioning someone who was not a non-naturalist at all, but who was what I shall call a *limited* naturalist. He is none other than Herbert Spencer, the man who identified 'good' with 'more evolved.' The problem with Spencer and other limited naturalists was that, although they attempted to see man as a natural entity within the universe described and presupposed by natural science, they neglected his natural function of taking a pro or con attitude toward things and events that affect him. Though they recognized the natural self, they didn't recognize the natural act of evaluating. (I call them *limited* naturalists to distinguish them from another kind of naturalism I shall discuss in section II, which does recognize the evaluative act). Spencer, for examply, by identifying 'good' definitively with 'more evolved,' ignored the evaluative meaning of good, and hence failed to see that man does not merely accept passively whatever events impinge on him. He reacts to them, sometimes positively, sometimes negatively.

G. E. Moore exposed the error of such definitions of 'good' by use of the open-question argument already mentioned. One can always ask of any such definitions of 'good,' which neglect man's evaluative function, 'Is that good?' Thus we may ask of Spencer's definition, 'Is it good to be more evolved?' Moore's conclusion as to the implications of the open-question argument is that 'good,' though a property of objects, is not to be confused with any of the natural properties of objects. It is a non-natural property, which can only be intuited. We know by intuition, both the meaning of 'good' and to which objects the word applies. He writes,

> Whenever (one) thinks of "intrinsic value," or "intrinsic worth," or says that a thing "ought to exist," he has before his mind the unique object—the unique property of things—which I mean by "good".[2]

Moore hopes in this way to rescue man's evaluative function from the limited naturalists. Although Moore doesn't use the phrase 'man's evaluative function,' the exercise of such a function is implied in the fact that minds have direct contact with the non-natural property of intrinsic value in things. They intuit this value.

This analysis rescues the evaluative function, but at the expense of introducing mysterious non-natural properties into things. It also makes the evaluative function a non-natural process. Value is not the result of a natural interaction between a man as a natural entity and his natural environment. Instead, Moore cuts value off from the evaluating subject and makes it the exclusive property of the object or objects evaluated. Value becomes a property of organic unities, and the evaluator considers these unities in isolation in order to discover, by intuition, their property of intrinsic value. The evaluator may, for example, imagine the existence of a very beautiful world and conclude that such a world would have intrinsic value even if it could never be contemplated by conscious beings. True, Moore says than an organic whole that included conscious beings in that beautiful world would be better, but this doesn't change the fact that Moore assumes that an intrinsic value such as beauty could exist in isolation from any evaluator. But this could not, even theoretically, be the case if values were the result of interaction between the evaluator and natural objects. Moore discounts any such interaction. For him, beauty could never be in the eyes of the beholder. On the contrary, beauty has nothing to do with the beholder; it belongs to the object. The beholder only discovers the pre-existent value. The fundamental objective of Ethics is then, according to Moore, to discover the intrinsic values of things. And this can be accomplished, theoretically, by isolating organic wholes and intuiting their goodness. Once this fundamental ethical task is accomplished, then science can tell us the means for maximizing the good we have discovered.

But what can be the nature of the self that performs the function of intuiting non-natural properties? The natural self performing the natural acts of sensing only discovers the natural properties of things, i.e. their color, shape, size, etc. The natural self discovers facts only. Therefore, the beholder who discovers the pre-existent intrinsic values of those same things must be endowed with a special non-natural faculty that enables him to intuit those non-natural properties— the values in things. So the assumption must be that of the alienated self that performs this non-natural function of intuiting non-natural properties. No psychological analysis of that self and it's evaluating act can be given. It simply intuits the good and no reason can be given for saying a thing is good. It just is and that is the end of the matter. The natural self studied by psychology, with needs, desires, sense perception, etc. is irrelevant to the determination of value. It can only discover facts. Moore has rescued the human evaluating process from the limited naturalists, but in so doing has given up the naturalist position of making the self that evaluates a natural entity within the universe described and presupposed by natural science. He has also created the sharp bifurcation of fact and value that always accompanies the theory of the alienated self.

R. M. Hare took another step in the trend I am describing by recognizing Moore's error in making 'good' a property of things. He pointed out that 'good' is not a property, but a word used to perform the verbal act of commending. He thereby avoided the necessity of talking about non-natural properties and shifted attention temporarily from the object being evaluated to the act of evaluating. It was an important step in the direction of recognizing the evaluating self as the natural entity described and presupposed by science, yet Hare didn't take the final step. He clung instead to the remnants of the presupposition of the alienated self and to it's correlate, the sharp bifurcation of fact and value.

As Hare discusses the evaluative act, we find the presupposition of the alienated self in evidence. Whereas Moore concentrated his attention upon the object being evaluated, Hare concentrates on the logic of the verbal act of commending. In *both* cases a psychological account of the evaluator is avoided. Therefore, both of them fail to see evaluation as a natural interaction between the natural biological and psychological self and it's environment. Instead, we have the enigmatic alienated self taking a random pro or con attitude toward his environment and the effects if his actions. For Hare, as for Moore, the state of the evaluator seems to play little or no role in the determination of that pro or con attitude. Either the evaluator can give no reason at all for his choices or, if he does give a reason, that reason says little or nothing about himself. Hare writes:

> But suppose that we were to ask such a man "Why did you choose this set of effects rather than that? Which of the many effects were they that led you to decide the way you did?" His answer to this question might be of two kinds. He might say "I can't give any reasons; I just felt like deciding that way; another time, faced with the same choice, I might decide differently." On the other hand, he might say "It was this and this that made me decide; I was deliberately avoiding such and such effects, and seeking such and such." If he gave the first of these two answers, we might in a

certain sense of that word call his decision arbitrary (though even in that case he had *some* reason for his choice, namely that he felt that way); but if he gave the second, we should not.[3]

I must give attention to both types of reasons (or lack of reasons).

Hare never returns to a fuller analysis of the first type of reason that he has given. There is only this parenthetical acknowledgement that, to say that one chose because one *felt* that way is to give *some* reason for the choice. Had Hare pursued this line of thought he would have been forced into a consideration of the state of the evaluator as an important factor in the determination of value. For to feel like choosing one way rather than another in this particular situation is to recognize, though perhaps vaguely, that there is something lacking in the present situation, and that this lack creates a desire to alter the situation. This realization would have led to the recognition of a two-way interaction between the evaluator, with needs and desires, and his environment, and hence to the acceptance of the self as described and presupposed by natural science. But Hare gives no further attention to the state of the evaluator.

He goes on to discuss the second type of reason a person might give for choosing a certain set of effects. This is the type of reason in which a person says 'I was deliberately avoiding such and such effects and seeking such and such.' Hare gives this analysis of such a reason:

> Let us see what is involved in this second type of answer. Although we have assumed that the man has no formed principles, he shows, if he gives the second answer, that he has started to form principles for himself; for to choose effects *because* they are such and such is to begin to act on a principle that such and such effects are to be chosen.[4]

There is a return in part to the Mooreian positions of concentrating on the objects of evaluation to the exclusion of the act of evaluating and the qualities of the evaluator. No reason can be given for calling those objects 'good.' Hare simply says they are to be chosen, and no further reason can be given for so choosing. There is a strained avoidance of the fact that the most common answer given to the question 'Why did you choose this set of effects rather than that?' would be something like, 'Because I had a need or desire for the effects I chose,' or 'I thought they would satisfy the requirements of the situation.' If the man were clairvoyant, as Hare hypothesized earlier, he might say 'I *knew* the effects I chose would satisfy my needs.' However, as Hare aptly points out, we are not clairvoyant. 'Our knowledge of the future is fragmentary and only probable.' Therefore, we are urged to act in accordance with principles which tell us 'do this rather than that, and the effects are most likely to be such as you would have chosen, if you had known them.'[5] So principles enable us to make better predictions about the effects of our actions. But how can they tell us that the effects will be such as we would have chosen, unless those principles are formed, in the first place, on the basis of people's original reasons for choosing, namely people's needs—biological, psychological, and social? It is these original and basic reasons for choosing which tell us about the properties of the *evaluator*. And it is this type of reason that Hare ignores.

> Whenever we commend, we have in mind something about the *object* commended which is the reason for our commendation.[6] (Italics mine.)

It is this continued concentration on the properties of the object to the neglect of the evaluator that is the best indication of Hare's commitment to the theory of the alienated self. Hare could not say, any more than Moore could, that beauty is in the eye of the beholder. The properties of the self apparently contribute nothing to the evaluation process. When we commend a thing or an action, the only reason we can give for doing so is that it conforms to a standard or principle, but we can give no reasons in terms of human needs and the requirements of situations to justify acceptance of the standards and principles in the first place. The evaluator is a blank slate that doesn't really know why it formulates and adheres to one principle rather than another.

In the next section I shall present the hypothesis that principles are empirical generalizations that have resulted from many instances of evaluating in conflict situations and observing the effectiveness of actions chosen in fulfilling human needs. The reasons for choosing our principles of action will be that actions in accordance with the principles generally satisfy the requirements of the situations in which they are applicable. But such an analysis will not work as long as the theory of the alienated self is retained, as I shall show later.

The result of Hare's implicit presupposition of the alienated self is, as always, the sharp bifurcation of fact and value. It is assumed that there are two mutually exclusive classes of words in our language, value-words and descriptive words. Descriptive words simply tell us the properties of things as they exist independently of the alienated self. That is, they tell us the brute facts. Value words are used by that self to commend things in accordance with principles and standards, these being determined apparently by the whim of the alienated self. Values can only be determined, in the final analysis, by such a whim, since to try to base them on the facts of human existence would be to commit the naturalistic fallacy (according to such non-naturalists).

In the following words, Hare sets up this bifurcation between facts and value and attempts to expose, once and for all, the fallacy of 'naturalism in ethics,' thereby committing mankind for all eternity to an ethics based on the whim of an alienated self.

> Naturalism in ethics, like attempts to square the circle and to "justify induction," will constantly recur so long as there are people who have not understood the fallacy involved. It may therefore be useful to give a simple procedure for exposing any new variety of it that may be offered. Let us suppose that someone claims that he can deduce a moral or other evaluative judgment from a set of purely factual or descriptive premises, relying on some definition to the effect that V (a value-word) means the same as C (a conjunction of descriptive predicates). We first have to ask him to be sure that C contains no expression that is covertly evaluative (for example "natural" or "normal" or "satisfying" or "fundamental human needs"). Nearly all so-called "naturalistic definitions" will break down under this test—for to be genuinely naturalistic a definition must contain no expression for whose applicability there is not a definite criterion which does not involve the making of a value-judgment. If the definition satisfies this test, we have next to ask whether its advocate ever wishes to commend anything for being C. If he says that he does, we have only to point out to him that his definition makes this impossible, for the reasons given. And clearly he cannot say that he never wishes to commend anything for being C; for to commend things for being C is the whole object of his theory.[7]

This is, in fact, a good refutation of someone who 'claims he can deduce a moral or other evaluative judgment from a set of purely factual or descriptive premises.' For if anyone makes such a claim he is assuming the same sharp fact-value bifurcation assumed by the non-naturalists he hopes to refute. He is assuming the theory of the alienated self, and if one starts with the premises of the non-naturalist he cannot avoid reaching their conclusions.

Hare first saddles the naturalist with his presupposition of a sharp bifurcation between fact and value, and the implicit theory of the alienated self on which that bifurcation is based, and then proceeds to annihilate naturalism in ethics so conceived. But in fact all he has shown is the impossibility of getting a naturalist ethics out of non-naturalist presuppositions. His refutation is final with respect to such *limited* naturalists as Spencer who ignored man's evaluative function. However, his refutation does not touch a naturalism such as the one I shall now present, which makes man's natural evaluative function central. This naturalism is free from Hare's criticism because it rejects the sharp bifurcation of fact and value and the theory of the alienated self on which that bifurcation is based.

II

The theory I shall now present rests upon a theory of the evaluating self as a natural entity performing the natural act of evaluating in the universe described and presupposed by natural science. In other words, it is assumed that evaluation is carried out by human beings as described by biology, psychology, and sociology, and that the evaluative acts of these rational beings form a link in the natural, determinate chain of events described by those sciences. The evaluating processes will be the natural acts of biological organisms with highly developed intelligence. The outcomes of these natural processes will be the institutions, the principles and standards of societies and individuals. These are the natural creations of the evaluating man. They are psychological and sociological facts as well as being values.

Given these naturalistic presuppositions, facts and values cannot be separated into opposing camps, for the institutions of society and the principles and standards of individuals are both! It is these institutions and principles that provide the implicit or explicit major premisses from which particular value judgments are derived. When used in this way, they function as *normative* judgments. This aspect of the theory does not differ from a prescriptivist such as Hare. Where this theory does differ is in the way in which the institutions, principles and standards are formed and revised. It is in this process of formation and revision that the naturalist theory treats them as empirical, sociological facts.

The naturalist view I am considering sees particular values arising out of conflict situation in which the individual with habits, needs and desires must deliberate to attempt to discover the action leading to effects that will satisfy the lack in the present situation. He will commend those things that fill the requirements of the situation. Institutions and principles will be empirical generalizations from these particular judgments of value. They will be sociological facts stating customs such as those making up the institutions of government, marriage, or of promising. Particular value-judgments may then be derived from these general principles which, as I have indicated, then function as normative judgments.

These institutions will, of course, always be subject to re-evaluation. We may always ask of them, 'Are they good?' Moore's open-question argument serves only to point out the permanent possibility of evaluating. The natural self can always re-evaluate any 'brute facts' or sociological facts previously commended. To say that something is 'good' is, as Hare pointed out, to perform an act of commending, but it is not, as Hare presupposed, the act of an alienated self, which merely commends an object if it conforms to a pre-established standard. Rather, in the naturalist theory, reasons can be given for accepting or rejecting the standards, principles and institutions in the first place. And reasons can be given for revising them.

The reasons for commending and choosing between effects must refer as much to the one who commends and chooses as they do to the objects commended or chosen, since evaluation involves an interaction between the evaluator and his environment. Any analysis of choosing and commending must include considerations pertaining to three elements: the evaluator; the objects being evaluated, i.e. the situation in which the evaluator finds himself; and the process of mutual interaction between that individual and his environment. Both versions of the theory of the alienated self that I have treated, i.e. Moore's and Hare's, left out considerations of both the nature of the evaluator and of the mutual interaction or reciprocal influence that takes place between him and his environment.

It should be noted that I do not make the naturalistic fallacy of reducing 'good' to any set of characteristics C within the situation being evaluated. 'Good' is, as Hare claimed, a term used to commend. My deviation from Hare lies in giving a naturalistic analysis of commending and choosing. And that is an important deviation.

An analysis of the natural act of choosing and commending shows the evaluator in a conflict situation, trying to decide what to do. The materials he has to work with are: his own needs and desires, the institutions of his society, his own principles and standards, and the empirical demands of the present situation. His decision to act or to commend one set of effects rather than another will be the result of weighing all of these factors with the aim of meeting the requirements of the situation. The action that he finally chooses will be whatever he feels will satisfy the requirements of the situation. But this is not the same as saying that 'good' means 'that which is satisfying.' 'Good' is still, as Hare pointed out, a term used to commend. The thing that will be commended will be whatever the evaluator decided will meet the requirements of the situation.

The importance of this analysis for the question of the relation of science to value inquiry is that the sciences become essential to the determination of values. For the sciences can give us the information that we need to know in determining the action that will best fill the requirements of the situation. Psychology can supplement our own immediate knowledge of our needs and desires, the various social sciences can tell us about the interlocking network of institutions in our society as well as in other societies, and all the sciences can tell us about the empirical demands, or brute facts, of the present situation. The more such information the individual has, the better will be his choice of the best action to meet the requirements of the situation. Yet the final decision about what to do, about which actions and which effects to commend will be up to the individual. He must still decide what he will call 'good.' Yet he will be in a position to give sound reasons for his choice. He will not have to rely entirely on intuition, whim, or a vague principle to the effect that these are simply the 'effects to be chosen.'

References

1. Edel, Abraham, 'The Relation of Fact and Value: A Reassessment' in *Experience, Existence and the Good*, I. C. Lieb, ed., pp. 215–29.
2. Moore, G. E., *Principia Ethica*, Cambridge University Press, 1903, p. 17.
3. Hare, P. M., *The Language of Morals*, Oxford Univ. Press, New York, 1964, pp. 58–9.
4. Ibid., p. 59.
5. Ibid., p. 60.
6. Ibid., p. 130.
7. Ibid., pp. 92–3.

A Preliminary Application of Ethnological Analysis to Ethical and Meta-Ethical Theory

H. ORENSTEIN

City University of New York

If ethical theory is analytic and nothing more, none of the scientific disciplines (considering 'science' in the broadest sense, as including all empirical, generalizing disciplines) can have much to say on the topic. Hence, unless I am to stop virtually before starting, I will assume that there *is* something more. I hope it is not a piece of chauvinism vis-à-vis my discipline that impells me to believe that if any empirical findings are relevant those of social anthropology are surely to be included.

I am not so presumptuous as to launch an assault on ethical theory in general; the problems I have chosen will surely seem sufficiently audacious. One is what the political scientist, Leo Strauss, referred to disapprovingly as 'the absolute heterogeneity of questions of fact and questions of value.'[1] I am not so foolhardy as to assert that I can establish universal ethical imperatives by inference from indicative propositions, yet I think the reader will agree that the descriptive hypotheses I will put forward, having reference to universal ethical imperatives, have consequences that reflect upon a universal ethics. Another matter that I will discuss in some detail will involve an inquiry into how far ethnology can contribute toward a definition of the terms 'good' or 'right.' In this regard my suggestions are in the nature of catharsis—to clean out, or perhaps, better, clear up, what I believe to be misleading ideas on the subject.

I hope to clarify these two problems by examining and analyzing how a people actually employ ethical rules—for the sake of the 'objectivity' that distance bestows, a people from a society quite different from our own. My data are primarily the rules given in the Dharmashastras, the Hindu 'law' codes—really ethical rather than legal codes. I will here simply outline my empirical findings; most, but not all, have been published elsewhere, and those interested can find the documentation there. I should forewarn the reader that the rules given here may not seem at all like ethical rules as we know them; but this, I think, will help to make my points; for they *are* the ethics of traditional Hinduism.[2]

The ultimate goal of the traditional Hindu ethical system is the maximization, not of pleasure but of spiritual purity.[3] The contribution of an activity to the purity of the actor is far the most important measure by which the goodness of an act is assessed in traditional India. Granted purity is difficult, if not impossible to define; but this state of affairs is not very different from that involved with the Western term 'happiness'—perhaps one of our most important ultimate ethical goals. What purity means might best be defined negatively, in terms of pollution. Pollution signifies involvement (any involvement) with life substance or process; polluted things or processes include birth, death, sexual intercourse, bodily excretions, actions harmful to life, and so on. Almost every action, according to the Hindu codes, is assessed as more or less polluting or purifying.

Pollution in the Dharmashastras falls into a number of implicit types, to which I have assigned what is largely my own nomenclature. (1) When a birth or death occurs in ego's kin group he is subject to *relational pollution*. He is defiled for a stipulated period of time varying with his genealogical distance from the deceased or newborn. Defilement is believed to 'spread' through the kin group, which is conceived, in the words of the Mitakshara, as 'connected by particles of the same body.' Relational pollution is incurred neither through ego's actions nor through the actions of others upon him; he is simply the recipient of defilement by virtue of his biological connection with others. (2) *Act-pollution* is brought about by some form of contact with biological phenomena. It is subdivided into (a) *internal pollution,* in which ego, as subject, acts upon objects, and (b) *external pollution,* in which ego is the object. One is defiled internally by injuring living things. External pollution is brought on if one contacts biological substance or process, for example, by touching or eating bodily secretions, one's own or another's.

Each of these types of pollution is associated with distinctive 'paradigms,' by which I mean orderly variations on rules not unlike the declensions of grammar. The paradigms for internal and external pollution are fairly obvious and easily explained. The amount of internal pollution ego incurs is proportionate to the purity of his victim's caste;[4] for example, the penance for killing a Kshatriya is less than that for killing a Brahman, and so on down in *varna* rank. Defilement is simply dependent upon the magnitude of the crime, which depends, in turn, upon the purity of the victim. The extent of ego's external pollution is proportionate to the defilement of the *varna* he contacts; for example, a Vaishya's corpse defiles more than does a Brahman's. Pollution here simply involves 'catching' defilement from someone or something; the more defiled the source, the greater the pollution.

The explanation of act-pollution and relational pollution is more complex. Ego's relational defilement is inversely proportionate to his caste rank; that is, the higher the rank the less the defilement in case of a birth or death. Brahmans are usually said to be polluted for ten days, Kshatriyas for twelve days. Vaishyas for fifteen, and Shudras for thirty. In contrast, the amount of act-pollution is proportionate to rank; if one touches a corpse or kills a cow, one's pollution is greater if one's caste is higher.

To explain this reversal, we must assume, first, that in the minds of the sacerdotal lawyers, all human beings, all living things, were conceived as to some extent polluted, and, second, that the amount of pollution 'normally,' 'naturally' associated with each caste was believed to vary with its rank; that is, low castes were conceived as naturally more deeply implicated with life substance and process than high ones. Any deviation from normal pollution requires a purifying process or period of time to return to the normal state. Since the latter differs among the castes, a different amount of purification is required of each.

Relational pollution was taken to be something that happens to a kinship group (people 'connected by particles of the same body'), something that 'spreads' throughout the group. 'Spreading' affects pollution in a manner analogous to multiplication. Holding constant such factors as degree of relationship, birth or death results in a 'multiplication' of normal pollution by the same amount for each caste. Because the normal condition of lower castes is to be more defiled, the increase in relational pollution for them is greater than for higher castes.

Act-pollution was conceived as impinging on the individual from without. Its extent was seen as determined, other things being equal, entirely by the phenomena with which ego interacts. To recover a normal state after act-pollution, a member of a high caste, hence, must

F

rid himself of more defilement than someone of low caste, for his normal state involves less defilement.

In order to make this position as clear as possible, I represent the distinction between relational and act-pollution graphically, exaggerating the precision of the rules.

Act-Pollution		: Normal : : Condition :		Relational Pollution	
Remainder	Object (=Abnormal Condition)		Event	Abnormal Condition	Remainder
		(Brahman)			
8	10	2	(x5)	10	8
		(Kshatriya)			
7	10	3	(x5)	15	12
		(Vaishya)			
5	10	5	(x5)	25	20
		(Shudra)			
2	10	8	(x5)	40	32

Of course, multiplication and subtraction did not take place in this precise fashion. The penances vary from code to code, and many of the paradigms are not given numerically. I suggest not an arithmetical model but rather a linguistic one.

I have restricted the discussion to caste thus far in order to simplify matters; yet caste is only one dimension along which pollution may vary, and the premises are applicable to all variations in defilement. For example, a man of low caste who is unusually diligent in his duties is thereby made purer, hence he suffers a shorter period of relational pollution; and if he is killed the murderer must suffer a greater penance than usual. Or a Brahman may, by serious neglect of his duties, fall from grace and permanently lose purity; then his relational pollution is much longer than others. In fact, the premises cover a very large slice of life. They apply to, among other conditions, the *ashramas* (the ideal life history of the individual), the differences between the sexes, different parts of the body, and the distinction between man and the supernatural.[5]

Let me add but one refinement to this rather incomplete presentation of my research. There is a special class of rules for which the paradigm is not quite like the others. This I call self-pollution, a subdivision of external pollution involving instances in which ego is affected by his own bodily processes; eating, for example, or menstruating. In ordinary circumstances the paradigms here are consistent with those of other kinds of external pollution. However, it is a quite different matter when this form of defilement is *compounded* with other forms of external pollution, *e.g.* if one touches an Untouchable under ordinary circumstances, one must merely bathe. But if one does so while one has the remains of a meal in one's mouth (a slightly defiled condition), one must fast for six nights. The two defilements taken together do not add up to a six-night austere purification. It is much the same with other bodily processes; when self-defilements are incurred jointly with ordinary external pollution, an extraordinary puricatory rite is required.

In order to explain this, we observe that there is similarity (but not identity) between self- and relational pollution. In the definition of relational pollution two conditions are involved. 1) It is incurred because ego shares 'particles of the same body' with the new-born or deceased. Thus, a part of one's own body pollutes the rest. Recall that it is the amount of *ego's* normal pollution that is crucial in determining the duration of his relational pollution, not the polluted condition of the deceased or new-born. He pollutes himself. 2) Yet, paradoxically, an alter is essential; the 'action'—birth or death—of another upon ego 'triggers' ego's defilement.

Viewing the process from ego's vantage point, then, relational pollution originates, at the same time, from within and from without. Now, self-pollution is similar to the first condition given in the definition of relational pollution. Ego pollutes himself through substances secreted by his own body. But there the similarity ends; and it is for this very reason that self-pollution is governed by the same principles as other forms of external pollution. It is so governed, however, only in the absence of an alter. An action of alter upon ego brings self-pollution into line with both terms of relational pollution; the inner and the outer aspects are now present. This resemblance in the structure of the categories engenders a concomitant similarity in the principles underlying their activity. I hypothesize that this process, which I call 'congruence,' is a general characteristic of 'grammars' of ethical systems: formal homologies among categories, whether implicit or explicit, will be accompanied by homologous principles of application to particulars.[6]

The analysis given here omits many of the qualifications and refinements of the original; yet I must be brief—as brief as possible with material so complex as this—in order to accomplish the task I set for myself: What does it all signify for ethical theory?

First of all it can have a cathartic function. It can help us to dispose of certain misleading notions, tell us what the term 'good' does *not* mean. First of all it can help us to lay to rest ethical utilitarianism and kindred doctrines.[7] Concepts like 'well-being,' 'happiness,' or 'pleasure' are surely not applicable to the Hindu 'good.' Pleasure, almost however defined, can be construed as rather more conducive to pollution than to purity. True, whatever a people assume to be good, whatever may be their ethical goals, can be *defined* as 'happiness,' etc. (whether that of ego or the general population makes little difference). The attainment of purity, thus, might be defined as the achievement of well-being, even if it involved a state of excruciating pain. But this is a purely analytic resolution; it 'solves' the problem by defining it out of existence.

More important, it ignores actual ethical usage. Thus, Hindus recognize not only *dharma,* but also, for example, the legitimate pursuit of pleasure (*kama*) and material gain (*artha*). These are among the goals of Hindu life; but they are not ethical goals. To define 'good' to be the same as 'happiness,' etc. is simply to blur over the distinctions people make between what is ethical (*dharma*) and what is not. Hence the utilitarian doctrine is either wrong or simultaneously whisks away, by verbal fiat, a legitimate empirical problem and does violence to the actuality of ethical discourse.

Other theories, generally advanced by logical empiricists, are more formidable. In particular I refer to the emotive theory and its positivistic variants. For the purposes of our discussion we can set aside many of the refinements that have been made in this approach; for example, many include exhortative and/or descriptive elements in the terms 'good' or 'ought,' but all insist on an emotive element, what might be called a 'pro-emotion' or a 'con-emotion,' as one fundamental constituent. For the sake of economy, I shall refer to all such theories as 'emotive,' although I recognize that there are differences of some importance among them.[8]

First of all, the emotive definition, as generally put forward, is too vague, even when qualified so as to include descriptive and exhortative elements. For even if the use of the term 'good' does express a positive attitude (among other things), it is not just any kind of positive emotion; an individual can have pro-emotions toward things that to him are not ethical—the Hindu *kama* and *artha* are examples. He may even have pro-emotions toward things he considers to be immoral. If the terms 'want' or 'positive emotion' are at all appropriate translations of ethical statements—I, for one, doubt that they are—there must be something about the wants that makes them different.

In contrast to some other kinds of choices, ethical judgments must be consistent, as R. M. Hare has indicated. But this point requires expansion; we must understand that, as our study of Hindu moral rules has shown, an ethical code comprises a *system*; the particular rules are (implicitly) deduced from general, though not quite conscious premises. Hence, when ego makes an ethical judgment, e.g. 'Stealing gold from a Brahman is polluting (bad)'—a rule that is, in fact, not infrequently mentioned in the codes—he does so on the basis of reason. He may, himself, despise Brahmans, feel no antipathy toward theft, and want very much to acquire gold; he may want to steal gold from Brahmans. Yet by virtue of deduction from his own implicit premises and definitions, he would know (not 'feel') that 1) Brahmans are elevated beings; 2) stealing is prohibited, especially from Brahmans; 3) gold is sacred and it, especially, should not be stolen. If he were, thus, to steal gold from a Brahman, he would be doing what he knew was immoral (polluting), whatever he might feel on the subject.

This is a non-fundamental ethical judgment. Such, it might be argued, are deducible from general premises; but what of the premises themselves? Does not the fact that one holds them indicate that one emotionally approves of them?

While this is not out of the question, I believe that to put it so distorts the issue. One takes on ethical rules, along with the premises involved in them, as *cognitions*—not unlike the way one learns pieces of information—with no necessary emotional attachment to them. This will, perhaps, be especially evident to a Western audience contemplating the ultimate Hindu good—purity. For it is clear that purity can be emotionally neutral, even something one dislikes. It can be something even Hindus are emotionally neutral about, even something they dislike; yet it can remain a standard to which they comply. It is surely not difficult to believe that many Hindus, like many Westerners, find their moral obligations irksome. The normal, traditional Hindu simply learns that he should not become more polluted than is prescribed for his status. True, he may become emotionally upset if he is polluted, but he need not be; emotion is incidental. (I have repeatedly witnessed the extent to which some Hindus are emotionally detached in their ritual observances.) Upon incurring extra pollution, one may simply be annoyed at the prospect of the ensuing rites; one may 'cleanse' oneself quite dispassionately and thus return to a normal state—and by these means, by one's own standards, be ethical.

The opposite of this occurs in non-fundamental moral actions every day, in India as well as in the West. Many Hindus are, *by their own admission,* 'lax' about purity. In order to avoid the inconvenience and discomfort of ritual purification they may allow themselves to remain defiled, especially in minor affairs. Similarly, out of self interest, a Westerner may cheat on his income tax returns, recognizing all the while that his action is stealing, that 'stealing is wrong,' but that, in this case, the crime is merely venial. Such actions may be called, in the terms of the participants themselves, 'immoral.'

It is possible, although not so frequent, for someone to go beyond this, quite consciously to set aside all ethical premises (putting no others in their stead), and act in what he believes to be his self interest. According to some reports, this may have been done by many leaders of the Nazi Party,[9] and according to some interpretations, this was advocated by Nietzsche.[10] Such actions may be labelled, in the terms of the actors themselves, as wholly 'immoral.'

In contrast, a people may have no ethical premises, or more likely weakly developed ones. They may tend, hence, either to follow their own interests or those among them who have the most power—as, perhaps, did many followers of Nazi leadership.[11] Of these, we may say that they are 'amoral.'

Now the use of the terms 'immoral' and 'amoral' in the immediately preceding paragraphs is, at least on one level, purely descriptive. 'Amorality' simply indicates a condition in which ethical rules are absent. 'Immorality' indicates that the actor is, so to speak, damning his own actions by reference to his own (cognitively ascertained) moral standards. Both terms, in this context, *indicate* something about other people's use of imperatives; we need not concur, for they are not necessarily our imperatives. However, there remains the possibility that the terms, in this context, have what I shall call 'meta-imperative' implications; that is, they are, in part, imperatives having other imperatives as referents. It is possible that all men hold (implicit) moral principles to the effect that 1) everyone should have a system of moral principles (i.e. should not be amoral) and/or that 2) everyone should, to the extent that it is feasible, follow his own moral principles (i.e. should not be immoral). I believe that most, if not all of us in the West hold these ethical meta-imperatives, but whether or not they are, in fact, universal can be decided only by extensive empirical study. We shall turn shortly to a problem allied to this.

If ethical systems are not matters of taste and feeling, why have emotive theories been so popular? This is, I contend, because emotions often do accompany moral thought. Not only does following one's ethical code often yield emotional satisfactions, but for highly ethical people, simply contemplating one's ethical system may result in a specifically moral emotion, Kant's *'Achtung für das Sittengesetz.'* Yet it should be evident to anyone who has observed or experienced moral problems that good conduct is often an outcome of a psychological struggle between a man's ethical standards and his tastes and feelings. The 'conflict between duty (which is unlike desire) and desire [is] a fundamental fact of moral experience ...'[12] Simply because we get emotional rewards from ethical thinking and activity does not signify that ethical systems, in any way or part, are to be defined as emotional. It is for this very reason that I selected the Hindu concept of purity for my illustrations; to most of us—and to some Hindus—purity is emotionally neutral. Kant's observation about the moral feeling accompanying the apprehension of morality is apropos; it does not, he says, 'serve as a means of judging actions or even as the ground of the moral law itself, but only as a motive to make it one's maxim.'[13] If we were to assert that because moral statements are motivated by emotion, they are composed of emotion then clearly—however absurdly—the same could be said of scientific truth, which is often involved with emotion, both as motive and as reward for its attainment.

Not being emotive, what then, can an ultimate ethical judgment be? I am not one of those who believes it is an immediate intuition of some unanalyzable characteristic, as, for example, redness.[14] Nor do I believe that an ultimate ethical premise is significantly comparable to a basic scientific hypothesis; the latter is verifiable, perhaps more properly falsifiable, *via* hypotheses deduced from them and tested against 'what is, in fact, the case.' While there are deductions in ethical thinking, there are no empirical tests; falsification is not possible.[15]

I do not pretend that the problem can be wholly explicated at this time from the position I have put forward; possibly it cannot be explicated at all. I will here venture some rather general, and I fear, vague suggestions. Terms like 'attitude' and 'want' are inadequate translations of 'good' unless they are defined in a cognitive rather than an affective sense. Ethical rules, first of all, are imperatives. They are, as it were, taken into the individual psyche, imbibed from without. Implied within the system of rules are ultimate ethical premises and ultimate goals—toward which one may or may not choose to strive. Such goals may be likened to pointers, 'objective' indicators of directions along which one learns to guide one's behavior—or, if one so wishes, to refuse to guide one's behavior. While such 'directions' are part of one's psyche, they need not be of one's personality—those of one's psychological characteristics that are 'person-defining.' They do not derive from a person's impulses, needs, or urges; they are inferred from particular ideas, particular ethical regulations, that he has taken onto himself and that he assumes have some binding force.

Ultimate ethical premises and goals, then, are objective—but not in the sense that they are non-mental, rather in that they may be and often are external to an individual's own wishes, in that they are not arbitrary (in the sense that dislikes may be), and in that they can be discovered dispassionately, through reason.

This is not to say that I am a 'conventionalist' or a 'public subjectivist.' Far from it. While imperatives are usually confined within the boundaries of a particular society and while they are, perhaps, largely brought into being through interaction with fellow-members of one's society, an individual's morality does not consist in what other members of his society, past or present, believe is moral. The ethical convictions of others may be the causes of our ethical beliefs; they do not, because of this, constitute our ethics. Once an individual acquires an ethical system, he reacts to it, not to others'. Indeed, out of sensitivity to others' opinions, one may act contrary to one's own ethical convictions, and, hence, look upon oneself as having been immoral for so doing.

At present I am skeptical that there is any way to 'justify' ultimate ethical premises or ideals. I am tempted to follow Hare's suggestion (similar—in this respect alone—to that of Hans Kelsen[16]) that such are justifiable—to the extent that it is possible—by reference to a 'complete specification of a way of life.' But I have my doubts. Ethical rules, as we have seen, comprise a system entailing basic premises, which in turn involve an ethical ideal. Now ethical ideals have properties peculiar to themselves, usually not shared with other ideals or with ethical duties. I would, for the present, hold, with the jurist, Lon Fuller, that ethical ideals constitute 'moralities of aspiration'[17] (so long as we understand 'aspiration' in a non-emotive sense). They are ideals toward which people tend to strive; but they are not standards in terms of which people 'want' to live, indeed in social reality they may be unlivable. This is especially evident in considering the Hindu ultimate ideal of purity. Purity serves well enough as a goal and a standard by which to measure right conduct; but absolute purity is, in fact, not attainable; living beings cannot circumvent life substance and process —not even in death, for, in Hinduism death itself is one of life's processes. Indeed, even if closely approached by a majority of the society, absolute purity would render individual and collective existence highly precarious.

Lest it be thought that this is peculiar to Hindu ethical ideals, or other similarly 'ascetic' goals, I would remind the reader of Michael Young's *Rise of the Meritocracy*[18]; equality of opportunity—surely one of the ultimate ethical imperatives of Anglo-American civilization —would, if fully achieved render day-to-day living virtually unendurable. If the term 'want' can be at all used in connection with ethics, ultimate ethical imperatives are not what people want, but what they want to want; they are targets we choose to aim at but choose not to hit. In this sense, then, ultimate ethical ideals, hence the ethical systems in which they are embedded, are not to be 'verified' by reference to the specification of an actual 'way of life.'

If I conclude that ethical systems are not verifiable, this does not mean that they are trivial or based on personal whim, and it in no way necessitates their being based on emotion. Systems of mathematics and logic are similarly, though of course much more rigorously, founded on 'arbitrary' definitions and rules of procedure and are similarly not empirically verifiable; yet few would call them 'emotive.'

As a fact, a given ethical system is bounded by a particular psyche while, as a tendency, its boundaries are those of a particular society. Yet I have just suggested that there may be universal ethical meta-imperatives, i.e. (second order) ethical imperatives that have as their referents yet other (first order) ethical imperatives. While most of us in the West might agree with these meta-imperatives, it is a matter for rather much empirical investigation to find out whether they are, in fact, universals. However, I do not think this is quite so necessary for universal first order imperatives; these, I hold, can be discerned in any ethical system, and once formulated will appear to anyone as ethically binding. The rules shortly to be adumbrated were formulated while analyzing the Hindu codes; but they could have been spelled out in the course of investigating any ethical code, or even without empirical study; for if they are, as I believe, universal ethical imperatives, they existed in my mind—as in others—before such study. Empirical research, in this case, merely stimulated me to set down explicitly what would have remained implicit in my own morality.

F*

The rules given below were suggested to me by my analysis of congruence in Hindu ethics. They are neither meta-ethical indicatives nor meta-ethical imperatives. They are descriptions of abstract ethical imperatives involved, I believe, in all ethical systems, that take on imperative force by virtue of the fact that they do, in fact, reside in all ethical systems, including, I assume, those of the reader.

I a) All ethical systems hold that, if people differ in relevant characteristics, they should be treated differently in proportion to their differences.

b) The converse of this is: in all ethical systems it is held that if people are similar in relevant respects their treatment should be similar in proportion to their similarity.

c) A corollary of this of much importance in the West is: in any ethical system it is held that people who are considered to be equal in relevant respects should be treated equally.

II a) All ethical systems hold that if equivalent people are to be punished for immoral actions, the punishment should be proportionate to the magnitude of the immorality.

b) A corollary of this is: in all ethical systems, given equivalent persons, the same crime—the same in relevant respects—is held to merit the same punishment.

III a) All ethical systems hold that if rewards are to be given for moral action, given equivalent actors, the reward should be proportionate to the merit of the action.

b) A corollary of this is: in all ethical systems it is held that if moral actions are to be rewarded, equally moral actions undertaken by equivalent persons should be equally rewarded.

Obviously I do not believe that all men *act* in accordance with these rules, only that the rules are, in more concrete form, involved in the ethical systems whereby they assess how they act.

These generalizations are universal, I believe, because of the way in which men's minds are constituted—*all* men's minds. Probably they will appear self-evident to many but this is precisely what I would expect. Indeed, their obviousness constitutes confirmation, for as has been intimated, their very universality—and their significance and immediacy—would make them appear so. Because significant and universal, they have, as one might expect, appeared here and there in religious and literary works of all kinds. Indeed they are in part similar to Aristotle's 'distributive justice.'[20]

At the outset of this paper I said that I would not be so foolhardy as to try to infer an ethical imperative from an indicative statement. I have more or less kept to my word, hedging only slightly; having formulated universal indicatives about imperatives, I only contend that the latter will, if the reader would examine his own conscience, be found there as cognitively living moral rules.[21]

Notes and References

1. Leo Strauss, *Natural Right and History*, Chicago: University of Chicago Press, 1953, Chs. 1–2, especially p. 39.

2. The frequently repeated assertion that Hinduism is amoral is pure, blind ethnocentrism. Ethical systems are sometimes not identified as such simply because their ideals and their fields of reference are radically different from ours.

3. It is possible to interpret virtually every endeavor of traditional India as religious. If one does, then, of course, the quest for purity is 'religion,' and, as such, some might exclude it from the domain of ethics. However, I believe this is an impudent imposition of the categories of our own culture onto India's. See note 2.

4. *Varna* and caste are different, in that the latter is an actual social group, while the former is, today at least, no more than an idea about social groups. However, as we are dealing with ways of thinking rather than forms of interaction and as the code-writers treat *varna* and caste in the same way, the distinction is of no importance for us.
The details of my analysis of pollution and caste are given in my article, 'The Structure of Hindu Caste Values: A Preliminary Study of Hierarchy and Ritual Defilement,' *Ethnology*, **4**, No. **1** (1965), pp. 1–14.

5. Most of my analysis of pollution in non-caste matters, along with some comments on ethical theory not mentioned here, is given in my article, 'Toward a Grammar of Defilement in Hindu Sacred Law,' in M. Singer and B. Cohn, eds., *Structure and Change in Indian Society*, Chicago: Aldine Publishing Co., 1968, pp. 115–31.

6. Documentation of this analysis is given in my 'Logical Congruence in Hindu Sacred Law,' in M. Zamora, J. M. Mahar, and H. Orenstein, eds., *On Culture*, publication pending.

7. To my knowledge, the most forceful and intelligent modern presentation of a view of the type I am here disputing is in Moritz Schlick's *Problems of Ethics* (New York: Prentice Hall, 1939). Of course, Schlick was not a classical utilitarian—see pp. 87–90. However, the criticisms given here apply with equal force to Schlick as to Bentham.

8. Perhaps the best known example of an unqualified emotive theory is in A. J. Ayer's *Language, Truth and Logic* (London: Victor Gollancz, 1950), Ch. VI. The foremost proponent of a qualified emotive theory is, of course, Charles L. Stevenson, *Ethics and Language* (New Haven: Yale University Press, 1944). An interesting variant on Stevenson is Paul Edwards' *The Logic*

of Moral Discourse (New York: The Free Press, 1955). I include in the category of emotive theories what Edwards calls 'naive subjectivism' (Ch. II), whereby the term 'good' is held to signify a *description* of the speaker's favorable emotional inclination. In this essay I have ignored many other distinctions usually made in ethical theory, for example, between 'good,' 'ought,' and 'right.' While I hope to discuss some of these in later publications none of the distinctions is important for the arguments of this paper.

9. E.g. see Hermann Rauschning, *The Revolution of Nihilism; Warning to the West*, New York: Longmans, Green and Co., 1939.

10. E.g. see Henry Sidgwick, *Outlines of the History of Ethics*, London: Macmillan and Co., 1954, p. 291.

11. E.g. see Peter Viereck, *Metapolitics, the Roots of the Nazi mind*, New York: Capricorn Books, 1961.

12. S. Körner, *Kant*, Harmondsworth: Penguin Books, 1955, p. 162.

13. Quoted in Körner, *ibid.*, pp. 162–3.

14. For an effective argument against intuitionism see R. M. Hare, *The Language of Morals*, New York: Oxford University Press, 1964, Ch. V.

15. Falsification is not possible except in disputes where, for example, there are differences over matters of fact or where rules are 'deduced' from different premises, some of which may be of a higher order than others. For different types of ethical disputes, see C. Stevenson, *Ethics and Language*, and P. Edwards, *The Logic of Moral Discourse*.

16. Hare, *The Language of Morals*, pp. 68–9; Hans Kelsen, *What is Justice?*, Berkeley: The University of California Press, 1960.

17. *The Morality of Law*, New Haven: Yale University Press, 1964.

18. *Rise of the Meritocracy, 1870–2033: an Essay on Education and Equality*, London: Thames and Hudson, 1958.

19. I use terms like 'equality' and 'the same' rather loosely throughout. If greater precision of usage is wanted the reader can substitute the appropriate terms, e.g. 'equivalance' for 'equality.' Obviously the matter of 'relevant respects' is of the utmost importance for social science, for the criteria of relevance are culturally determined in each particular society.

20. *The Nicomachaen Ethics* (J. Smith, transl., Everyman's Library, New York: E. P. Dutton, 1911), V, iii, 1131b; pp. 107–8.

21. The general ethical imperatives suggested here surely do not exhaust all that exist. Indeed, one other was long ago hinted at by anthropologists and sociologists, the norm of reciprocity. All men hold that it is morally right always to return a favor and, moreover (my rule III), that the return should be equivalent to the favor. This rule, like the ones I have suggested, appears self-evident once formulated; yet a considerable body of data had to be studied over a long period of time in order to arrive at it.

Ethical Naturalism and Biocultural Evolution

CHARLES FAY

California State College, Dominguez Hills

The end of this conference is to integrate or at least re-examine the relevance of natural science to human value. A non-empirical concept of human value would not seem adequate to this end. But any effort to develop an empirical concept of value is immediately challenged in the name of 'Hume's law' which asserts an unbridgeable gulf between fact and value. The proper interpretation of Hume's ethics and a reconsideration of the naturalistic fallacy are occasioning second thoughts on the part of some ethicians at present. I find myself in essential agreement with MacIntyre's position that moral experience is unintelligible apart from notions such as desiring, needing, pleasure, happiness, and health—notions that transcend the dichotomies of analytic philosophers in regard to the descriptive and the normative. In MacIntyre's interpretation of Hume,[1] a transition from 'is' to 'ought' can be made by means of the notion of wanting. This bringing to bear of human wants and urges on human values is of special interest to those naturalists in ethics who seek a foundation for ethics in the sciences of man and is one way of accomplishing the end of this conference. For the natural and behavioral sciences sometimes concern themselves with what people want, and in considering what people want these sciences also concern themselves with particular instances of what is. The frequently complex, problematic connection between actual wants and what is desirable requires a great deal of practical reflection. However, it is reason, rooted in the actual experience of need, which makes the judgment that x is good. And a concept of value which is in this sense empirical can be related to the humanities and to the sciences and in the process can further extend its basis in human experience and acquire both general perspective and immediate application to contemporary moral and social problems.

This paper in particular deals with the problem of situating a need theory of value in the context of contemporary evolutionary theory. Quite recently, A. G. N. Flew[2] and Anthony Quinton[3] have reconsidered the possibilities of an evolutionary ethics. These thinkers recognize that there is a logical distinction between judgments of value and the neutral, strictly theoretical statements of fact. Nevertheless, they agree with Julian Huxley's observation: 'It makes a great difference whether we think of the history of mankind as something wholly apart from this history of the rest of life, or as a continuation of the general evolutionary process, though with special characteristics of its own.'[4] Huxley's qualification, 'though with special characteristics of its own,' suggests that human evolution differs from organic evolution. Unfortunately, neither of these contemporary authors seems to have pondered the differences when they take the position that ethics involves considerations that transcend genetics and natural selection as these processes ordinarily operate in evolutionary biology.

Quinton asserts that language may in fact relate to objects or states of affairs which occasion satisfaction or enjoyment and at the same time this language can be established as true or false.[5] Concepts such as health and social welfare have cognitive significance in medicine or social work; yet they also refer to human needs and they provide good and sufficient reasons for actions which are empirically verifiable. In an examination of the alleged autonomy of ethics, Dorothy Emmett also questions whether a social fact such as parenthood can be understood apart from an appreciation of what is appropriate behavior for parents.

> The notion of *role*, therefore, I suggest provides a link between factual descriptions of social situations and moral pronouncements about what ought to be done in them. It has, so to speak, a foot in both camps, that of fact and of value; it refers to a relationship with a factual basis, and it has a norm of behavior built into it which is being explicitly or tacitly accepted if the role is cited as a reason.[6]

The facts of the behavioral sciences are ethically neutral only when considered in abstraction from their relationship to human needs; when seen in relationship to human passions and interests, these facts involve value. When we speak of interlocking roles which involve rights and duties, or of efficiency or the economical, we are dealing with social, technological, and economic systems independently of the evolutionary process. What interests us especially is the relevance of evolutionary theory and data to morality. And for our purposes we welcome the suggestion of Quinton that we find in evolutionary biology concepts such as adaptation, progress, and genetic or biological efficiency which apply to all living beings, which are verifiable, and which pertain to goals that human beings generally desire.[7] Such values are subordinate and defeasible. However, the biological efficiency of some policy or institution is certainly a good and sufficient reason for choice, other things being equal, just as efficiency or economy or healthiness are. Quinton would argue, however, that before arriving at an ethical conclusion in regard to any course of action, one would consider many other goods besides the biological; consequently, other facts besides evolution must be taken into account, with the result that evolutionary ethics is inadequate.

In my view, the major shortcoming of current re-evaluations such as those of Flew and Quinton is the abstract and truncated view of evolution that figures in their arguments that evolutionary considerations are irrelevant or subordinate to higher values. The nature of the evolutionary process as it is currently conceived by anthropologists and biologists is of crucial importance to any re-evaluation of an evolutionary ethics by philosophers. What is called for is not a rehearsal of nineteenth century theories but philosophic reflection on the current scientific doctrine that the evolutionary process insofar as it pertains to the origin and continued evolution of man is biocultural and not simply biological. According to Quinton, evolutionary theory consists fundamentally of genetic theories of inheritable characteristics and chance variations and the theory of natural selection.[8] Also for Flew, 'the obvious and right place from which to begin a study of evolutionary ethics is Charles Darwin.'[9] There is a tendency on the part of philosophers not only to distinguish organic evolution from cultural change but even to separate them. It is as though human beings somehow emerged as the result of a purely biological process. When their nature was complete they then produced culture, and ethics is restricted entirely to what man has produced since his evolution was completed.

But the process of human evolution is bio-cultural. These two factors are indeed formally distinct but they interact in human origins, and the resulting holistic process must be analyzed in terms of concepts that cut across the organic and the cultural. In fact, the dominant factor in human origins is culture. Reflecting on the role of culture in the ecological situation of early man, Sherwood Washburn contends that it is probably more accurate to think of much of our structure as the result of culture than it is to think of men anatomically like ourselves slowly developing culture.[10] When culture begins to operate in hominid evolution, we have to do with a rudimentary form of the social nature which is also an ethical nature. And the further development of this nature is not wholly due to chance. According to Goudge, it is precisely the point of the theory of evolution that selection is an anti-chance factor that tends to produce systematic and orderly change in a population.[11] While the genetic factors operate in a random manner, the selective factors do not.

Certain anthropologists emphasize, and I believe rightly, the adaptive value of spontaneous cooperation and friendship in the course of human evolution.[12] These factors can be related to the same psychological and social nature that characterizes the primitive tool maker. Leslie White maintains that the *sui generis* character of culture is accounted for by man's symbolic mentality which transforms and elevates the tool use and social life of non-human primates.[13] The very act of communicating tool-making traditions involves initiative, shared experience, and cooperation. If this is the case, freedom and justice are 'writ large' in the evolutionary process. And inasmuch as natural selection operates in a non-random fashion in hominid evolution, that is, inasmuch as an ecological situation endures which places a premium on these moral factors, they become better established in man's psycho-biological nature. An evolutionary view of the human situation would indicate that man is as much committed to the values of freedom and justice as he is to an upright posture. The fact that he suffers from moral conflict and perplexity is analogous to the hazards of an incomplete adaptation to an upright posture, namely, backache, fallen arches, and sagging mesenteries. The moral nature in question is still inchoative, and this helps to explain the celebrated enigma stressed by de-ontologists in ethics: obligation sometimes seems to clash with our immediate desires. The fact that aggression and conflict also have adaptive value in various stages of hominid evolution further complicates the picture.

Now inasmuch as culture and the needs of an ethical animal become essential to the evolutionary process, cultural and ethical factors are both emergent and yet intrinsically dependent on the organic processes of reproduction, growth, and evolution. That human culture is more than organic has been maintained by American anthropologists since A. L. Kroeber's article 'The Superorganic' appeared in 1917.[14] Biocultural evolution cannot be reduced to purely biological evolution, just as organic evolution cannot be reduced to chemical changes in non-living materials. Biocultural evolution includes the 'higher values,' those relating to what Maslow has called self-actualization,[15] as well as the lower.

There is, however, some confusion in anthropological theory concerning the exact meaning of the superorganic character of culture. Sometimes it is merely a methodological convenience; that is to say, culture is viewed as if it were something more than organic, but this is nothing more than a convenient fiction for many anthropologists. Others speak of the superorganic as something both superindividual and real, in a way reminiscent of Plato's world of ideas. However, there is no doubt that culture is real and not a Platonic idea. Psychotherapists have always been interested in the cultural dimension of human conflict and suffering. In many studies, culture and its value orientations are related to what existentialists and phenomenologists call man's subjectivity. By means of a theory of the self as social, it is possible, I believe, to show that all of culture, considered ontologically, is reducible without remainder to something manifest in the behavior and consciousness of individuals. George Herbert Mead provides some indication of how this reduction is achieved with his account of the social self and his theory of role and symbolic interaction.[16] If one understands the human individual properly, he is seen to be an individual whose normal maturation involves what the anthropologists call enculturation. This means not only becoming socialized but also acquiring all the outlooks and attitudes that the higher values imply. And if one understands culture ontologically, it is not something that exists apart from individuals. To be sure, the way people live can be considered in abstraction from individual humans and viewed as a functional system of interdependent customs and institutions. When so considered, concepts which apply to organic evolution also apply analogously to the culture system. Many definitions of culture emphasize adjustment or view it as a problem-solving device. The following definitions illustrate the adaptive function of culture in relation to basic needs of individuals.

> The culture of a people may be defined as the sum total of the material and intellectual equipment whereby they satisfy their biological and social needs and adapt themselves to their environment.[17]
> The culture of a society may be said to consist of the characteristic ways in which basic needs of individuals are satisfied in that society . . . .[18]

The concept of adaptation

> ' . . . provides a unifying theme that makes it possible to bridge the seemingly disparate interests of anthropologists—from the emergence of Homo sapiens out of his nonhuman primate ancestry to the development of huge metropolitan areas in modern states. . . .
> Among nonhuman animals, adaptation takes place principally by means of genetic mutation. In man, on the other hand, adaptation is accomplished by cultural means, principally through the harnessing of new sources of energy for productive ends and through the organizations of social relations that make it possible to use these energy systems effectively.[19]

However, to abstract a mode of life from the concrete human individuals who live it is not to deny the ontological dependence of the former on the latter. Let us recall that man's adjustment requires not only the harnessing of new sources of energy but, as Marx explains, in acquiring new productive forces men change all their social relations. Consequently, adaptation on the cultural level involves an ethical system by means of which the social relations are organized. Whether the cultural system is in a state of equilibrium or disequilibrium will be of utmost consequence for the moral and social problems of individual human beings. In short, given a proper understanding of the human individual on the one hand and of culture on the other, it should be evident that there can be nothing in the whole field of value, including what is most private and unique, which transcends a biocultural view of the evolution of man.

We have already acknowledged that culture frustrates human needs as well as satisfies them. In a recent analysis of socio-cultural systems, the anthropologist Morris Freilich concludes that even though these systems tend toward states of balance, they exist most frequently in states of imbalance.[20] The conflict that exists in the California educational system with its three-way split between a conservative governor and state legislature, a liberal faculty and administration, and an increasingly radicalized student body is merely illustrative of the sort of situation that obtains generally in human evolution. It is therefore incumbent on me to show how a functional and even progressive view of evolution can be maintained in spite of all the conflict and suffering, and it hardly seems enough to point out that there are overall trends toward equilibrium in social systems. I think I can show this by reflecting on a great cultural revolution in the past which was clearly progressive yet paradoxical in its effects upon individuals. Prior to the Neolithic, man's social life was integrated exclusively on the basis of kinship ties. There was accordingly no state, no market, no rationalizing man of classical economic theory. But after some millions of years of biological and cultural change, hunters and gatherers, at least in some instances, created socio-cultural systems that not only tended toward balance but actually were balanced.

> The economic system of primitive peoples is identified largely with the kinship system and is therefore characterized by cooperation, mutual aid, and sharing. . . .
>
> Private and personal property are institutions· of primitive society as they are of our own, but use is emphasized rather than ownership in the sense in which the latter term is used in our culture.[21]
>
> The Agricultural Revolution transformed primitive society, based upon kinship, into civil society, founded upon property relations and territorial organization. Class structure and class division replace lineage and clan; competition and conflict take the place of mutual aid. From the standpoint of the needs and satisfactions of human beings, this transformation meant a great loss: the loss of kinship, which, as Tylor pointed out, means 'kindliness' and mutual aid.[22]

In a sense, things have never been as good as they were in the Old Stone Age. Yet the average life expectancy was some twenty-two years; unless a human being was a relative he was a non-human being and therefore not a subject of rights. That moral as well as technological progress is accomplished in this great revolution is argued at some length by Robert Redfield in *The Primitive World and Its Transformations*.[23] The emergence of the agricultural state involved a new mode of integration of economic and political activity which must be viewed as progressive. The result is an increase in social efficiency analogous to the increase of biological efficiency entailed by organic evolution. Aristotle's naturally political animal is the product of changes that took place for the most part from the Neolithic on. The industrial revolution has been a continual source of upheaval and social dislocation, culminating in the economic and political structure described by Galbraith in *The New Industrial State*.[24] At present, a system of power and social control seems to have emerged in which anonymous bands of specialists determine the priority of questions of social policy and the best means of implementing policy. It is easy to understand the feeling of alienation on the part of humanists and the radical left. Nevertheless, the new industrial state, like the old agricultural state, has a functional and adaptive value for the reason that it makes possible the solution of problems that involve man's relation to his total environment, problems that can be solved in no other way. The nostalgic appeal of participatory democracy is regressive in the current redefinition of the locus of power and responsibility. If the great problems that concern the quality of human existence are ever to be dealt with, it will be through Galbraith's technostructure rather than by the contemporary Thoreaus who reject any system that curtails individualistic freedoms. In the Cenozoic, the thing to be was a mammal rather than a reptile. Today, freedom and responsibility are realized through the emergent organization, or not at all. New opportunities for creativity and responsibility exact a heavy toll in moral suffering and frustration. And this is the sum and total of the consolation offered by the evolutionist in the face of the problem of evil.

An evolutionary ethics will provide some light by means of its functional and adaptive analysis of human value. Some of the arbitrariness that relativists and non-cognitivists rest their case on will be diminished. However, to borrow an observation from Abraham Edel, 'Some indeterminacy will always remain.'[25] Complexity in an evolutionary ethics centers on the relationship between the needs of an individual and a biocultural system whose conflicting elements only approximate an equilibrium. Moral conflict is universal in human experience not because human nature has been corrupted by original sin but because it is unfinished. The 'is' from which we argue in ethics is not a stable, universal, and necessary entity but something in process, in transition. An evolutionary view of the human situation both preserves the ambiguity of the practical life which is the universal testimony of thoughtful persons and further provides an explanation of this irreducible irrationality. Such an ethics will not provide all the light we crave but what it does make available is tied in with the evolution of human science, and this limited understanding is especially crucial in periods of cultural transition.

Notes and References

1. A. C. MacIntyre, 'Hume on "Is" and "Ought",' in *Hume, A Collection of Critical Essays*, ed. V. C. Chappell, New York: Doubleday Anchor Book Original, 1966, 240–64; reference to 257–8.
2. A. G. N. Flew, *Evolutionary Ethics*, London: Macmillan, 1967.
3. Anthony Quinton, 'Ethics and the Theory of Evolution,' in *Biology and Personality*, ed. I. T. Ramsey, Oxford: Basil Blackwell, 1965, 107–31.
4. Julian Huxley, *Evolution in Action*, 1953, New York: Mentor Book, 1957, vi.
5. Quinton, *op. cit.*, 111.
6. Dorothy Emmett, *Rules, Roles and Relations*, London: Macmillan, 1966, 41.
7. Quinton, *op. cit.*, 113.
8. Quinton, *op. cit.*, 123.

9. Flew, *op. cit.*, 1.

10. Sherwood Washburn, 'Tools and Human Evolution,' *Scientific American*. **203**, No. 3, Sept., 1960.

11. T. A. Goudge, *The Ascent of Life*, Toronto: University of Toronto Press, 1961, 109–13.

12. Marshall Sahlins, 'The Origin of Society,' *Scientific American*. **203**, No. **3**, Sept., 1960; 'The Social Life of Monkeys, Apes and Primitive man,' in *The Evolution of Man's Capacity for Culture*, ed. J. N. Spuhler, Detroit: Wayne State University Press, 1959, 54–73. Leslie White, *The Evolution of Culture*, New York: McGraw-Hill, 1959, especially ch. 4, 'The Transition from Anthropoid Society to Human Society.'

13. Leslie White, *The Science of Culture*, New York: Farrar, Strauss and Cudahy, 1949, especially ch. 2, 'The Symbol: the Origin and Basis of Human Behavior,' and ch. 3, 'On the Use of Tools by Primates.'

14. A. L. Kroeber, 'The Superorganic,' *American Anthropologist*, **19**, April–June, 1917, 163–213.

15. 'Furthermore, *all* these basic needs may be considered simply steps along the time path to general self-actualization, under which all basic needs can be subsumed.' Abraham H. Maslow, 'Psychological Data and Value Theory,' in *New Knowledge in Human Values*, ed. Abraham H. Maslow, New York: Harper & Brothers, 1959, 123; *Motivation and Personality*, New York: Harper and Brothers, 1954, especially ch. 4, 'The Instinctoid Nature of Basic Needs.'

16. For an Interesting comparison of Mead and Buber, cr. Paul E. Pfuetze, *Self, Society, Existence* (New York: Harper Torchbooks, 1954), especially ch. 2 and ch. 4. For our purposes, this study indicates how culture and its evolution could be related to what the existentialists call subjectivity. For Mead's concepts can serve as a connecting link between the so-called objective realm of biocultural evolution and the lived experience of existing in the world that is interpreted in contemporary existentialism and phenomenology.

17. A. L. Kroeber and Clyde Kluckhohn, *Culture: A Critical Review of Concepts and Definitions*, Papers of the Peabody Museum of American Archeology and Ethnology, Harvard University, **XLVII**, No. **1**, 1952, 56.

18. *Ibid.*

19. 'Introduction,' *Man in Adaptation: The Biosocial Background*, ed. Yehudi A. Cohen, Chicago: Aldine, 1968, 1, 3.

20. Morris Freilich, 'The Natural Triad in Kinship and Complex Systems,' *American Sociological Review*. **29**, No. **4**, Aug., 1964, 529–40.

21. Leslie White, *The Evolution of Culture*, 260.

22. Leslie White, *The Evolution of Culture*, 141.

23. Robert Redfield, *The Primitive World and Its Transformations*, Cornell: Cornell University, 1953.

24. John Kenneth Galbraith, *The New Industrial State*, Boston: Houghton Mifflin, 1967.

25. Abraham Edel, *Ethical Judgment*, Glencoe: Free Press, 1955, 336.

Why the Gap is Under Attack

J. O. WISDOM

State University of New York, at Fredonia

As chairman, I have been asked to give my 'summary and evaluation.' My summary will be factual (so far as it is accurate); my evaluation will no doubt be objective and a logical consequence of facts about the papers!

One of the handful of 'truths' that have been claimed to have been established in philosophy is that a value-judgment cannot be deduced from statements of fact. Alas, even this 'truth' is now being questioned!

1) Dr. Walter went in to bat first. To the following effect.

Hume asserted that value-judgments do not follow from statements of fact. Why? Because value-judgments are not subject to reason, which is passive, but are subject to emotions which are active (I suppose 'subject to' means 'the product of'). Walter does not, at this point, discuss whether the contemporary acceptance of Hume's conclusion is based on the same premiss or whether it considers an alternative justification. He points out that reason and emotion are not separated in our lives, are not two separate processes (which is true, though hardly momentous); he claims that there are reasons for regarding reasoning as preferable to non-rational methods for altering attitudes (one wonders if he is not *ipso facto* separating reason from emotion, but let that pass); he holds that emotions cannot lead to understanding (*pace* perceptive women and the emotional expression he gave vent to in this context); he aims to *prove* that the 'is cannot entail ought' 'fallacy' is not a fallacy, but is based on an uncritical acceptance of the Humian view (without making it clear how he would prove this); he discusses the difficulty of resolving moral disagreements with the aim of showing that agreement can in principle be reached by rational means, des-

pite the practical impossibility of resolving them (evidently to leave
the path of rationality open) (without pointing out that, even if disagreements could be resolved, i.e. a *consensus gentium* achieved, this
would not establish a conclusion beyond the fact that people as a whole
might agree, even though wrongly); and further he claims that a
rational method can be used to arrive at an evaluation in all cases
(presumably meaning 'in principle,' but no indication is given about
how this might be established).

My factual summary is accompanied by an evaluation insinuated in
my parenthetic comments. In brief, though Walter has provided an
interesting paper, he has not put over a clear argument to show that
the 'naturalistic fallacy' is not a fallacy. Moreover, his overall position
is undermined by his assuming that the denial that value-judgments
can follow from statements of fact is supported by no new argument
but rests solely on Hume's premiss; this is contrary to historical fact,
as is clear from the next paper.

2) It is not that Dr. Leavenworth (or subsequent speakers) disagrees
with Walter's rejection of the naturalistic fallacy; but she recognizes
that the assertion of the fallacy has other support than Hume's. Indeed
she accepts the standard argument that, whatever naturalistic account
of 'good' is offered, one may ask of it whether it is good.

May Leavenworth provides an interesting approach to the problem
of the Gap. Her way of bridging it is to find that, if we look at it from
the right angle, it has been full all the time. First we are to note that
the ethical philosopher, if not involved in the world, is 'alienated' from
his self as a person-in-the-world; in that case, a natural self cannot
value and an alienated self must perform the non-natural function of
intuiting non-natural properties (nicely put). But if not alienated, then
values become institutions. In short the trick is that: eliminate alienation and then fact and value live happily ever after (but *ought* we to
eliminate alienation?). For, with alienation overcome, evaluative processes are natural acts of a biological entity possessing intelligence, or
alternatively put institutions will embody principles and values and
will be natural processes; thus we cannot separate facts and values, for
institutions, by involving principles and values, are both. (I confess to
some doubt about how this merger is manipulated.) She makes some
appropriate comment on Hare, with a view to showing that his powerful method of exposing the naturalistic fallacy does not damage her
approach. Her thesis is this: moral principles are empirical generalizations that satisfy needs/situations; in a natural world, institutions

provide normative standards (how? is this true for non-alienated selves? The thesis is obscure at this point); 'commending' (from Hare she takes over that 'good' = 'commended') is directed at what satisfies these standards.

Paradoxically, I find this fascinating, and only wish I could understand it.

Further, it would seem open to the devastating criticism that it would be wrong to alter standards. Nonetheless, May Leavenworth is perfectly alive to this point, but she admits it holds only for an alienated self and audaciously denies that it holds for a natural self (this denial I do not understand—no doubt because of my alienation).

Be these things as they may, May Leavenworth's thesis boils down to this: What is 'good' = What satisfies requirements = What has 'utility' = What is a suitable *means*. Thus is would seem that the Gap she has filled is that of *means;* but the problem of fact and value concerns *ends.* Otherwise thus: she turns her trick by covertly excluding the *deontological* point at stake.

3) An ally follows. Dr. Orenstein provides some equally arresting material. This in the shape of an excursion into Hindu notions of 'purity' and 'pollution.' From there he launches on to the still higher plane of meta-imperatives, which he claims are objective, i.e. can be discovered dispassionately through reason, at least they can be found in all ethical systems.

Perhaps Orenstein's ideas are arresting *because* they are irrelevant. At all events, his ending is inconclusive—or rather he candidly admits that he cannot establish his disbelief in the Gap, in the naturalistic fallacy.

One cannot be blamed for failing to solve a fundamental problem; it eases the listener's burden to be told candidly that there is no solution insinuated behind a smoke screen; there remains, however, the practical consideration, whether to hand in a blank sheet of paper when one has nothing to say about a problem or to write interestingly about something else (personally I am glad to have read this irrelevant paper).

I will add a comment on an irrelevancy. Orenstein writes of the notion of 'purity'; and this is interesting because it has dropped out of western culture (for interesting reasons). One thinks of man's aim as being, e.g. happiness, pleasure, duty-no-matter-what, self-sacrifice, etc., but who in the west bothers about purity? Yet it is an understandable notion. And it is not in fact peculiar to the east, for it is surely also Jewish and Christian (cf. the notion of washing away sin). However, in bringing in this notion, Orenstein in effect makes the point that an ethic dominated by the notion of duty is narrower than and different from one dominated by the notion of sin. The contrast underlines the fact that twentieth century man, while full to bursting with the importance of duty, on the whole does not take sin very seriously. (Wherein he may be overlooking something, if Bertrand Russell is right—he thought the world would be nothing like such fun without sin.)

4) Dr. Fay's general attitude is pretty well identical despite difference of content.

He takes over that 'is' and 'ought' are linked by *wanting* and by *role;* evidently agrees with May Leavenworth that 'role' involves the value concept of appropriateness; contends that evolution is not merely biological but biocultural (which is very well put); notes that culture and ethics are both 'emergent' and 'dependent'; makes a (confused) claim that the social self is reducible individualistically on the grounds that culture does not exist independently of individuals; expresses a 'naturalism' in claiming that nothing concerning value transcends a biocultural view of man; and concludes in an obscure discussive fashion that, because of evolution, we are in an unfinished state (true) and that nothing about values can be said with definiteness (which is opting out), but that conflict has its place, having previously pointed out that it can have adaptive value, and that there can be an overall adaptation.

No doubt there is an overall adaptation, or we shouldn't be here— not a very smooth one as the world's troubles show but one that just gets by. Let me give you a report of my field-work on *homo holywoodicus* among the Antids. A great prophet arose and converted the people; the times had been fraught with profligacy; and the prophet, who was popularly acclaimed, though she never admitted it herself, to be a re-incarnation of Queen Victoria, won the people over to an unusual form of ethics, for they held that sexual relations were intrinsically wrong; celibacy was extended from the priesthood over a great part of the population, who extolled its virtues with much fervor and righteousness; there were some dissidents, but they were a small minority and feared congressional persecution; some of them practised their cult only during the 'safe' period; the rest took for breakfast a form of orange-juice that contained the pill. In the course of one generation, i.e. what might have been a generation, the community ceased to be. And their ethical doctrine, defeated by a mere science, the Darwinism theory, ceased to have adherents. Some archaeologists, digging north of Los Angeles, came to the tentative conclusion that ethics and evolution have a bearing on each other. Fay, however, more far-seeing, noted that some moral attitudes have evolutionari-wise become built into the social structure, thus in effect following the spirit of May Leavenworth in holding that value is built into insti-tutions.

However this overall functional view, drawn from one of his men-tor's, would seem to be restricted to ethics concerned with the notion of a part with a function, the function of subserving the whole, and so has at most value of a utilitarian or efficiency kind—means to end; it thus sweeps under the carpet the notion of value-appropriateness. The paper makes a definite contribution but does not meet the fact-value problem. So we are back, as usual, at square one.

There are two issues: (i) is there a broad ethical issue to which we want to have a certain sort of answer, which will almost certainly com-mit the naturalistic fallacy, (ii) is the 'is' to 'ought' inference really fallacious?

(i) This would seem to be indicated by the growing unwillingness to accept the naturalistic fallacy. All four speakers have tried to get round it, either by logical argument or by side-stepping it; and recent literature also reveals a war of attrition against it, even though not an open attack.

What in fact is the point these four symposiasts are trying to make or to protect? (1) Walter wants to preserve rational discussion of moral issues. Very reasonable. Also very interesting. Because one would have expected a naturalistic ethic to have drained ethics of its rationality; yet here he is, saying that an ethic rooted in deontological concepts can-not be rational, presumably because there is no way of establishing the validity of one deontological theory over its rivals. A strong point. (2) May Leavenworth wants people to be whole persons. Good. And she wants us to see values embedded in our society. Good. But isn't she mixing up two things? Some values are values of individuals, but some are values that belong essentially to communities. Justice, for example, is not a value that characterizes transactions between two persons; nor even a collection of persons; it involves a society or at least a group. So some values are institutional. But she need not hold (as she seems to) that institutions (necessarily) provide normative standards. But she is doing a service in drawing attention to the fact (which I first came across stressed by Clara Williams[1]) that some values are institutional or societal. (3) Ornstein wants to remind us that peoples hold very different codes of values, but nonetheless that mankind is somehow one as regards what underlies their codes. Good. This may even be true. (If so, it poses an interesting task for committees for international education: is it possible for *homo americanus* to communicate with swarm-man?) (4) Fay wants to relate ethics not only to evolution as a biological process but to culture as an evolutionary product. Presumably the message is that if we want to solve our moral problems or understand change, we should have a better chance if we see them in the setting of cultural evolution (rather than in terms of absolute values).

These philosophers evidently do not want anarchy or a free-for-all subjectivism. They want to be able to solve moral problems; they want values to be regarded as immanent in society, not transcendent (as deontological concepts might be regarded as being); they want such values to unite man; they want to allow for change. (I have said 'they,' I believe correctly, though these clauses obviously correspond respectively to the four speakers.)

Good.

Does this aim *require* the naturalistic fallacy to be validated? In my opinion, no.

(ii) Is the naturalistic fallacy really a fallacy? The standard reasons for this, repeated in this symposium, seem conclusive. So how do we handle the situation? What may need to be denied is that deontological concepts are really relevant to ethics. If this could be shown, the procedures of our symposiasts, their ideas of appropriateness of role and of biocultural evolution might find a home. Let us explore this briefly.

I begin by admitting the overwhelming force of the need for objectivity in ethics, and by admitting the overwhelming force of the subjectivist position. It is no use turning a blind eye to these two factors just because they are inconsistent, because we want to back one of them, and because we want to sweep the other under the carpet. We begin soberly, therefore, by realizing that we cannot accept one of these alternatives, however powerful an argument we find for it, unless we at the same time satisfy the force of the other alternative.

I. Being a person means at least having desires and needs—say, having vital interests. Further it involves recognition of interests in others, where 'recognition' conveys the possibility of toleration of another's interests. Thus you cannot be a person unless you recognize others as persons and tolerate their interests.

II. Consider Leonard Nelson's version of the categorical imperative: (*a*) 'In deciding between alternative actions, take into account the interests of others who are affected by your action *equally* with your own'; and (*b*) 'Do not carry out an alternative you could not consent to if you had in mind not only your own interest but *equally* the interests of those others.'

III. Corresponding to this, let us construct a *hypothetical injunction*: *if* you wish to be even in part a person, which involves treating others as persons, *then* you can do this only by taking account of their felt interests.

IV. This hypothetical injunction does not tell us we *ought* to recognize the interests of others—it does not include categorical obligation. It involves only a form of utility-appropriateness: recognizing the interests of others is what you should show *if* you wish to be a person—but if you do not wish to be a person, the hypothetical does not tell you you ought to.

V. The extent to which men take into account the felt interest of others is the extent to which they succeed in being persons.

VI. Thus the *categorical* imperative—apart from exhortation and the like—has no ethical role. Otherwise expressed, deontological concepts are otiose.

VII. But given the intention of being a person then certain rules become obligatory—thus explaining the appearance of absoluteness pertaining to ethics.

VIII. The hypothetical injunction is a compound of psychological fact about recognition and of philosophical theory about personhood. It would seem to provide a basis for the appearance of universality that characterizes moral imperatives, while at the same time allowing variation and change. For, the appearance of universality, or the sense of objectivity, would stem from a common conception of personhood, while variation (or cultural relativism) would reflect variation and development in the awareness of others.

IX. An extreme form of change occurs if a person decides to opt out of recognition of the interests of others; but if he opts out, he ceases to be a person.

Thus I conclude by supporting the symposiasts in their search, not however by denying the naturalistic fallacy, but by denying the relevance to ethics of deontological concepts or categorical obligability.

Reference

1. Williams, Clara, Values as Structural Principles: a comparison of two societies, *M.A. Thesis*, University of Southern California, June 1961.

Recommended Reading—
Naturalistic Facts and Human Values

Ackerman, Robert. 'Normative Explanation,' *Philosophy and Phenomenological Research*, January, 1964.

Aiyar, N. C. *Mayne's Treatise on Hindu Law and Usage*, Higginbothams Ltd., 1953.

Albert, Ethel M., and Kluckhohn, Clyde. *A Selected Bibliography on Values, Ethics, and Esthetics in the Behavioral Sciences and Philosophy, 1920–1958*. Glencoe: Free Press, 1959.

Baier, Kurt, and Rescher, Nicholas, (eds.). *Values and the Future*. New York: The Free Press, 1969.

Cohen, Yehudi A. 'Introduction,' *Man in Adaptation: The Biosocial Background*. Yehudi A. Cohen, (ed.). Chicago: Aldine, 1968.

Dobzhansky, Theodosius. *Mankind Evolving*. New Haven: Yale University Press, 1962.

Dumont, L., and Pocock, D. 'Pure and Impure,' *Contributions to Indian Sociology*, **3**, pp. 9–39.

Edel, Abraham. *Ethical Judgment*. Glencoe: Free Press, 1955.

Edel, Abraham. 'The Relation of Fact and Value: A Reassessment,' in *Experience, Existence and the Good*, I. C. Lieb (ed.).

Edel, May, and Edel, Abraham. *Anthropology and Ethics*. Springfield: Charles Thomas, 1959.

Ehrmann, Jacques (ed.). *Structuralism (Yale French Studies*, Nos. 36–67).

Emmett, Dorothy. *Rules, Roles and Relations*. London: Macmillan, 1966.

Foot, Philippa, (ed.). *Theories of Ethics*. London: Oxford University Press, 1967.

Frankena, W. K. 'The Naturalistic Fallacy,' *Mind*, **XLVIII**, 1939.

Fuller, Lon L. *The Morality of Law*. New Haven: Yale University Press, 1964.

Hare, R. M. *The Language of Morals*. Oxford: Clarendon Press, 1952.

Harper, Edward. 'Ritual Pollution as an Integrator of Caste and Religion,' *Journal of Asian Studies*, **23**, pp. 151–97.

Hutton, J. H. *Caste in India*, Oxford University Press, 1951.

Huxley, Julian. *Evolution in Action*. New York: Mentor Book edition, 1957.

Huxley, Julian. *Knowledge, Morality, and Destiny* (original title: *New Bottles for New Wine*). New York: New American Library Mentor Books, 1957.

Kane, P. V. *History of Dharmashastra* (5 vols.). Bhardarkar Oriental Research Institute, 1930–62.

Lévi-Strauss. *Structural Anthropology*. New York: Basic Books, 1963.

Lévi-Strauss. *The Savage Mind*. Chicago: University of Chicago Press, 1966.

MacIntyre, A. C. 'Hume on "Is" and "Ought",' in Hume, *A Collection of Critical Essays*, V. C. Chapell, (ed.). New York: Doubleday Anchor Book Original, 1966.

Maslow, Abraham H. (ed.). *New Knowledge in Human Values*. New York: Harper, 1959.

Moore, G. E. *Principia Ethica*. Cambridge: University Press, 1960.

Nunokawa, Walter D. (ed.). *Human Values and Abnormal Behavior*. Glenview: Scott Foresman, 1965.

Northrop, F. S. C. *The Meeting of East and West*. New York: Macmillan, 1946.

Northrop, F. S. C., and Livingston, H. H. (eds.). *Cross Cultural Understanding: Epistemology in Anthropology*. New York: Harper and Row, 1964.

Pepper, Stephen C. *The Sources of Value*. Berkeley and Los Angeles: University of California Press, 1958.

Quinton, Anthony. 'Ethics and the Theory of Evolution,' in *Biology and Personality*. I. T. Ramsey (ed.). Oxford: Basil Blackwell, 1965.

Redfield, Robert. *The Primitive World and Its Transformations*. Ithaca: Cornell University Press, 1953.

Rosenfeld, Albert. *The Second Genesis*. Englewood Cliffs: Prentice-Hall, 1969.

Searle, John R. 'How to Derive "Ought" from "Is",' *Philosophical Review*, January, 1964.

Sesonske, Alexander. *Value and Obligation*. New York: Oxford University Press, 1964.

Scheffler, Israel. 'Anti-Naturalistic Restrictions in Ethics,' *Journal of Philosophy*. L, July, 1953, pp. 457–66.

Scheffler, Israel. 'On Justification and Committment,' *Journal of Philosophy*. LI, 1954, pp. 180–90.

Srinivas, M. N. *Religion and Society Among the Coorgs of South India*. Oxford University Press, 1952.

Stevenson, C. L. *Ethics and Language*. New Haven: Yale University Press, 1962.

Waddington, C. H. *The Ethical Animal*. London: George Allen & Unwin, 1960.

Young, J. Z. *Doubt and Certainty in Science*. New York: Oxford University Press, 1960.

Science, Freedom, and Determinism

The Verification of the
Free Will Hypothesis

MARY CARMAN ROSE

Goucher College

By the free will hypothesis I mean the hypothesis that some—but, of course, only some—human decisions are genuinely free. Being free, they are not to be understood solely in terms of efficient causality; and being responsible, deliberate, and rational, they are not to be understood by appeal to a-causality.[1] If what I have called the free will hypothesis is an authentic hypothesis, then it is neither a postulate nor a 'convention' to which truth and falsity are irrelevant nor a derivative conclusion whose truth depends solely upon the truth of more fundamental propositions.[2] In what follows I wish to explore the possibility of providing an empirical investigation of the free will hypothesis.

Clearly, empirical investigation requires public experiential verification of hypothesis, since empiricism's most significant criterion of truth[3] is verification in inter-subjective experience of predictions derived from a hypothesis in conjunction with other relevant previously established empirical conclusions as well as assumptions of which the investigator may be unaware or which he has deliberately accepted because they appear to be obviously true. On the other hand, working hypotheses, hypotheses, and the concepts used in the formulation of hypotheses may have a variety of origins. They may, of course, be carefully derived from a considerable array of inter-subjective data. They may also be deduced from well established hypotheses and, being deduced, they may be intended to pertain to the same area as the latter. They may represent the tentative extension of a conclusion already demonstrated to be true of one area to another area significantly different from the first. They may be imaginative and speculative, having initially very little inter-subjective data to support them. Or, finally, the individual may have found them fruitful in the interpretation of his own subjective experience.

These observations have an immediate relevance for the present inquiry. For example, even though efficient causality has been demonstrated to be the most fruitful category for the interpretation of the flux within some areas of empirical investigation (e.g. classical physics), we may not without specific inquiry accept it as adequate for the interpretation of all aspects of flux within the human self. Also, the fact that 'free will' is not initially clearly definable by appeal only to inter-subjective data is not a deterrent to the empirical examination of the free will hypothesis. In fact, in recent years we have discovered that some of our empirical investigation of nature require the use of concepts which are not derived from and which have no analogue in sensory data. And, as I shall emphasize below, it is a likelihood that some human concerns, decisions, and affective states, with their profoundly important subjective aspect, require the use of concepts that are not exemplified in sensory experience.

'Free will' is initially present in this inquiry as a working concept. A working concept is a concept used at the outset of an empirical investigation because it is judged to be potentially fruitful and the meaning of which is purposely left unclear and incomplete. The working concept possesses a suggested meaning rather than a carefully worked out definition, and in empirical investigation it is no less useful than the working hypothesis—which a few generations ago some analysts of the empirical method rejected as having no legitimate role of the structure of empirical inquiry. In mid-twentieth century, however, it has become clear that very often empirical inquiry proceeds by the verification of the hypothesis that a particular working concept will be fruitful in the interpretation of a particular set of data. Complete and precise definition of such a concept will be one product of the demonstration of the usefulness of the concept. Thus, free will—defined initially as a category for the interpretation of the character of some human choices, different from both efficient causality and a-causality, and by virtue of which the individual is capable of genuine autonomy in the shaping of his future—is a legitimate working concept.

Of course, empirical investigation requires from the outset experiences which can serve as evidence in support of the hypothesis we seek to verify. And, recalling that there is no proscription of an initial appeal to subjective experience, we may initiate the search for data relevant to the free will hypothesis by asking whether among human decisions there are any of which it may be said that if the individual does, indeed, possess the capacity for a free choice, then surely these decisions are free. We may stipulate three characteristics which must be possessed by the decisions chosen as a source of relevant evidence. First, these decisions must not be any which from the point of view of our present knowledge of the self seem to be easily explained as the product of efficient causality alone. It would not do, for example, to select decisions which apparently derive from sub-conscious pressures. Second, these decisions must be deliberate. Even though the free will hypothesis may be true, we need not interpret the unreflective or purely reflexive act as free. Third, the decision must be made with reference to a principle—or what is more likely, perhaps, to a number of principles. The moral decision, for example, is made with reference to whatever moral principles the individual accepts. By virtue of its relation to such principles the free choice is not random; and, hence, it differs from the a-causal event; and it is carefully worked out, and hence it differs from the irresponsible choice.

While there are a number of types of decisions which satisfy these requirements, I choose for anlysis what I shall call the 'difficult moral choice.' This type of decision is especially relevant to inquiry concerning the free will hypothesis because historically significant discussion of the free will-determinism problem has often derived from the concern with man's relation to a moral law. Also, and as I shall emphasize below, when the individual makes a difficult moral choice he must exert some effort—sometimes a very great effort—in which he either believes or pretends that he believes that he makes a genuinely free choice. If the difficult moral choice is free, then the individual who makes such a choice knows at first hand something of the nature of free will, although since not all aspects of the self are directly observable, he will not be able to observe all aspects of the free choice. As a first step, then, we may pose a traditional question: Can the individual by inspection of his own acquaintance with the difficult moral choice find any evidence that the choice is free? Examination of that kind of choice discloses several distinct elements.

There are the moral principles according to which the individual makes the choice; his conviction that these principles are relevant to this particular situation; whatever he envisages as possible choices in that situation; that one of the possible choices which he is convinced is the right (or most nearly right) choice; his desire to make the morally right choice; the conflicting desires which he must silence in order to make the choice; all that he believes to be his knowledge of himself and of the particular situation by virtue of which he is able to make the choice effectively; and, finally, the effort required for him to make the choice as well as to sustain the effort which is necessary for him to see the choice through. This effort is a *sine qua non* of the difficult moral choice. Some of the other elements—e.g. which moral principles the individual accepts or which additional choices occur to the individual as possibilities—may be the products of efficient causality; but if the choice is free, then this effort must have an ingredient of freedom, and in making the choice the individual knows the free choice at first hand.

The difficulty of this choice derives from the allure of other possible choices—choices which may be initially less difficult to make and less difficult to carry through, but which also are not compatible with what the individual judges to be the moral choice. Hence the effort of the difficult moral choice is an effort which the individual makes against those aspects of himself which respond to the allure of possible choices which are also found to be lesser goods when they are judged by his moral principles. The difficult moral choice requires the effort to make one's desires, concerns, thoughts, and overt acts conform to a standard; and hence it requires the two-fold effort of the denying of competing lesser choices and of compliance—to the extent that one is able—with the requirements of one's moral principles. This two-fold effort is common to all difficult moral choices, though the quality and the degree of effort required will depend upon the moral capacities of the individual; upon the particular circumstances of each choice; and upon the content of the individual's moral principles.[4]

Undeniably the difficult moral choice is a deeply significant recurrent human experience. In the inquiry concerning the free will hypothesis this kind of experience with its decisive effort has a two-fold function: it is one source of the free will hypothesis and it is also a source of evidence concerning the possible truth of the hypothesis. In an empirical investigation any one set of experiences may have this dual role, since the experiences which are the source of the hypothesis simultaneously provide a clue to its fruitfulness. Hence, on the one hand, the effort of the difficult moral choice yields the insight that some category other than a-causality or efficient causality may be required for the interpretation of that experience; and, on the other hand, it also provides some evidence that a category that bestows the capacity for genuine autonomy upon the individual may be a fruitful mode of interpretation of that experience.

This initial appeal to the investigator's first-hand acquaintance with the difficult moral choice, along with the logic of the empirical investigation, provides a complex mode of verification of the free will hypothesis. Empirical investigation proceeds by the prediction of future experiences which are compatible with our hypothesis; and, as I have already indicated, these predictions derive not only from the hypothesis, but also from previously empirically derived relevant beliefs and fundamental assumptions concerning the area of inquiry. Relevant to the present area of inquiry are four widely accepted, experientially derived beliefs which together with the free will hypothesis yield the type of predictions requisite for empirical investigation. First, there is the belief that in proportion as any particular aspect of the self is brought into play the individual acquires increased facility in its use. Examples of such increased facility are provided by the development which takes place in most (and perhaps all) learning processes, although the mode of achievement of the increased facility will vary with the type of learning. It will be different, for example, in learning a language; in learning to solve differential equations; in learning the motor responses useful in driving an automobile; or in learning to make the difficult moral choice. Second, there is the belief that development or atrophy of a particular capacity will be accompanied by a change in related aspects of the self. Once more, this pertains to a great many types of change within the self, depending upon which capacity has developed or atrophied. Obviously, I am interested here in the kind of change within the self which will accompany the increased facility to make a difficult moral choice, this change being a common phenomenon in moral experience. Third, there is the belief that if one's moral principles are genuinely relevant to the human self, then, if they are appropriated, they will provide a quality of satisfaction that is not present where they are rejected. For example, if we urge as moral principles the cultivation of integrity, courage, and charity, we are at least tacitly assuming that they provide a quality and depth of satisfaction not provided by dishonesty, cowardice, intolerance, or hatred. Fourth, there is the belief that when the individual possesses true insight concerning himself and acts in terms of that insight his decisions are more fruitful and beneficial for him than when he acts in terms of what is false or only partly true. Some of these insights will pertain to the individual alone. They will, for example, pertain to his fears, hopes, frustrations, or talents which he by no means shares with all men. On the other hand, some of his true insights will pertain to him because they pertain to most or, perhaps, to all men. If the free will hypothesis is true, then such is the insight that he possesses a capacity for making a difficult moral choice which is genuinely free.

It will be fruitful to illustrate this step in the verification of the free will hypothesis by using as an example of the choice made in accordance with a set of moral principles the choice made in accordance with the individual's present understanding of the ideals of integrity, courage, and charity. Then we may pose this question: if these ideas are relevant to the self; if the capacity for the difficult moral choice develops as it is called into play; if this development brings with it development of other aspects of the self; if the individual's decisions which are made in accordance with true insight concerning himself have effects within himself which are fruitful and beneficial; and if the free will hypothesis is true, then when an individual repeatedly makes the difficult moral choice in the appropriation of these ideals, what can he expect to find in his future experience by way of verification of the free will hypothesis?

At least a part of the answer is that he can expect to find that his moral nature by no means remains unchanged; that his capacities to act in accordance with what he believes to be the dictates of integrity, courage, and charity will develop; and that, in a variety of ways, these choices become less difficult. And, in general, the individual who consistently tries to make such choices, does, indeed, find these redictions verified in his experience. He finds that his capacities for acting in terms of these ideals have increased; that there is an increase of his insight into the content and the demands of these ideals; that he becomes acquainted with the effects within his character structure of the acts that are honest, courageous, and charitable; and that he gains facility in the making of what he believes to be a free choice—perhaps in the sense that the allure of competing goods has lessened.

Clearly, the epistemological structure of this investigative step is analogous to that of empirical inquiry; the individual has asked a question which derives from his experience; he has developed a tentative answer to that question; and he has verified the answer in his experience. Since, however, the experience to which he appeals as evidence has been for the most part (if not wholly) subjective rather than inter-subjective, the conclusion that the free will hypothesis is probably true cannot be expected to be persuasive to the scientific community. What, then, of the possibility of proceeding finally to a public verification of the individual's conclusion pertaining to the probable truth of the free will hypothesis? There are several preliminary points to be noted here.

First, even though public verification requires sensory data, almost never are the sensory data themselves our objects of inquiry. In most empirical investigations the objects concerning which we seek knowledge cannot be observed directly: they may be too far away or too small; or they may not be spatially located so that we can have direct access to them. In large part empirical science is a matter of learning to read our sensory experience as symbols of our objects of inquiry.[5] Our difficult moral choices are among the possible objects of empirical investigation which are not open to direct inspection by the senses and which can be given a public investigation only in so far as we can learn to correlate them with sense data. The effort of the difficult moral choice; the allure of competing goods; the effort of denying these goods; the recognition that one now comprehends more of the demands of charity, integrity, and courage as ideals than one did formerly—all these are to be distinguished from whatever overt behavior may accompany them. The effort of making the choice; the overt acts necessary to seeing the decision through; the growth of the comprehension of the content of an ideal—these are all distinct from each other; they call into play different aspects of the self and have different functions within the complex process in which the individual makes a choice and completes whatever action follows upon that choice. If we are able to investigate the free will hypothesis by means of successful public inquiry concerning the difficult moral choice and its effects upon the individual's experience and character structure, it will be because we have learned to interpret the sense data (e.g. overt behavior) which symbolize them and are correlated with them but are not identical with them.

Second, although we have no choice but to seek verification by appeal to sense data as the ultimate demonstration of the truth of our hypotheses, nonetheless, it is contrary to the ethos of empiricism to set a priori or arbitrary limits to the potential investigative usefulness of sensory data; to those kinds of objects for which we may seek to devise an empirical investigation; or to the concepts or insights we may examine for their scientific or philosophical fruitfulness. We cannot say what categories we will in future find fruitful in the comprehension of the structure of the human self or in the investigation of subjective experience. And we may not stipulate *a priori* what kinds of categories will be found useful in our empirical investigation; nor restrict future investigation of the human self to a limited set of categories; nor cease to try the fruitfulness of new categories. The concept of free will is, of course, a case in point. If when it is used as a working concept it should prove fruitful, then with the evidence thus obtained, we can

G*

begin to develop an empirically adequate definition of 'free will.'
Clearly, however, unless we take these first steps toward seeking evidence of the relevance of free will as a category for the comprehension
of human subjective experience, we will not achieve either an adequate
definition of it or knowledge of its fruitfulness.

Third, it may be that some of the categories which ultimately will be
found essential to our comprehension of the self are not exemplified
in sensory data. In fact, given the qualitative differences between our
subjective experience and our overt activity—between, for example,
the deep concern of the difficult moral choice and the overt behavior
which accompanies it—it is to be expected that it will be so. Surely,
as a rule, it is appropriate to conceive of the overt activity and the
physiological activities which accompany joy, sorrow, deep anxiety,
and the difficult moral choice as part of these highly significant human
experiences. Nonetheless, the overt behavior and the physiological
processes, on the one hand, and the subjective experiences, on the
other, are distinctive elements within the whole complex situation
where the experiences are present and they have distinct functions
within it. And if the free will hypothesis is true, then it is likely that
the concept of free will would be among those categories which are
useful for the interpretation of flux (i.e. in this case a type of human
decision-making) and not discernable in sensory data. Yet it is to be
expected that the difficult moral choice and its freedom would have
effects on overt behavior; and our problem is to learn to recognize
these effects. I shall emphasize this point below.

Fourth, what the individual observer finds in any particular set of
sense data depends upon what interpretation he is able to give them,
and this in turn depends upon what capacities he brings to his inquiry.
Certainly each of the natural sciences requires in the investigator the
presence of cultivated specialized capacities. Analogous comments are
to be made concerning the free will hypothesis. For example, to be
prepared for inquiry into the evidential value of the difficult moral
choice, the investigator must be acquainted with the dynamics of that
type of choice. Also, he must have some understanding of the significance for the human spirit of the moral life; of the difficult moral
choice; and of the possibility that that choice is free. Further, the
investigator's finesse in examining the free will hypothesis will be increased if he knows at first-hand what it is to make or to endeavor to
make the difficult moral choice. A corollary of this last observation is
that in the investigation of the free will hypothesis, the character of the
investigator's moral committment and capacities has an investigative

role—a role which is qualitatively distinct from any role it might have in the natural sciences.

So far as public verification of the free will hypothesis is concerned what, then, of the problem of learning to interpret another's overt behavior as a symbol of the content and the structure of his choices? There are at least three possibilities: it may be that all; some but only some; or no difficult moral choices have specific, identifiable correlates in overt behavior. Obviously, it is contrary to the ethos of empiricism to choose among these possibilities without adequate investigation or to assume a priori that the investigation of any one of these possibilities will not be fruitful.

If our attempts to cultivate a set of moral principles (e.g. to act in terms of the requirements of such ideals as integrity, courage, and charity) have effects on our moral capacities and character structure, then it is to be expected that these latter will in turn have their effects on our overt action. We will do well, however, to emphasize the distinction between the overt activities which accompany or follow immediately upon the making of a particular difficult moral choice and the overt activities of which the individual eventually becomes capable because, as a result of his repeated effort at making the choice, his moral capacities have developed and he has acquired new insight into his ideals and has become capable of making and of carrying through new kinds of decisions. Hence, although the content of the difficult moral choice may not be immediately and decisively revealed in the individual's overt behavior, there may be a discoverable and predictable relationship between the new content of subjective experience which is the product of the developed capacities and the overt behavior which in one way or another expresses this new content.

Thus the free will hypothesis may receive a partial—although a most significant—verification by the prediction of progressive changes in the individual's character structure which eventuate in decisive, permanent changes in his overt behavior following upon his appropriation of a set of moral ideals. It is to be expected that the length of time required for an individual's moral concerns and moral effort to work their changes in his moral capacities and subsequently in his overt activities will vary from individual to individual, for individuals differ not only in their moral capacities but also in their perseverance in what they believe to be their use of their capacities for a free choice. Hence, it would be unwise to stipulate initially that any particular length of time would be sufficient for the cumulative effects of the individual's difficult moral choices to make discernable differences in his overt behavior. Perhaps the complexities of the human self and the diversities among persons are such that the conclusion that eventually the difficult moral choice will have observable results in overt activity will have to be left open-ended not only in respect to the particular kind of overt activity that will represent positive verification but also in respect to the length of time that would be required for the changes to appear.

In the foregoing I have intended to suggest that in the verification of the free will hypothesis we have a uniquely important opportunity to achieve clarity concerning the de facto present-day usefulness of subjective data in inquiry which has the epistemological structure of empiricism; that the concept of free will provides a valuable example of a category specifically useful for the interpretation of human experience as opposed to the non-human aspects of nature; that in the process of verification we will be interpreting the human personality as a complex unity and not taking an interest only in its behaviorial aspects; and that in this inquiry new investigative roles will be given to the investigator's valuational capacities. If these suggestions are true, it follows that in the verification of the free will hypothesis we have an opportunity to achieve increased understanding of the very logic and potentialities of empiricism itself.

Notes and References

1. The view that all human decisions can be explained by appeal to efficient causality alone is, of course, the perennial position known as determinism. Since the development of the Principle of Indeterminacy in physics the appeal to a-causality as a way of explaining the free choice has come into fashion again, although, of course, Epicurus in his own way tried this also. In twentieth century a-causality has been judged to have at least two types of relevance to the free will-determinism problem. It has been suggested that the possibility that there is indeterminacy at the heart of matter provides an argument against the determinism which was widely accepted at the end of the nineteenth century. And, on the other hand, it has been argued that the alternative to efficient causality is randomicity and, hence, that the free choice must be irresponsible. (See, for example, Max Planck, *Where is Science Going?* trans. by James Murphy [London: George Allen, and Unwin: 1933], Chapters IV and V.) In this essay I am taking the point of view that causality and a-causality are not exhaustive of the possibilities for the interpretation of flux and that what has traditionally been known as free will is a third possibility. The relations among the three may be described thus: in efficient causality there is a closed future and the flux is governed by natural law; in a-causality there is an open future and freedom from natural law; and in free will there would

be an open future the content of which the individual decides by virtue of his making a decision in accordance with principles (of whatever kind) which he accepts.

2. This is different from Immanuel Kant's point of view that the belief in free will is an irresistible postulate of the moral nature; from the point of view that our fundamental beliefs which inform our areas of inquiry are conventions even though we find it convenient to articulate them in propositional form; and from the medieval rationalist's view that man's freedom can be established with logical certainty because it can be deduced from logically certain premisses pertaining to the human self and to man's moral nature.

3. I have said that verification in experience is the most significant criterion of truth in empirical inquiry. A secondary criterion of truth derives from the fact that in any one area of empirical investigation, particular conclusions are mutually coherent. At the very least this means that they do not contradict one another, and an additional meaning would be that they illumine and supplement each other. This criterion of truth, however, has itself been empirically determined. Verification in experience is the only criterion of truth which derives from the very epistemological structure of empiricism.

4. The more a particular moral principle demand that not only the overt action but also the feelings, thoughts, desires, and concerns conform to a standard, the more is it the case that certain individuals may accept the principles, be convinced of their relevance to them, desire to conform to their requirements, but be genuinely incapable of doing so. If they are permanently unable to become the kind of persons who can conform to the requirements of the principle, then for them the ideal is unattainable. Most moral principles require some transformation and development of the self before the individual can fully appropriate them.

5. Obviously this analysis presupposes a non-positivistic distinction between sensory experience, on the one hand, and all those real entities, events, and situations which are known to us only through experience but which are not to be identified with experience. In the very asking whether the free will hypothesis is true, however, non-positivistic interpretations of reality and the human self are implied. Neither have I written this paper from the point of view that 'reality' and 'human self' are phenomenological 'intentions.'

Psychology, Moral Philosophy, and Determinism

JOHN O'CONNOR

Case Western Reserve University

Many philosophers have argued that human freedom is necessary for morality. They have then been led to frame their accounts of human actions, decisions, behavior, etc., so as to allow for some degree of freedom, which they feel is necessary for men to be moral. In this paper, I will argue, however, that freedom is not a necessary condition for morality, that even if determinism—in a sense incompatible with human freedom—is true and men believe that it is true, it is still perfectly possible for men to be moral.

I undertake this investigation in part for its own sake, but in part to illustrate one way in which scientific theories can be put to use in answering questions in moral philosophy, particularly in meta-ethics. Many philosophers would grant that anthropoligists and sociologists can supply them with interesting examples of moral behavior and moral standards, and that psychologists can give intriguing account of moral motivation and of moral development. How this material is to be used by the philosopher, however, is less easy to be clear about.

I suggest that one of its primary roles is to assist the philosopher in his conceptual investigations, by helping him to form concepts which are useful and indeed necessary if his investigations are to be fruitful. That is, scientific results are of interest to the philosopher not only as a stimulus to his imagination, but also as playing an important role in concept formation. The consideration in this paper of the relation between freedom and morality will be used to illustrate this.

Let us assume that the question 'Does morality presuppose freedom, or at least a belief in freedom?' is primarily a conceptual question. (I do not mean to suggest that there is a sharp line between conceptual and so-called 'empirical' questions.) That is, it is to be answered by laying out what it is to be free and what it is to be moral, and seeing if the latter requires the former. On this view of the question, the chief problem is sketching out the two concepts.

(Since my concern in this paper is primarily with the concept of morality, little discussion will be undertaken of the notoriously tricky notion of freedom. I use the term 'freedom' as the opposite of 'determinism,' where for a person to be determined to do something in this sense is for him to be unable to do anything else. When I say that all men are determined, I mean, therefore, that no one could do other than he in fact does on any occasion.)

We all have some intuitive notion of what it is to be moral: it involves at least acting in certain ways, being disposed to have certain 'moral' feelings (guilt, shame, etc.) in certain circumstances, and judging the behavior of oneself and others in certain ways. However, to be able to pick out moral men or moral behavior is not yet to have a concept clearly enough in mind to carry out philosophical investigation. The philosopher's job is to articulate that concept. It is here that psychology can play an important role.

One might try to give behavioral descriptions of moral human beings, but this is unlikely to be sufficient, since what the developmental factors which produce the behavior are we would not have made clear, and it is these factors which very likely might involve freedom (or a belief in it). Developmental psychology, however, suggests another way of formulating the concept of being moral, and, in fact, supplies a large part of the content of the concept:

Men are moral because they have become moral, and they have become moral by having undergone a certain development which is describable by psychological laws. Hence to find out what is presupposed by being moral, find out what is involved in the process of moral development. Hence a psychological theory of moral development (if it is the correct one) supplies to the philosopher a workable and fruitful concept of being moral.

The special value of forming the concept in this way is this: Not only will the philosopher be talking about moral human beings, since they are the ones who have undergone the process, but also he will be made aware of the various developmental factors which produce moral human beings. Such knowledge will make the conceptual investigation much sounder, since no 'hidden' features which might presuppose human freedom or a belief in it will be likely to have been omitted.

In this paper I will attempt to show that morality does not presuppose freedom, and hence that men can be moral, even if determinism is true, by characterizing being moral in terms of a psychological theory of moral development, and showing that there is nothing in the developmental process which requires either that men be free or that they believe themselves to be free. Of course, it is important to note that even if this argument is unsuccessful, the methodological point still stands: one of the benefits to be obtained from applying science to moral philosophy is that of concept formation.

Part I of this paper is a sketch of a psychological theory of moral development which derives mainly from the work of John Rawls and Jean Piaget. In Part II it is shown that the truth of the relevant psychological laws would be unaffected by the truth of determinism and that there is nothing in the statement of the antecedent conditions for the application of these laws which requires that men be free or believe themselves to be free. Part III treats of possible objections to this view; Part IV is summary.

I

The psychological theory which I will present is drawn from John Rawls' 'The Sense of Justice.'[1] Two things should be noted: Rawls points out that this theory is only meant as a hypothetical account. However, I feel that it is close enough to the results of, for example, Jean Piaget, that it represents a plausible account of moral development.[2] It may need modification in detail, but the modifications should not affect my argument. Second, the theory deals with the sense of justice only. However, I see no reason to assume that a more general theory might not be worked out to cover all moral development. I use Rawls' theory because it represents a plausible account in which the philosophical implications of moral development are made clear. As noted above, however, even if the psychological theory turns out to be incorrect, the method which this paper embodies of using a scientific theory to form a concept for philosophic investigation, is still sound.

Rawls gives three laws which describe the development in a person of the sense of justice. They are (I list them in the order in which (they apply to a person in the normal course of things):

a) A child, moved by certain instincts and regulated (if at all) by rational self-love, will come to love, and to recognize the love of, the parent if the parent manifestly loves the child.

b) If a person's capacity for fellow-feeling has been realized in accordance with the first law, then, where another, engaged with him in a joint activity known to satisfy certain principles of justice, with evident intention lives up to his duty of fair play, friendly feelings toward him develop as well as feelings of mutual trust and confidence.[3]

c) Given that the attitudes of love and trust, friendly feelings and mutual respect have been generated in accordance with the two previous psychological laws, then, if a person (and his associates) are the beneficiaries of a successful and enduring institution or scheme of cooperation known to satisfy certain principles of justice, he will acquire a sense of justice.[4]

It should be added, to complete the account, that persons with a sense of justice so formed will in general do their duty in particular cases. To substantiate this, a more detailed account of the sense of justice would be needed, but even without it it is plausible to assume that the psychological mechanism described here would be an adequate account of moral motivation.

Of course, this is not the only plausible set of laws which would describe moral development. For example one might use Piaget's more general formulations.[5] These, however, being limited to children, do not take into account so explicitly the final stage. Similar sorts of laws might be worked out to govern the acquisition of a sense of shame, and these would involve notions like self-respect. The force of my argument, however, would not be affected by this.

II

Two questions must be answered. First, does the truth of these laws (or of some set closely related to them) presuppose either that men are free or that men believe they are free? That is, is determinism or a belief in determinism incompatible with the truth of these laws? Second, is it a necessary condition for these laws to be applicable to a given person that the person be free or believe that he is? If the answer to both of these questions is no, then it follows (given the correctness and adequacy of the laws) that men can be moral even if they are not free and believe that they are not free.

With respect to the first question, the answer is obviously no. These laws might be true even if everyone has a true belief in determinism, they are scientific laws, and therefore would have the status of any scientific laws.[6]

The second question is more difficult; for it can be argued that while the laws would be true in a world inhabited by people who have a true belief in hard determinism, yet no person could ever be such that the laws would apply to him unless he were free or at least believed he was free. That is, the law may be of the form 'Whenever C then D,' but a necessary condition for C obtaining is that the person in question be free or believe he is.

To show that this is not the case, each of the statements of initial conditions in the three laws will be examined.

In the first law, it is clear that a child can be determined to have certain instincts and rational self-love. That is, there is no contradiction in saying that a child loves himself and has certain instincts because of certain causal conditions. Perhaps the ultimate explanation would be in terms of neurophysiology; in any case a child can be such that law (a) applies to him even if he is determined.

The second law is a bit more complicated. Certainly a person can be determined to engage in an activity with others. Even if he believes he is determined to engage in it, this need have no effect on the fact that he does engage in it.[7]

One might object that no *action* can be determined, but I find this highly implausible. Whether a person does something or not is one question, whether it is determined that he do it is in general another question. If one should argue that should a child be determined to engage in the activity, he is not responsible for engaging in it, this may well be true. It is however irrelevant. All that is in question is whether or not he could engage in it, and I do not see that determinism would be a barrier.

Two further points remain with respect to law (b). First, can a person who is determined come to recognize that an activity satisfies certain principles of justice?[8] The answer is yes, since there is nothing incoherent in supposing a person can be caused to recognize that some activity is fair. Second, can the person know that the other fellow has an intention to live up to the duty of fair play? The answer here is also yes, since whether a person is determined to recognize an intention or not does not affect the recognition of the intention. Hence, in the case of law (b), there is nothing in the statement of initial conditions which would preclude the law from applying to a person who had a true belief in determinism.

The first two laws state that, given certain conditions, a person will acquire such feelings as love, trust, mutual respect. Of course these are not morally neutral, for, as Rawls has shown, a person who loves will be liable to feelings of guilt should the bond be breached.[9] The same obtains with regard to mutual respect. Hence it might be argued that the discussion so far has not taken into account the moral aspects of these feelings, and that if these are taken into account, the need for freedom (or at least for a belief in freedom) will be shown. I will discuss this point below.

The third law yields no new problems, for a person can certainly come to enjoy the benefits of a system which he knows is fair even though he is determined to do so and he knows that he is so determined.

The preliminary result so far is that there is nothing with respect to the laws or the initial conditions embodied in them which would preclude a person developing morally in accord with them even if the person is determined to do so and knows that he is.

III

Before the thesis of this paper is fully substantiated two objections must be dealt with. The first is that implicit in the operations of the psychological laws is the assumption that a person commits himself to one or another course of action, pattern of behavior, etc., and that commitment presupposes freedom or at least a belief in freedom. The second is that all of the laws will apply only to persons who accept moral principles or have intuitive moral beliefs or are capable of certain moral feelings. From this it follows that morality must not be an empty notion, and in particular since moral responsibility is a central notion in morality and moral responsibility presupposes freedom, that the men to whom the laws apply must be free. If either of these objections is successful, then the argument of this paper fails.

The first objection can be expanded in this way: With respect to law (b), the mere intellectual recognition of the fairness of an activity is not sufficient to explain why a person would develop feelings of mutual trust and respect. It must be that the person has adopted the principles of fairness or justice, and this is something that requires freedom. Similarly with respect to law (c), a person with a sense of justice is one who, among other things, will accept those institutions which he believes are just and from which he has benefited. But acceptance in this sense presupposes freedom. The argument is that one who commits himself, say, by uttering the phrase 'I promise,' is excused if it is found that he was determined to utter the words because, e.g. of a drug administered to him. Hence, if determinism were true, all commitments would be void, and therefore no one could be such that law (b) or law (c) ever applied to him. That is, the correctness of the psychological account presupposes that men are free.

This argument fails for two reasons: First, if it is designed to show that no person is morally responsible for becoming moral, it may be correct, but then it is irrelevant. Not until a person acquires a sense of justice (and other comparable degrees of moral maturity) is he a fully moral being. Hence, to morally blame someone for not achieving this state would be quite inappropriate. One is not morally responsible for becoming a being who is capable of being morally responsible. Second, it is false to say that one is never responsible for doing something if he is determined by antecedent conditions to do it. For example, I may promise to meet you for lunch tomorrow, believing (perhaps correctly) that I am determined causally to promise, and yet feel responsible to meet you. Of course, I probably would not feel that way if I discovered that I had been drugged. The point is that I have taken responsibility for my meeting you in the one case and not in the other. Whether a person has taken responsibility may be discovered—not by looking into him to see if the act is really free in some metaphysical sense—but by seeing how he reacts if he fails to meet his self-imposed obligation. For example, does he apologize, does he attempt to make up for any damage his absence may have caused, etc? That is, does he feel guilty? If he does, then he has taken responsibility; if not, barring a special explanation, he has not. It is a contingent fact that most people most of the time fulfill their commitments. The psychological laws (a)—(c) describe the mechanism through which this occurs. So far, we see that there is no incompatibility between this psychological account and determinism. It is possible to commit oneself, even if one has a true belief in determinism, since to do so is to become disposed to act and feel in certain ways. Hence, the fact that the laws involve commitments does not affect the question of the truth of determinism.

The second argument is that the psychological account presupposes certain moral principles adopted (at least intuitively) by the persons in question since one cannot have a morality without being free (or at least believing oneself free), the psychological account presupposes freedom. It is tempting to reply that this argument begs the question, since if the view presented in this paper is correct, morality does not presuppose freedom. Hence to assert that it does is to disregard the argument already presented. However, matters are not quite so simple.

For moral development does involve a person's recognizing certain moral notions, e.g. that of justice or fairness, as applicable in certain situations. (Cf. laws (b) and (c).) If these moral notions presuppose some system of moral principles, and this system was applicable only if men were free or believed they were, then moral development would not be compatible with a true belief in determinism.

One may, however, give three other replies to the argument: First, the burden is upon the objector to show that every set of moral principles which could make up a satisfactory moral system presupposes freedom. Second, as was shown in the reply to the first argument there is an important sense of responsibility, namely taking responsibility, which is compatible with a lack of freedom; therefore even if morality does presuppose responsibility, it does not presuppose freedom. Third, one could sketch a system of moral principles which does not presuppose that men are free. I imagine that several moral systems from the history of philosophy satisfy this condition. An ideal contractarian system embodying Rawls' principles of justice would be a good candidate.[10] I conclude then that it is possible to find a system of moral principles which would not presuppose that men are free, and would, in particular, satisfy the demands for moral principles implicit in the psychological laws.

IV

I have argued that whether or not men have a true belief in determinism, there will still be moral men, for the psychological laws which govern moral development will remain true in such a world, and there is nothing in the antecedents of the laws which would prevent the inhabitants of this world from becoming moral in the manner described by the laws. The fact that commitments are involved in the workings of the laws, and the fact that certain moral principles must be adopted (at least intuitively) in the course of moral development does not affect the argument.

As noted previously, the laws considered here relate primarily to justice. It is plausible to conclude that whatever the laws of psychological development are which govern the remainder of the phenomenon of moral development, a similar account can be given. Hence morality does not presuppose freedom. Therefore, studies of morality can be freed from the perplexing questions of determinism, and those philosophers who have been driven to say that man is free for fear of finding that morality is empty unless he is free, need not, for that reason, fear determinism.

Furthermore, this investigation has indicated the value of using scientific results in moral philosophy. While some moral questions may not be so easily treated by examination of concepts formed in this way, it is obvious that moral philosophy in general can only benefit from the results of science. Often the scientist can supply the material the philosopher needs to formulate his own questions in an answerable form. In this way at least, moral philosophy is no different from any other field of human inquiry.

Notes and References

1. *Philosophical Review,* **LXXII** (1963), pp. 281–305.
2. *The Moral Judgment of the Child*, New York: Collier Books, 1962. Recent work by Lawrence Kohlberg has indicated that Piaget's account may require supplementation. See Kohlberg's 'Development of Moral Character and Moral Ideology,' *Review of Child Development Research*, **I**, 1964, and his 'The Development of Children's Orientations Toward a Moral Order,' *Vita Humana*, **VI** (1963), pp. 11–33.
3. These first two laws embody roughly Piaget's two moralities of the child: the one founded on unilateral respect for authority, and the other founded on mutual respect and cooperation. Cf. *The Moral Judgment of the Child*, 194–96.
4. 'The Sense of Justice,' pp. 287, 289, 292.
5. *The Moral Judgment of the Child*, pp. 103, 335, *et passim*.
6. A compatibilist might argue that, while these are deterministic laws, they do not conflict with freedom. I will not attempt to give a critique of compatibilism here. Rather I will assume that it is an unsatisfactory account of the facts, and therefore will assume that determinism is incompatible with freedom.
7. It is not clear that a child at this stage can even formulate a belief in determinism. If he cannot, there is no problem for my view with respect to belief. Cf. *The Moral Judgment of the Child*, pp. 188–89.
8. Rawls' principles are (i) that each person participating in the activity or affected by it has an equal right to the most extensive liberty compatible with a like liberty for all, and (ii) that inequalities are arbitrary unless it is reasonable to expect that they will work out for everyone's advantage, and provided that the positions and offices to which they attach, or from which they may be gained, are open to all. ('The Sense of Justice,' p. 283.) It is not crucial for my purposes whether or not these are exactly right. All that matters is that the participants know in some intuitive sense that the activity is fair.
9. 'The Sense of Justice,' pp. 293–98.
10. Cf. John Rawls, 'Justice as Fairness,' *Philosophical Review*, **LVXII** (1958), pp. 164–94.

Determinism, Responsibility, and the Person

NEIL W. MacGILL

University of New Brunswick

The problem of the Freedom of the Will—the problem which develops from the apparent conflict between responsibility and determinism—has a long history. In part this is because there is not just one problem falling under this title, but rather a number of problems, each related to a particular variety of determinism, a particular way in which it has been believed that human actions are the unavoidable consequences of factors outside the agent's control.

There seem to be three main varieties of determinism:

1) Logical Determinism: typified by the claim that what will be, will be; that what a man does is unavoidable because it has been true for all time that he will do it.

2) Religious Determinism: the view that a man's actions could not be other than they are because they are controlled by God's will (or by fate, nature, history, etc.)—or simply because God knows what they will be.

3) Scientific Determinism: the claim that a man's action are, in theory, completely predictable on the basis of a full knowledge of the state of affairs prior to the action, in conjunction with the appropriate scientific laws.

In this paper I want to consider the relationship between responsibility and scientific determinism, though some of the things I shall say would be relevant also to religious determinism.

There are, of course, a number of distinct theories which fall under the heading of scientific determinism, but even without discussing them in detail I think it can be claimed that in each case the theory allows that choices and decisions occur, phenomenally at least, and that, by one process or another, they are followed by the appropriate actions. I shall return to this point later, but first I should like to consider the two extreme solutions to the paradox of Free Will—the paradox created by the two apparent truths; that a person is only responsible for what he could have done, or could have avoided doing, and that no one could act in any way differently from the way he did, since his actions are determined.

On the one hand, we could deny the truth of determinism; as is in effect done by those who regard the efforts of the psychiatrist and the psychologist as misguided in principle. This position is not a difficult one to adopt, for the principle of determinism is essentially the principle of the uniformity of nature, and it can never be proven within any science. There will always be the possibility that any range of phenomena may in fact be irreducible to scientific laws. But determinism is, rather, an essential metaphysical presupposition of all science. The very attempt to establish scientific laws presupposes that there exist such regularities in nature, or at any rate in that area of nature with which the particular science is concerned.

To deny determinism, then, is to deny the very possibility of science. And to deny that human behavior and action is determined is to abandon much of the hope of improving it.

On the other hand, therefore, we might adopt the second alternative of denying that man is responsible for his actions. Again, this is a position which has been taken up, at least in part, in modern times. In an extreme case, where we regard a man as insane, we do not regard him as being responsible for his actions; and this seems, in some cases anyway, to be because we feel that his actions are determined by factors outside his control. But even in less extreme cases a person is often treated leniently, whether in court or in day to day life, because of his environmental background—'because he didn't have a proper chance in life.' In effect his responsibility is held to be diminished because his actions are regarded as the effects of his upbringing—factors outside his control. (It is interesting to note that the effects of heredity seem to be less acceptable as an excuse in most contexts.)

But, it may well be asked, is this partial absolution from responsibility consistent? If determinism is accepted, then it must be accepted that *everyone's* behavior is determined by factors, of environment and of heredity, which are outside their control. However 'normal' a person may appear, his actions are as much the result of these factors as are those of the hardened criminal or the mixed-up kid, and if we excuse the latter, then we should excuse everyone. To be specific; not only should we absolve the mixed-up kid from responsibility, but also his parents, whose inadequacy in bringing him up was equally the result of their own background; and so on.

It is this universal absolution, without even a demand for penitence, which tends to stick in the throat. Is there, then, a third alternative?

In the ordinary case where we say that someone is not responsible for something because he could not help it, we say this because he literally *had no choice*: perhaps he was physically forced, so that it was beyond his strength to resist; or perhaps the event was something over which he simply had no control—the weather, or the actions of someone who refused to listen to him.

It is often suggested that we also absolve a person from responsibility when he *does* have a choice, but chooses under duress—with a gun in his back, for example. But it would seem that in this case we do not absolve him from responsibility, but rather accept that he chose the lesser of two evils, since we agree that him being shot would be an evil. This interpretation is supported by the fact that if the choice he is being 'encouraged' to make is sufficiently important the gun in the back will not excuse him. It would not excuse him, for instance, if his finger were on the proverbial button.

As far as the determinist thesis is concerned, we have already noticed that it does not preclude choices and decisions; they occur, and they are followed by the appropriate actions. To that extent they are relevant to the actions. But let us continue with a closer look at the concept of responsibility.

I would suggest that, in one of the senses of 'responsible' that is relevant here, it is self-contradictory to assert that a man is responsible for an action X, that X is wrong, and that the man ought not to be blamed for the action. Such an assertion could only be understood by giving some unusual sense to one or more of the terms involved. In other words, responsibility, in this sense, is essentially connected with the way in which a man *ought* to be treated; it is a normative concept. When we say that someone is responsible for his actions, we are not *describing* him, or his actions, in any way: we are rather *prescribing* how he ought to be treated. In doing so, we rely, of course, on descriptive criteria, as we do in applying any normative term. We call a painting good, or beautiful, because of certain physical characteristics which it possesses; we call an action right because it falls under a certain description: but to call the action right or the painting beautiful is not to state that it falls under that description or has those characteristics, any more than making a choice is the same as giving reasons for a choice.

To say that someone is responsible for an action is to say that he *ought* to be blamed (and possibly punished) for it if it is wrong, and praised (and possibly rewarded) for it if it is right. Responsibility is thus intimately connected with the notion of blame and, in more serious cases, with that of punishment. We can carry this paper-chase a stage further, therefore, by turning our attention to the concept of punishment.

There are four aspects of punishment. The first is that of retribution: the Old Testament view—an eye for an eye, a tooth for a tooth. Punishment balances the crime on the scales of justice; 'Let the punishment fit the crime,' and the best punishment is the one that best fits the crime.

Secondly, there is punishment from the reformative aspect. Punishment is regarded more and more nowadays as a device for improving the punishees behavior. The best punishment is then the one which most effectively stops that person from repeating his offence—the punishment fits the criminal.

Thirdly, punishment may be regarded as a deterrent, a device for improving other people's behavior. It is *'pour encourager les autres.'*

Fourthly, punishment also has the function of protecting society, either by locking away the wrong-doer, or by killing him.

The term 'punishment' is sometimes reserved for the first of these three headings—Retribution: the second is referred to as 'Treatment,' the third, deterrence, is regarded as oriental and unmentionable, while the fourth, protection, is merely an advantageous by-product. It seems to me that, though this trend reflects a valid dichotomy, none the less all four aspects have to be weighed together in reaching a final decision about what ought to be done in a particular situation.

If we consider the relationship between determinism and the last three aspects of punishment, there appears to be no obvious incompatibility involved; indeed determinism would seem to underwrite the possibility of effective action with these ends in view. And when we consider certain common practices from the point of view of the reformative and deterrent function of punishment they seem somewhat more reasonable. We noticed earlier the apparent inconsistency of our dealings with the insane criminal, or the kid from a broken home, in contrast to more 'normal' people; but from these points of view the distinction between punishment and treatment disappears. In trying to reform the criminal we properly use our knowledge of psychology where such is available, while in its absence we fall back on less scientific but better tried methods.

Another common practice which is clarified on the reformative view is the tendency to hold people other than the agent responsible for an action. If we can do more to improve the behavior of those concerned by dealing with the parents, for example, then we tend to hold them responsible. It is sometimes suggested that responsibility can be 'divided up' between the parents and the child, but this arithmetical analogy is hardly appropriate; it is probably an unfortunate effect of the necessity of awarding damages in the law courts. A joint murder does not halve, or even necessarily reduce, the responsibility of each murderer; responsibility is not arithmetically dependent on the number of people involved.

It is when we turn to the problem of reconciling retribution with determinism that the difficulties start to increase. It is perhaps because of these difficulties, as well as the inclination, on reformative grounds, to ascribe responsibility to people other than the agent, that the notion of retribution seems to be going out of favour these days, with the word even taking on a pejorative note. But we cannot therefore ignore this retributive aspect of punishment, if only because its negative side is still central to our conception of punishment. By this I mean that, although we may feel that punishment cannot be justified *solely* as retribution for a certain action, nevertheless *no* punishment can be justified in the *absence* of a fitting crime: we are not justified in punishing the innocent (And I do not assert this merely as a tautology), or in overpunishing the not so guilty. I illustrate this point with a quotation from a B.B.C. TV discussion between Barbara Wootton, Lord Devlin and Robin Day (*The Listener*; Aug. 18th., 1966, p. 226):

> 'Robin Day: When you were looking at a man in the dock, and deciding what sentence to give him, what was first in your mind, the nature of the crime, the protection of the community, the effect on the man himself, or the effect on other people who might commit such an offence?
> Lord Devlin: I would start this way. I would say broadly, what does this man deserve? And that's what I would mean by punishing wickedness. After all, you are going to take away his liberty; you are not entitled to take away his liberty unless he has offended in some way. And therefore the first thing to find out is: does he deserve some sort of punishment? And the only punishment we have now is the deprivation of liberty. Does he deserve it? If so, broadly, and in a rough way, how heavy should it be? So that if

somebody came to me and said, give us this young lad and we can
reform him in three years, my first thing is, does he deserve to have
his liberty taken away for three years? Because if not, then I will
not do it.'

Lord Devlin goes on to emphasize that this notion of desert is
'generally a limiting factor' on the punishment that is appropriate:
retribution, then, sets an *upper* limit to the punishment, but the other
aspects of punishment are needed to justify its use in the first place.

We might meet our problem, therefore, in this way: retribution as
a positive justification for punishment *is* incompatible with determinism; but as a negative limitation on punishment it is not incompatible
with determinism. This opposition of principles in the justification of
punishment stems, I think, from the fact that punishment necessarily
conflicts with the status of the person punished as an agent—a being
who acts, and who in acting creates values. I shall try to show at the
end of this paper that this notion of the person as agent is not itself
incompatible with determinism, but is, if anything, enhanced by it. If
this is correct, then it is always our attempts to control human beings
—to reform or deter them—that calls for justification, not our refusal
to do so.

However, I would like to leave this problem for a moment, and consider further the notion of retribution as setting a limit. I have already
referred to our tendency to feel that there is sometimes a justification
for holding people other than the agent responsible, even when we
cannot establish that the effects they had on the agent were the result
of deliberate or neglectful actions on their part. It seems clear that the
principle of retribution would exclude such an allocation of responsibility.

But at this point we should remember the point I made earlier:
'Responsibility' is a normative term, and the criteria of responsibility
are therefore dependent on our moral beliefs, and not the other way
round. Consequently, if we have grounds for changing our moral beliefs, we may well, *ipso facto,* have grounds for changing our criteria of
responsibility.

I would suggest that we do have such grounds at the present time:
grounds based on our increasing recognition of the facts of personal
interdependence and interaction which are being established by psychology, sociology and the other social sciences. Our knowledge of the
ways in which people's actions and conduct affect other people's behavior is limited at the moment; but it is steadily growing, and as it
changes our moral concepts should change with it.

I would propose that we accustom ourselves to a new metaphysic of morals by altering our criteria of responsibility in a fundamental way; namely, by redefining the concept of the moral individual.

In *Individuals,* P. F. Strawson refers to the possibility of a conceptual scheme based on the notion of a group person—a person consisting of a group of what we now call individual people who all act and think together in a systematic way. He points out that we actually use such a conception in part when we talk about teams, armies, classes or nations: we speak of the team doing this or thinking that, and we only refer to the members of the team *as* members—quarter-back, pitcher, and so on. It is only because people do not always display such a degree of togetherness that we normally use the concept of the individual that we do. On the other hand, if people's bodies were less coordinated than they usually are, we might well have developed a concept of the body as consisting of a number of persons, each associated with a particular limb. Strawson mentions the ambiguity of the phrase 'a body and its members.'

I propose that a new concept of the moral individual, the moral person, be developed, so that the person comes to be identified with a certain social group, the group which we now regard as having a high degree of formative effect of the individual in our old sense. We could then retain our concepts of responsibility and retribution, but now, instead of our punishment being restricted to the actual body that performed the wrong action, it is only limited to members of the social group of which that body is a member. Just *which* members would be decided on grounds of reformative and deterrent efficiency.

To make this proposal less indigestible, I might point out that our present concept of the moral person is not coextensive with that of the physical person. We do not hold people responsible for what they did in childhood, or even for what they did in adulthood after a certain passage of time. For instance, many people feel that the American custom of sending men to the electric chair a couple of decades after their crime cannot be altogether justified by the need for a due process of law. In other words, the moral person is more limited in the time dimension than is the physical person.

What is more, when we look into the past, or even the murkier parts of the present, we find conceptions of moral responsibility which extend the concept of the moral person far beyond the spatial limits of the physical person. It is only recently that the Roman Catholic church decided that the Jewish race was not collectively responsible for the crucifixion of Christ, and history is full of family or clan feuds which seem to reflect a conception of a group moral person. Most of these concepts differ from my proposal in a fundamental way, however, in that the group consists of the *descendents* of the acting member, whereas I propose groups consisting rather of the ancestors of the acting member. His descendents would normally be excluded.

One effect of this proposal which might seem unfortunate is that we would always find it difficult to specify the membership of the group person with any precision, especially as each physical person would be a member of a large number of different groups even in relation to cases in which he was the acting member. It can only be pointed out that this sort of problem already exists in specifying the temporal limits of our present concept of the moral person: we are often uncertain whether to hold someone responsible for something he did sometime in the past, and we also tend to hold someone responsible over a longer period for more serious actions.

I should like to end this paper by making some remarks about the 'first person' sense of 'responsibility': responsibility for a before the event decision. In what sense can the individual regard himself as a free agent, responsible for his future actions, if determinism is true? Should he not abandon himself to his fate?

Here I might tell you a story about my late Aunt Elsie. Aunt Elsie, when young, was notoriously pigheaded. So her sisters would wait until she was about to go out of the room and then say 'Elsie, leave the room at once!' In order to avoid doing what she was told, Elsie would stay right where she was. The prediction implicit in her sisters' order actually led Elsie to behave in a way other than that predicted. This phenomenon is, of course, widely recognized: even sociologists speak of 'self-fulfilling prophecies'; though in this example the prophecy is self-refuting rather than self-fulfilling. D. M. MacKay has used the expression 'logical indeterminacy' in much the same way.

The point to which these terms draw attention is that on most theories of scientific determinism the agent's knowledge of the situation, including his knowledge of the predictions that have been made concerning his behavior, is one of the main factors determining his behavior (either directly, or indirectly through its physiological correlates). Consequently, any prediction that is made about a person's behavior will, once it is known to that person, change the facts on which the prediction was made, and hence invalidate it. If a new prediction is made on the basis of this new situation then it will, on discovery, modify the situation once again, so that the process can continue *ad infinitum*.

It may be possible to make some predictions which would not be affected by the agent's knowledge of them, because (a) this knowledge would not lead him to change his mind, (b) the knowledge that it had been predicted that he would not change his mind would not lead him to change his mind, and so on. An example of such a prediction would be that I shall not jump out of a top floor window in the next ten minutes: it seems likely that most such predictions would pose as little threat to human responsibility as that one. There may, however, be some cases where we must regard human freedom as being limited on this criterion. A person might be said to be suffering from a neurosis precisely when his behavior in some area is unaffected by any knowledge he may acquire of the predictions of that behavior. Yet even in such a case a person will often be able to take indirect steps to change his behavior—by going to a psychiatrist, for example. (In the value-free world of psychology, my inability to jump out of the window might be said to be due to a neurosis.)

Thus determinism does not, in general, destroy man's position in the world as an agent confronted with decisions. If the agent does not know what his predicted behavior is, then his decision may be as predicted; yet it still has to be made by him. If the agent does know of the prediction, then this knowledge undermines the prediction and becomes merely another piece of information which he may use or ignore when he makes his decision.

Indeed, determinism suggests that the scope of human responsibility is in fact wider than has sometimes been supposed. People often seem to assume that their responsibility is ended when actions of other people are interposed among the consequences of their own actions. To take a contemporary example, student revolutionaries occasionally claim that their movement is not responsible for violence since they merely provoke it in others. Yet on a determinist view other people's actions may be as much a consequence of my actions as anything else is: I share in the responsibility for their actions, just as those whose actions have an effect on mine share in the responsibility for my actions.

There is another sense in which human freedom and responsibility can be increased by accepting the truth of determinism. It *may* be true that there are some things that we think we could choose to do which we may discover are in fact beyond our choice. If so, it is helpful for us to know what these things are, just as it is useful for me to know that I cannot fly down to the ground from the top floor window. If our freedom *is* limited in this way, it is limited whether we know it or not:

H

it is then important that we should be in a position to allow for this limitation.

For the most part, if it *is* a fact that our actions are determined, it only limits our freedom for as long as we remain in ignorance of the particular ways in which they are determined. The more men know about the laws of human behavior, the more they will be able to allow for them in their decisions, and thus achieve what they wish to achieve, for good or ill. As in other fields, we must be prepared to act on our discoveries. We may blame grandma for what we did yesterday, but the decision what to do tomorrow is ours alone.

Responsibility, Freedom, and Statistical Determination

GEORGE L. KLINE

Bryn Mawr College

I

The recent attack of the 'hard' determinists upon the 'soft' determinists has helped to clear the air[1]. With the clearing, the hard determinists have emerged as both candid and hard-headed (although—in my opinion—fundamentally wrong), while the soft determinists have emerged as either disingenuous or soft-headed (and equally wrong). The soft determinists misleadingly claim that the proper opposite to freedom (in the moral sense) is not necessity, but coercion; and they unconvincingly claim that strict determinism is fully compatible with moral responsibility.

In contrast, such hard determinists as Edwards and (with qualifications) Hospers maintain that, if determinism is true, it makes no sense to hold anyone responsible for any act, or failure to act, since no one could have done other than he in fact did, or failed to do. (Hospers is unequivocal in his rejection of the notion of moral responsibility, but equivocal in his acceptance of determinism, which, as a theory, he finds 'not empirically verifiable.')

Two of the papers in the present symposium suggest that the warning of the hard determinists has been ignored and that the soft-determinist line of Hume, Mill, Schlick, and Ayer is being partially revived—with what success I shall inquire in a moment. Both Mr. O'Connor and Mr. MacGill assert, or assume, the truth of (strict) determinism, and both consider the determinist position incompatible with the assumption that men act, or choose, freely in the morally relevant sense(s). This last appears to be a gain, at least in candor, over the 'classical' soft determinists, whose position was marked by what James impatiently dubbed a 'quagmire of evasion.'

Mr. O'Connor claims that responsibility at least is compatible with determinism. Mr. MacGill goes further, attempting to mitigate the opposition between determinism and moral responsibility by classifying the statement (1) '*A* is responsible' or (1.1) '*A* is responsible for *x*' as a value-judgment rather than a description or assertion. He would presumably admit that the statement (2) '*A* is free' or (2.1) '*A* is free to do *x*'—although he would consider it false, since he considers determinism true—is a descriptive or constative statement, and that its falsity is compatible with the truth or validity of value-judgments (1) and (1.1). In other words, for Mr. MacGill the ascription of moral responsibility is compatible both with the denial of moral freedom and with the assertion of strict determinism.

Mrs. Rose takes a more traditional line on these questions, denying (at least implicitly) the truth of determinism, and defending the ascription to moral agents of both responsibility and freedom. I am in closer sympathy with her assumptions than with those of the other two symposiasts (since I reject strict determinism), but I have some reservations about the evidence which she offers for what she calls the 'free will hypothesis.'

I am struck by the fact that not one of the three symposiasts—nor for that matter any of the hard or soft determinists—has had anything to say about *statistical* determinism (or determination) as distinguished from strict determinism. I shall return to this topic, since it seems to me to offer a plausible way out of what would otherwise be a theoretical dead-end.

II

Mrs. Rose wants to distinguish freedom in the sense of free will from both (deterministic) efficient causality and a-causality (causelessness). She asks: 'Can the individual by inspection of his own acquaintance with [i.e. experience of] the difficult moral choice find any evidence that the choice is free?' (p. 183). Her answer appears to be affirmative; what counts as 'evidence' is the experienced decrease in difficulty of 'difficult moral choices' on the third, fourth, and nth occasion, as contrasted to the first or second occasion. This is sound Peripatetic doctrine. Aristotle said—savoring the whiff of paradox—that 'we become courageous (just, generous) by performing courageous (just, generous) actions'; he meant that the non-courageous man, the neophyte in the difficult task of facing danger without fleeing or flinching, may act courageously, i.e. may knowingly and deliberately stand his ground, even though he quake inwardly. Through practice and experience such a man may develop a 'fixed disposition' to be courageous, and a capacity to take pleasure or satisfaction in courageous actions. The flavor of paradox vanishes once the two senses of 'courageous' (or 'just' or 'generous') are distinguished. (Let us call them 'courageous₁' and 'courageous₂'.)

The process by which a man 'becomes courageous₂ by performing courageous₁ actions' might appropriately be described as one in which an initially 'difficult' moral choice becomes progressively 'easier,' i.e. more habitual, more satisfying, and—in a broad sense—more pleasant or pleasurable. Aristotle, of course, assumed that moral agents were free to act, to choose, and to develop moral habits. I am not persuaded by Mrs. Rose that the process by which a difficult moral choice becomes easier has a special relevance to the question of moral freedom (pp. 184, 186). Does this experience in fact offer more convincing evidence for the 'freewill hypothesis' than the experience of acting, or choosing, freely in a single case? Or does a difficult moral choice offer more convincing evidence on this point than an easy moral choice?

Mrs. Rose admits that the experience in question is 'for the most part (if not wholly) subjective rather than intersubjective' (p. 186) and that it is qualitatively distinct from the 'overt behavior which accompanies it' (p. 188), which would seem—from the determinist's point of view—to place it under the same pall of subjectivist suspicion as the obviously 'non-intersubjective' experience of choosing or acting freely in a single case. Toward the end of her paper, Mrs. Rose goes further, suggesting that 'there may be a discoverable and predictable relationship between the new content of subjective experience which is the product of the developed [moral] capacities and the overt behavior which . . . expresses this new content' (p. 189).

Unfortunately, Mrs. Rose gives no examples, and the Aristotelian examples that come to mind do not seem to support her case. The courageous₁ action of a not-yet-courageous₂ man might be behaviorally indistinguishable from the courageous₂ action of an already-courageous₂ man—the (subjective) difference being that the courageous₂ man, unlike the non-courageous₂ man, acts from fixed dispositions and takes pleasure in his courageous₂ action.

The generous₁ act of a not-yet-generous₂ man differs from the generous₂ act of an already-generous₂ man in that the latter, but not the former, takes pleasure in bestowing gifts and does so from a fixed disposition. We might expect the generous$_2$ man to smile or 'appear jovial' while performing his generous act, and the ungenerous$_2$ man to frown or grit his teeth. But surely the ungenerous$_2$ man might hide his displeasure (and he would have strong social-psychological reasons for doing so), forcing a hospitable smile, while the generous$_2$ man might hide his pleasure, keeping a straight or sober face.

But we are in imminent peril of being sucked into the quicksands of the 'problem of other minds'—a problem which, in the present context, would be both digressive and distracting.

III

Mr. O'Connor begins with the strong claim that 'even if determinism—in a sense incompatible with human freedom—is true and men believe that it is true, it is still perfectly possible for men to be moral' (p. 193). He adds that such determinism entails that 'no one could do other than he in fact does on any occasion' (p. 194). Would he also accept what seems to me the clearer and more radical claim that 'no one will be able to do other than he in fact will do on any occasion'? Tense-distinctions might help to clarify at least some of the issues involved here.

Puzzlingly, Mr. O'Connor denies that his hard-determinist position is incompatible with moral responsibility, in the sense of an agent's 'taking responsibility,' although he admits that it is incompatible with moral freedom (cf. pp. 199, 200). His discussion of a 'psychological theory of moral development' inspired by Piaget and Rawls, while interesting in its own right, does not—in my judgment—support his claim that determinism and responsibility are compatible. (On the question of compatibility, I would side with such hard determinists as Paul Edwards, although I do *not* share the Edwardsian commitment to strict determinism.) Mr. O'Connor asserts: 'the fact that the [psychological] laws [of moral development] involve commitments does not affect the question of the truth of determinism' (p. 199). And he adds: 'The fact that certain moral principles must be adopted . . . in the course of moral development' is no argument for moral freedom (p. 200).

Mr. O'Connor thus seems to have taken a long step away from soft determinism in the direction of hard determinism. I am sorry to say that I find in his paper no theoretical justification for this move.

IV

Mr. MacGill's defense of determinism strikes me as rather rigid, especially since he makes no distinction between strict and statistical determinism. He says that 'to deny [strict] determinism' is 'to deny the very possibility of science. [Is quantum mechanics then not a science?] And to deny that human behavior and action is determined is to abandon all hope of explaining and understanding it. . .' (p. 204). Strict determinism, he argues, is compatible with moral responsibility in the sense that 'when we say that someone is responsible for his actions, we are not *describing* him, or his actions, in any way; we are rather *prescribing* how he ought to be treated' (p. 205). But even if we grant this distinction, surely the prescription or value-judgment that a man is responsible (i.e. should be called to account, punished or rewarded, for his acts) presupposes the descriptive or constative judgment that he is free (i.e. that he might have acted otherwise than he in fact did).

Mr. MacGill's discussion of punishment is interesting in its own terms, but does not—it seems to me—throw light on our central issue. And I am unable to follow him (perhaps this is due to my obtuseness) when he asserts that 'retribution as a positive justification for punishment *is* incompatible with determinism; but as a negative limitation on punishment it is not incompatible with determinism' (p. 208). I am also puzzled by his claim that the 'notion of the person as agent is not . . . incompatible with determinism, but is, if anything, enhanced by it' (p. 208). Presumably Mr. MacGill wishes to maintain that a person, as moral agent, is both unfree in the sense of unable to do other than he does and yet responsible for what he (necessarily) does.

Mr. MacGill's introduction—following Strawson—of the 'new concept' of the 'group moral person' is not so much puzzling as alarming, and for moral rather than theoretical reasons. (See pp. 209-210). The 'group person' is to be limited, he suggests, to 'the ancestors [presumably only those still living] of the acting member [of the group]'; the descendents 'would normally be excluded' (p. 210). This smells entirely too much like the amorphous 'collective responsibility' with which totalitarian regimes of both right and left have underpinned their campaigns of terror and intimidation. In 1918–20 Lenin and Trotsky rounded up the elders of Russian villages and, when the young men refused to deliver the grain demanded by the Bolsheviks, arbitrarily shot 'every tenth' elder. The Gestapo did the same thing with French partisans during the occupation of France (1940–44). The execution or exile of whole families for the misdeeds of one member, especially a junior member, appears to have been standard Chinese communist practice.

Surely, it is *individuals,* not groups or families, who are morally responsible, however cohesive the social unit of which they are members. The principle of group or collective responsibility and guilt is designed to play upon the loyalty and affection that binds family members together, and particularly upon the horror which children feel at the prospect of the torture or killing of their parents, torture or killing which they can prevent, even if at dreadful cost. It is reported that when Stalin's secret police ordered Nikolai Bukharin to confess (in open court) his 'crimes against socialism,' he refused categorically, declaring his willingness to die or face torture rather than debase himself. But when he was informed that his aged father was in police custody and would be tortured, he immediately agreed to 'confess to anything.'

I am not, of course, ascribing to Mr. MacGill approval of either the motives or the methods of Stalin's (or Hitler's) security police. I have no doubt that he finds them quite as repugnant as I do. But I fear that his—and Strawson's—concept of the group person is open to just such despotic abuses.

V

Finally, a word about the bearing of statistical determinism or 'determination' upon moral responsibility and freedom. At least one hard determinist has asserted that even 'irreducibly statistical laws' (i.e. those the 'statisticality' of which is not due to human ignorance or 'relevant hidden parameters') preclude the 'kind of freedom required by the philosophical indeterminist for the assignment of moral responsibility.'[2] I am not convinced.

Kant, who was just as 'hard' a determinist as Grünbaum, once suggested in passing (although he left the suggestion undeveloped) that the kind of determinism or natural necessity that is compatible with individual moral responsibility may be statistical rather than strict. (He did not use the term 'statistical' but he clearly had the idea.) Kant's example is the statistical predictability—in sufficiently large populations—of the rates of marriage, birth, and death, despite the element of free (and responsible) choice involved in such human actions—and, we might add, especially in those of the first class, i.e. marriages[3].

More recently, the Polish philosopher Leszek Kołakowski, at a stage of his intellectual development which I have characterized as 'Kantian-existential Marxism,' made a similar point.

> The fate of an individual cannot be determined by the generalized laws of the class struggle [or any other general social laws], any more than the behavior of an individual [gas molecule] can be predicted from the general laws governing the mechanics of gases [i.e. statistical mechanics], although the latter remain valid with respect to aggregates.[4]

There may be a very high probability, even a 'statistical quasi-certainty,'[5] that at least one of the thousand people standing by a river bank will leap into the water to save a drowning child, but Kołakowski insists—anyone who actually *does* so must have made his own (free and responsible) decision. And no one who *fails* to do so has any right to appeal to historical, social, or even biological necessity as an excuse for his inaction.

I cannot develop this point here.[6] I admit that it involves certain difficulties: e.g. it appears to commit one to the view that *all* laws of nature are ultimately statistical (a view to which I am drawn not only on moral but also on metaphysical grounds). The position needs to be worked out more carefully than anyone has yet done—although Whitehead has, I think, made an impressive start in this direction. In any case, I would insist that the kind of regularity provided by statistical or probabilistic laws is entirely sufficient for purposes of 'understanding, predicting, and influencing' human behavior. Hard and soft determinists alike, of course, contend that such understanding, prediction, and influence presuppose strict, non-probabilistic laws.

Notes and References

1. The terms were first used by William James in his essay, 'The Dilemma of Determinism' (1884). For a sampling of the recent literature, see Sidney Hook, ed., *Determinism and Freedom in the Age of Modern Science* (New York, 1958; paperback edition, 1961), especially the essays by Paul Edwards and John Hospers.
2. Adolf Grünbaum, 'Free Will and Laws of Human Behavior,' unpublished manuscript, 1969, p. 19.
3. 'Idee zu einer allgemeinen Geschichte in weltbürgerlicher Absicht' (1784) in *Immanuel Kants Werke*, ed. A. Buchenau and E. Cassirer, Berlin, 1922, vol. 4, p. 151.
4. Leszek Kołakowski, 'Istota i istnienie w pojęciu wolności' ('Essence and Existence in the Concept of Freedom'), in *Światopoglad i życie codzienne* (World-View and Everyday Life), Warsaw, 1957, p. 117.

H*

5. Leszek Kołakowski, 'Odpowiedzialność i historia' ('Responsibility and History'), originally in *Nowa Kultura* (Warsaw), 1957. English translation in L. Kołakowski, *Toward a Marxist Humanism: Essays on the Left Today* (trans. by Jane Zielonko Peel), New York, 1968, p. 140 (the quoted expression is misleadingly rendered as 'quasi-statistical certainty').

6. I have discussed it, and other aspects of Kołakowski's position, in 'Leszek Kołakowski and the Revision of Marxism' in G. L. Kline, ed., *European Philosophy Today* (Chicago, 1965), pp. 113–56; reprinted, without footnotes, in *New Writing of East Europe*, ed. G. Gömöri and C. Newman (Chicago, 1968), pp. 82–101.

Recommended Reading—
Science, Freedom, and Determinism

Adler, Mortinmer. *The Idea of Freedom*. Garden City: Doubleday, 1961.

Beardsley, Elizabeth. 'Determinism and Moral Perspectives,' *Philosophy and Phenomenological Research*, 1960.

Berofsky, B. (ed.). *Free Will and Determinism*. New York: Harper and Row, 1966.

Broad, D. C. 'Determinism, Indeterminism, and Libertarianism,' *Ethics and the History of Philosophy*. London, 1952.

Devlin, Patrick, Wootton, Barbara, Day, Robin. 'How Should Criminals be Sentenced?' *The Listener*, **LXXVI**, no. 1951 (British Broadcasting Corporation).

Edwards, Paul. 'Hard and Soft Determinism' (1958), in *Determinism and Freedom in the Age of Modern Science*. Sidney Hook (ed.). New York: Collier Books, 1961, pp. 117–25.

Hospers, John. 'What Means this Freedom?' (1958), in *ibid*., pp. 126–42.

James, William. 'The Dilemma of Determinism' (1884), in *The Will to Believe and Other Essays in Popular Philosophy*. New York: Longmans, Green, 1989, pp. 145–83.

Kant, I. *Groundwork of the Metaphysic of Morals*. Trans. by H. I. Paton. New York: Barnes and Noble, 1967.

Kołakowski, Leszek. 'Responsibility and History' (1957), in *Towards a Marxist Humanism: Essays on the Left Today*. New York: Grove Press, 1968, pp. 85–157. (The British edition of this book has the more accurate title: *Marxism and Beyond*.)

Kołakowski, Leszek. 'Determinism and Responsibility' (1959), in *ibid*., pp. 188–210.

MacKay, D. M. *Freedom of Action in a Mechanistic Universe*. Cambridge: University Press, 1967.

Meldon, A. I. *Free Action*. London: Routledge and Paul, 1961.

Morris, H. (ed.). *Freedom and Responsibility*. Stanford, Cal.: Stanford University Press, 1961.

Piaget, J. *The Psychology of Intelligence*. Totowa, N.J.: Littlefield, Adams, 1966.

Rawls, J. 'The Sense of Justice,' *Philosophical Review*. 1963.

Strawson, P. F. *Individuals*. London: Methuen, 1959.

Taylor, Richard. 'Determinism' in *Encyclopedia of Philosophy*. (Ed. Paul Edwards), New York: Macmillan: Free Press, 1967, vol. 2, pp. 359–73.

Toward a Science of Values

An Abstract Definition
of the Good

JOHN G. GILL

Central Michigan University

I   The Problem

> The great advantage of the mathematical sciences above the moral consists in this, that the ideas of the former, being sensible, are always clear and determinate, the smallest distinction between them is immediately perceptible, and the same terms are still expressive of the same ideas, without ambiguity or variation. An oval is never mistaken for a circle, nor an hyperbola for an elipsis. The isosceles and scalenum are distinguished by boundaries more exact than vice and virtue, right and wrong.[1]

David Hume contrasts the precision of geometry with the vagueness of ethics. His keen observation, however, falls short of stating a universal law. Whether we accept Hume's words as an ultimate authority or as a stimulating challenge, determines our response. No demon compels us always to remain where Hume left us.

This paper contends that a clear definition of good is possible if the work meets certain conditions. Following the example of mathematics, it must break away from special cases. The definition must have no empirical conditions to prevent it from being universally generalized.

II   Axioms and Primitive Terms

We take for granted the rules of logic. These apply both to natural science and to human affairs. Every field of inquiry assumes logic. Logic contains principles by which we must think if we think at all.

The usual concepts and rules of logic are considered postulates for our purpose. In particular, we require four axioms.

Postulate One: *An inconsistency cannot be affirmed.* An affirmation claims that something is true or valuable. A contradiction cannot be either. Whatever sentence is represented by 'p,' it is false that p and not-p can be asserted. In logical terms p and not-p strictly imply not-p: CKpNpNp. An inconsistency is necessarily false. If an inconsistency were true, everything would follow, and truth itself have no meaning. Affirmation implies consistency.

Postulate Two: *A concept and its complement exhaust the universe of discourse.* This rule makes possible indirect proofs. Euclid demonstrates that the number of primes is infinite, relying on this postulate. The number is finite or infinite. If it is finite, there is a largest one. Using this unknown 'largest prime' and familiar rules of arithmetic, he constructs a still larger prime—one larger than the largest. Thus he shows a contradiction in the assumption that the number is finite. Considering the number finite, leads to contradiction. Therefore, the number of primes is infinite.[2]

Postulate Three is the axiom of decidability: *Between any two elements, it is possible to decide.* Postulate Three suggests that complex evaluations can be broken down to atomic decisions. In a different context it repeats the resolve to carry analysis to its conclusion. If the criterion is clear, any relevant element can be classified.

Postulate Four adds: *A decision having been made, the objects can be ordered.* If all atomic instances are decidable, molecular units can be arranged in a sequence.[3] Since each element is 'good' or 'not-good,' complexes can be placed with good on top, evil on the bottom. 'Better than' an *asymmetric, non-reflexive transitive, ordering relation,* yields a lattice.

Definition of the good, in addition to four postulates, requires five primitive terms. These must be the simplest discoverable, which can be used to define the concept. They appear with their every day connotations. The definition starts from ordinary speech. The primitives are restricted as they assume their place in the theory. Their narrower meanings must not conflict with common usage. In effect, the system itself defines them. The five primitives are: *affirmation, negation, life, individual* and *society.*

Adding to ordinary rules of logic four axioms and five primitive terms, gives us the technical apparatus necessary for a definition of the good.

III Extension of Good

A common catalogue of goods includes: *health, wealth, happiness, fame* and *power*. Most desirable objects can be classified under one of these headings. The arrangement may vary. A person frustrated in some experience might exclude this or that. The list expresses the values of most people.

While other lists might be drawn up, these five headings certainly contain the good. We have, at least, boxed our subject. Can we then close in on it? Can we shorten the list without losing its truth? Can any headings be eliminated or included in others?

Examining health, remembering that it includes the psychological, we see that it expresses a fundamental truth. Other objects lose their appeal if health is lacking. Almost everyone desires physical health. Most want mental health as well. If there are any who do not care to be healthy, they may be considered twisted souls who are very sick indeed. Health, however, cannot be a defining characteristic of good. Health is not a complete concept, and cannot be well-formed in our theory.

By Postulate Two: *A concept and its complement exhaust the universe of discourse.* Disease is the opposite of health. But disease cannot be a true contradictory. Both health and disease appear to be only parts of ideas. Disease is related to death, to which in all extreme cases it leads. Pure sickness would be death. The contradictory of death is *life,* one of our primitives. Death can be defined as the complement of *life,* and the classification can be made exclusive and exhaustive. Everything in the universe is either alive or dead. Our list of goods is strengthened if, instead of health, we write *life.*

The next item is incomplete in much the same way as *health.* The opposite of wealth is poverty, and the two can be made exclusive by placing a figure on annual income as 'the poverty line.' But like health and disease, wealth and poverty are not exhaustive. Wealth, by itself, represents only so much paper or metal. The meaning of wealth is power. Total poverty would be complete impotence. Power is another heading on our list.

Bernard Bosanquet has pointed out that beauty and ugliness, are not opposites.[4] On the contrary, they are closely related. Pleasure and pain, happiness and misery also require each other. We are hardly ever conscious of one without the other. Each of the pairs represents experience. The contradictory of each is no experience at all, but plain dullness. Dullness itself is only part of a concept and is closely kin to death. Complete dullness would be the absence of experience which is death. The contradictory of death, once again is *life*.

Careful examination of our five headings shows that each of them, in so far as it is good, represents *life*. Each has for its opposite death. We have only one pair of contradictories, *life* and death. *Life* is one of our accepted primitives. Death is defined as the *negation* of *life*. They are exclusive and exhaustive. Together they describe a universe of discourse which is the Universe itself. They also reveal an interesting structure.

Death includes all that is inert, unconscious matter. Opposed to it is the highly complex substance—protoplasm—which forms the basis of all living beings. *Life* is structured and creative. It occurs in many forms, from the simple bacterium, or amoeba, to the jellyfish, the oyster, the salmon, the elk, the ape and the man. *Life* in its myriad present manifesations is still not exhausted. It also includes all past forms in which it has appeared—the trilobite, the pteraspis, the pterodactyl, the brontosaurus and the mastodon. To get the full meaning of *life,* we also include future forms, perhaps infinite in number.

Here the concept *life* reveals a significance which we may not have considered. Essential to life is possibility. The contradictory of inert matter counts capacities as well as achievement. Death is an end of possibilities. *Life* includes the past, the present, and all that the future may be. *Life* contains 'Point Omega' which the brilliant priest and scientist, Pierre Teilhard de Chardin postulated, as the still unknown high water mark of evolution.[5]

If *a concept and its contradictory exhaust the universe of discourse,* then the contradictory of death goes far beyond mere achievements. It means possibilities as well. This is obviously more than we consciously include in the word *life,* but so far from contradicting everyday usage, it brings out an implied sense. Part of the meaning of *life* is possibility. Among the possibilities are consciousness and growth. The primitive word *life* is defined by its place in the system. Compared to this fuller sense of life, the facile notion 'the good is individual survival' appears a truncated version of a more profound and exciting idea.

Extensionally, the good is an enriched and deepened concept of *life,* counting as part of its meaning—possibility. All of our list of goods are included in this idea of *life*.

IV Intensional Meaning of Good

In looking for the intension of *good,* we return to our five conventional classifications. Seeking an idea which would draw together the positive content of each heading, we found the meaning of good in the primitive term *life,* as reinterpreted in the theory. Now we ask what these five headings have in common. What is the intension of good? What is there that distinguishes *health, wealth, happiness, approval* and *power*?

In accepting this list and ruling out other claimants, we asked of each: 'Is this desirable?' The natural basis for counting any object good, is its desirability. This clue leads to the meaning of good. Every child takes for granted that what he wants is good. The good is the desirable. The notion of desirability carries intuitive validity. The objects we want appear good to us. No matter who the speaker, it seems to express a truth for him to say: 'The good for me is that which I desire.'

This *prima facie* definition conforms closely to ordinary speech. Beyond any doubt it expresses an important characteristic of the good. *The good for me is that which I desire* represents at least a surface view. Many thoughtful people have not gone beyond this. However, certain limitations make it unsuitable for a definition. The most obvious difficulty lies in the word 'desire.' Being subjective, it can never yield an objective test. We have no way to compare desires. We cannot measure how much anybody desires anything. While the first glance definition conveys an element of truth, it also carries a flimsy, fairy godmother quality. It makes the object of every wish good while we wish for it.

If, for the subjective word 'desire' we substitute the word 'choose,' we can relate our definition to an objective criterion, decidedly strengthening it. *The good for me is that which I choose,* makes the act of selection, rather than the feeling the *fundamentum divisionis*. It separates objects of deliberate selection from momentary wishes. Our revision identifies the good with the object of choice.

We can further increase precision without losing the force of our intuitive definition by substituting the logical word *affirm* for the informal, less clearly demarked word 'choose.' To *affirm* means to accept as valid, to consider true or valuable. The definition now contains a tautological element. It suggests: 'The good for me is that which I accept as good.' Since the act of affirming makes the object affirmed to be good, the defining character is found, not in the object, but in the affirmation. *The good for me is that which I affirm.*

This settles some old debates, with one danger. It risks treating philosophers as computers treat engineers. Engineers design computers. Computers do engineers out of jobs. Over the head of each philosopher, hangs the sword of Damocles. A thoroughgoing definition of the good threatens value theorists with technological obsolescence.

The schools of Greek and Roman philosophers, and the medieval Scholastics who followed them, never succeeded in convincing each other. Their work lacked the permanent achievement of their contemporaries, the mathematicians. They remained divided. They developed consequences of various definitions of good, but could not resolve differences between the schools. They failed to find principles strong enough to convince all serious students.[6] Now we understand. Each was right in his way. *The good for me is that which I affirm.* Affirmation determines the good. Beginning at the wrong end, they tried to select the object first. They should have started with their own choices.

V Logical Development

My good is relative to me, yours to you. Man's good is related to himself. In more general form, *the good for an individual is that which he affirms.* Appearing as a propositional function, the definition connects two of our primitive terms, *affirmation* and *individual.* It remains tautological, but carries interesting implications. It is a fruitful definition. The theory already restricts the meaning of its primitive terms.

The good for an individual is that which he affirms, implies that the individual can affirm. Not every organic unit meets this requirement. Our definition, relative to the individual, assumes that the individual is able to decide. He must have well-formed desires. His affirmations must proceed from a single point. To be an agent requires unity. For the word *good* to have meaning, the concept of individual is restricted. It presupposes organization and central direction. The extension of the primitive term *individual* is narrowed. Its intension increased.

Where knowledge is cut up, in amnesia or schizophrenia, we have a divided personality. We cannot speak of 'good' any more than we can speak strictly of *individual.* We have two or more persons moving a single body. The nerves and blood vessels are integrated, the mind is not. An *individual* must be a harmony, a unity of desires, for the good to be meaningful. This follows from the definition.

The ordering of *affirmations* extends through time. The individual must continue to *affirm* his choice for his good to be significant. Principles by which affirmations are made or altered, become second-order concepts. The good has enduring meaning in so far as the *individuals* have continuing principles and have decided how they will choose. The good can have no content under conflicting principles, because a contradiction implies everything and nothing. This conforms to experience. It also follows from the definition: *The good for an individual is that which he affirms.*

The definition can now be clarified by application of Postulate One: *An inconsistency cannot be affirmed.* This severely cuts down its extension. Many acts that at first glance appeared to be affirmations, are eliminated. This operates like a definition in geometry.

Few concepts outside mathematics have achieved the clarity of a triangle, a hyperbola, or an ellipse. Fewer still have been tested for consistency. Probably, up to now, ethics and sociology have been dealing with 'apparent goods' and have not made the first step toward a science of values.[2] Until a concept is proved self-consistent, we do not know whether it can be affirmed.

Alexander Meiklejohn, in a too little known essay pointed out that most human tragedies grow out of man's failure to find out what things *really* are. For centuries men bowed before bricks and stones. They sacrificed their firstborn children and their dearest treasures. Because they did not know what things were, they threw away objects of priceless worth.[8] Nowhere is the lack of reality more costly than in a superficial and untested idea of good.

Postulate Two clarifies our definition: *A concept and its complement exhaust the universe of discourse.* This expresses the determination to create classes which are exclusive and exhaustive. A self-contradictory notion like a round square cannot exist. Attempting to find it, leads to frustration. Self-consistency is a necessary criterion of the good. In it we have a standard. Seeming goods can be tested and some of them eliminated. The self-contradictory belongs to the class of not-good, that is to say, *evil*. Here an interesting parallel to Thomism appears. Thomists insist that evil does not exist, but is real. To them, evil has a negative being, like darkness, a wound or a scar. Evil is compared to the noise an orchestra makes when the players fail to follow the conductor. Evil is a missing harmony.[9] We may add precision to their insight. A contradiction is real, but a contradictory object cannot exist. Men place their hopes in it only to go wrong, and to be disappointed.

Postulate Three: *Between any two elements it is possible to decide,* in adding decidability, expresses the resolve to break molecules down into parts. In complex situations no simple judgment is adequate. The decisions with which we are confronted will not be made easy by a postulate. In Postulate Two we provided that our classes should be exclusive and exhaustive. Postulate Three goes further. The analysis is not complete until the atoms are distinguished. Once recognized, elements are classifiable. They are good, or if not good, then evil.

Postulate Four adds: *A decision having been made the objects can be ordered.* With the elements classified, a partially ordered system or lattice, can be constructed. We can build such a lattice because *Better than* turns out to be a typical *asymmetric, non-reflexive, transitive, ordering relation.*

The levels of values appeared at first glance to be arbitrary. On the surface, we could choose anything for first, second, or third. Values appeared as confused as human desires. Now we see that the good is not subject to our varying whims. The arrangement is structured. Some elements can meaningfully be affirmed. Others cannot. Some situations are better than others. Postulate Four asserts the possibility of an ordering of values.

If *the good for an individual is that which he affirms,* what becomes of our definition when we universalize it? The logical operation Universal Generalization (U.G.) can be performed on any propositional function which is not 'flagged'—i.e. subject to particular limiting conditions. What holds for a triangle, applies to any triangle, provided the description has been completely general. By Universal Generalization it is asserted of all triangles.[10] Our definition contains no empirical limitations.

The good for an individual is that which he affirms. With Universal Generalization this becomes: *The good for all individuals is that which each affirms.* We cannot generalize the remaining 'each' without risking the fallacy of composition, inferring from the accepted fact of individual desires, some possible universal agreement.

Even as it stands, the proposition is interesting. *The good for all individuals is that which each affirms* can be recognized as a form of the Golden Rule: 'What you desire for yourself should be your rule in treating others.' That this formula should appear in all advanced religions,[11] takes on a new and obvious explanation. Only a familiar logical step separates this advanced insight of ethics from an intuitive definition. *The good for me is that which I affirm,* becomes: *The good for all individuals is that which each affirms.* The demonstration can be written as a one-step theorem:

The good for an individual is that which he affirms.

The good for all individuals is that which each affirms.

VI   Basic Theorem and Definition

We have found that the objects men consider good can be classified under: *health, wealth, happiness, approval* or *power.* Other arrangements might serve, but this expresses the accepted meaning of good. Analyzing each of the headings, we found a single idea which covered them all, though no existing word was adequate. *Life* when interpreted to include past achievements and future possibilities expressed the concept most nearly.

Turning again to our catalogue of goods, we asked what the recognized goods had in common. We found a first glance answer. The good is the desirable. *The good for me is that which I desire.* By substituting increasingly precise terms and universally generalizing the result, we reached a relative definition of the good: *The good for all individuals is that which each affirms.* Substituting our synonym for the good, we obtain a basic theorem: *Life is that which each individual affirms.*

To speak of all living beings affirming life at first glance appears absurd, as if a chestnut tree desired water, or a crab chose sand. The same absurdity would have struck a seventeenth century philosopher if a modern physicist had told him of invisible light or inaudible sound. These would have appeared contradictory. However, freeing light and sound from their matrix of sense has let us deal with wavelengths beyond the visible spectrum or the auditory range. The extension exposes many interconnections. The concepts deal more powerfully with reality. They reveal hidden structures. The theorem: *Life is that which each individual affirms,* clarifies the terms it uses.

Since a single negative example suffices to disprove a theory, more difficult questions ask about suicide and war. Some individuals choose suicide. Almost every human being and some animals dearly love war. Suicide involves us in the Freudean 'death wish.' To what extent is suicide a choice? Could suicide be a perverted affirmation of life's possibilities, involving total rejection of some form of 'mere existence?'

War may not be the negative example it first appears. The slogans of recent wars raise the question. 'Make the world safe for democracy,' and 'This is a war to end all war,' or 'the defense of the free world' and even 'national aggrandizement,' may be distorted manifestations of life-affirmation.[12]

The theorem: *Life is that which each individual affirms,* corresponds closely to Dr. Albert Schweitzer's observation: 'I am life that wills to live, surrounded by life that also wills to live.' From this, he derives the basic principle of his ethics: 'Reverence for life.' Dr. Schweitzer's argument moves from his own 'will to live' through a mystical experience of universal life-will.[13] We reach the same point from postulates, omitting the mystical step. Considering *life* as including its possibilities, we have come to the conclusion: *Life is that which each individual affirms.*

We can now define the good. If the good for all individuals is that which each affirms, and *life* is that which each individual affirms, then *the good is life-affirmation.*

VII   Conclusion

The argument shows why so-called 'normative theory' as the game is usually played, is unlikely to produce scientific results. Questionnaires which try to find out what people value are often phrased in different words or different contexts to get beyond the merely 'approved' response. Each answer is written down. The researcher goes on to the next question or the next respondent. We see that this procedure cannot get beyond 'apparent good,' and hence cannot be called science. It finds what the individual thinks he affirms, remaining ignorant of whether the object can be affirmed or not.

Socrates had a better way. He also asked people what they considered good. Then he cross-questioned them to find whether their opinions were self-consistent and therefore made sense. Even then he did not stop until he had found whether the affirmations were consistent with other objects which the individual thought he chose. Only if the answers passed the tests of self-consistency and consistency with each other could the respondent be considered as holding a scientific view. The criterion was set. No opinions met Socrates' standard, not even his own.

Our inquiry has shown that the good can be defined. If, in the primitive term *life,* possibilities and consciousness are included, then *the good is life affirmation.* We have seen that 'good' yields an ordering. Complex situations can be arranged from the best to the worst.

The resultant lattice, when the detailed work has been done, will be, in the mathematical sense of the words, a *value theory*.

Notes and References

1. *An Enquiry Concerning Human Understanding*, Section VII, Part i. David Hume, *The Philosophical Works*. 1964 reprint of New Ed. London, 1882. Vol. IV, p. 50.
2. *The Elements*, Euclid Bk. Trans. with commentary by Sir Thomas L. Heath, Dover Press, N.Y., 1956. Vol. II, pp. 412–3. IX Prop. 20. Summaries are to be found in almost any advanced algebra.
3. *Introduction to Logic*, by Patrick Suppes, N.Y., 1957, p. 220–3. See *A Survey of Modern Algebra* by Garrett Birkoff and Saunders MacLane, N.Y., 1953, pp. 348–55.
4. Bosanquet's view, suggested in a number of his lectures, is capable of much greater development. *The Principle of Individuality and Value*, London, 1927, p. 5. *The Value and Destiny of the Individual*, London, 1923, p. 176. *A History of Aesthetic*, N.Y., 1957, p. 417–19. *Science and Philosophy*, N.Y., 1927, p. 423. *History*, pp. 433–4.
5. *The Phenomenon of Man*, Intro. Sir Julian Huxley, N.Y., 1961, p. 257 ff.
6. 'Règles pour la direction de l'esprit.' *Ouvres et Lettres*, Pleiade ed. Bruges, 1952. Règle II, p. 40.
7. However, interesting work is being done by Prof. Robert S. Hartmann in: *The Structure of Value*, preface Paul Weiss, Carbondale, Ill., 1967; also 'The Measurement of Value, Set Theory as Value Theory,' *XIV International Congress of Philosophy*, Vienna, 1968.
8. *Philosophy*, Chicago, 1926, p. 31–2.
9. *Evil and the God of Love*, by John Hick, N.Y., 1966, pp. 53–4. *God and the Permission of Evil*, Jacques Maritain, Milwaukee, 1966, pp. 33–5.
10. Suppes, 60–2. *Natural Deduction the Logical Basis of Axiom Systems*, by John M. Anderson and Henry W. Johnstone, Jr., Belmont Cal., 1962, pp. 162–70.
11. Christianity: Matt. 7:12, Lu. 6:31. Judaism: Tobit 4:15, or *Talmud*, Shabath, Fol. 31, Col. 1, *Hebraic Literature*, N.Y., 1943, p. 4. Hinduism: *Bhagavad Gita* (c. 1 A.D.), trans. Nikhilananda, N.Y., 1944, p. 171. Also *The Wisdom of China and India*, ed. Lin, N.Y., p. 831.
12. *Eros and Civilization* by Herbert Marcuse, N.Y., 1955, esp. p. 46.
13. *The Philosophy of Civilization*, N.Y., 1949. Esp. pp. 307–15.

How Intrinsic Values
Interdepend

ARCHIE J. BAHM

University of New Mexico

Ethics is a natural science. Probably the best way to overcome its neglect is to locate the basic values natural to man and to expose their nature in a way which will make clear for anyone who investigates how obvious are the foundations of an adequate theory of ethical practice. Ethical theory, in which obligation is doubtless the key concept (obligation consists in the power which an apparently greater good has over a lesser good in compelling our choices), rests upon axiology. Axiology, despite its long history and sound achievements, remains an area of controversy, partly because ordinary experience normally presents values as aspects of knowledge-complexes which often can be understood only through intricate and delicate epistemological analyses, and partly because sectarian schools vigorously persist in their reductionistic contentions. Limiting discussion to intrinsic values, I propose as non-reductionistic the following theory of the nature of intrinsic values and of their interdependence as both necessary for and adequate for axiology and ethics as sciences. Only a summary is possible here.

Four kinds of intrinsic value are distinguishable. Each is directly intuited by persons experiencing them. Each has been recognized by theorists for centuries. Each is advocated by sectarians as the most ultimate, if not the only, kind of intrinsic value. The four are feelings of pleasure, as advocated by Hedonists, feelings of satisfaction, as advocated by Voluntarists, feelings of enthusiasm, as advocated by Romanticists, and feelings of contentment, as advocated by Hindu Anandists. Each kind has as its paradigm a distinguishable aspect of ordinary experience. Awareness of pleasant feelings occurs most obviously in the presence of sensory stimulation and can be illustrated most easily by tasting something sweet. A feeling of satisfaction may be observed most clearly while experiencing achievement of something intensely desired, as when one begins to swallow a cool drink after feeling thirsty for a long time. A feeling of enthusiasm, or of desireousness, may be less easy to typify for those not already appreciative of its nature. It manifests itself as exuberance, eagerness, zest, gusto, thrill, excitement, anxiety, urgency, earnestness, willfullness, conviction and commitment. Contentment, epitomized in yogic intuition, may be enjoyed by anyone experiencing a feeling of complete satisfaction; but its paradigm requires contentment felt as so self-contained that all traces of the desire which has been satisfied have been forgotten. A person who feels contented when he awakes in the morning will have no desire to get out of bed.

Four kinds of intrinsic evil, intuited by everyone, oppose the four kinds of intrinsic good respectively, as follows: People suffer feelings of displeasure, paradigmed by sharp pain or severe ache, of frustration, epitomized by anger, of apathy, experienced most annoyingly as boredom, and discontentment, characterized most generally by anxiety, which reaches pinacles alike both in frustration and in greed, lust, dogmatic insistence, insatiable ambition, with pleasures as well as pains and hopes as well as doubts exemplifying disquietude.

All intrinsic values, both goods and evils, are alike in many ways. All are intuited, and thus their intrinsic value is present in consciousness and is available for observation as such by anyone who can attend to discern end-in-itself aspects of experience gestalts. All may be properly spoken of as 'felt,' and as either 'enjoyed' (goods) or 'suffered' (evils). All may be talked about factually, as when one says 'I feel hungry,' 'my tooth aches,' 'I feel full.' All can be distinguished from those aspects of experience which appear as instrumental values, although their fusion in gestalts, resulting from their intimate interdependence, may involve more discriminating insight and effort than occurs normally. All are biologically based and are such that many of the causal conditions of their nature and variations can be traced and generalized about. Although the biological foundations of value experiences are not intuitively obvious, common sense, psychology, biology, a long history of literature, including both fiction and philosophy, Oriental and Western, and multitudes of recent studies in the behavioral sciences, confirm this assumption. All of the four kinds of intrinsic goods and evils may be experienced by degrees, i.e. as more or less, pleasant, painful, satisfying, frustrating, enthusiastic, apathetic, con-

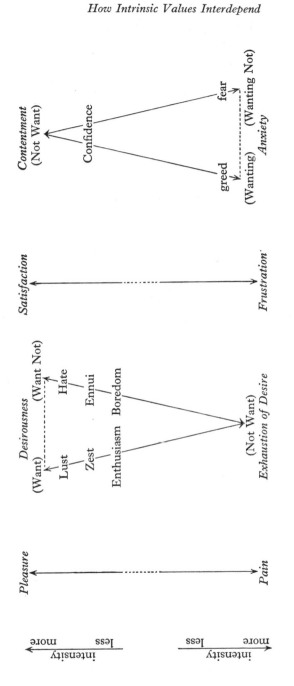

Four theories (kinds) of intrinsic value (good and evil)

tented or anxious. And doubtless many kinds of correlations between variations in the degree of enjoyment or suffering and variations in physiological conditions can be measured.

Intrinsic values interdepend. By 'interdependence' I mean that two or more things interdepend when each is partly independent of and partly dependent upon the others. Limiting discussion here to the four kinds of intrinsic goods and evils, I wish to call attention first to ways in which each is independent of the others. Not only is each independent in the sense that it can be clearly distinguished from the others, as exemplified by paradigms, but each can occur in experience in such a way that it can occupy attention, or awareness, completely to the exclusion of the others. One may enjoy a sensation as pleasant, whether a flavor, odor, color, tone, or tactile sensation, without having his desire aroused for more such enjoyment. One may experience having his desire aroused as a result of burgeoning energy, exemplified in desires to yawn or stretch or in tumescence, without either prior sensory stimulation or consequent satisfaction. For desires, even intense and enthusiastic desires, may subside, or be forgotten, without being either satisfied or frustrated. One may experience a feeling of satisfaction, or completion or achievement, without previous awareness of desire and certainly without being aware of previous desireousness. One may enjoy a feeling of contentment without awareness of desires having been satisfied, either through successful yogic endeavors or when awaking some morning before his desires have been aroused.

On the other hand, each of the four kinds of value depends upon the others in various ways. (1) Simplest, perhaps, is the observation that, since all are constituents in experiences, each is needed to supplement the others in constituting all of such experiences. Insofar as each is a part or aspect of experience, each is needed to complete the whole of such experience.

(2) We can observe tendencies of each to involve the others. When sensory experiences are enjoyed as pleasant, they tend to arouse desires for more such enjoyment; and the more pleasant the sensation the more likely it is to arouse desire for continuance or recurrence of the sensory pleasure. Desire, once aroused, usually cannot be satisfied apart from experiencing some sensory pleasure. Desire is always, by nature, desire for satisfaction, so most feelings of satisfaction, at least, depend upon the desires being satisfied. Without prospect of satisfaction, desires are much less likely to arise or persist. Yet, satisfaction also often depends upon the enjoyment of desiring itself, for, especially when the satisfaction is anticipated as far in the future, if desiring

is experienced as unpleasant, we are likely to try to suppress or neglect it. Anticipatory satisfaction accompanying desiring promotes such desiring, and the more intensely the desiring itself is enjoyed the more likely the desire is to continue on toward satisfaction. Motivation experts exploit this fact. Feelings of satisfaction tend either to give rise to more desires for such satisfaction, in which case the enjoyment of such desires depends upon the enjoyment of such satisfaction, or to pass into contentment, in which case the satisfaction is so complete that it eliminates all feeling of need for further desiring. Contentment, although ideally antithetical to any disturbance, whether by pleasures and satisfactions or by pains and frustrations, tends to provide the body with rest which, except perhaps in the weak or aged, is conducive to replenishment of energy which eventually engenders desire. Feeling energetic without opportunity for activity begets a feeling of boredom which in turn generates desire for activity. Hence, each of the four kinds of intrinsic value often depends for its existence upon influences by the others.

(3) In addition to contributing to experience as a whole and tending to cause each other, our four kinds of intrinsic value intermingle in particular experiences. In the flux of experience, pleasant sensations so automatically give rise to desires that usually no awareness of distinctness occurs. The arousal and satisfaction of a single desire often is experienced as a single event, especially when the event is short, as when glancing at a beautiful object or drinking a sip of wine. Enjoyment of enthusiasm and of anticipatory satisfaction are seldom distinguished from each other. A feeling of satisfaction usually is clearly felt as the satisfaction of a specific desire, with the content of the desire, and even the complexity and intensity of the desire, continuing as ingredients in the feeling of satisfaction. Satisfaction, when complete, fades imperceptibly into contentment; and enjoyment of contentment and enjoyment of mild pleasures and slowly emerging desires may be experienced as an unbroken continuum.

Consider a more complex example. Enjoyment of a gay garden party may, at any moment, involve a mixture of pleasant sounds of voices and music, the fragrance of flowers, the delicious flavor of food, enthusiasm for sharing in the excitement, satisfaction at having arrived, anticipatory satisfactions regarding what is planned for the evening, feelings of pride, gratitude, generosity, and interestedness in conversation and games. Many particular values thus participate in and contribute to the enjoyed experience as a whole in which intricate gestalts kaleidoscopically glide on and on without analysis of distinctions between each kind of value. In experiences at weddings, where several long-range and deeply-embedded desires contribute pervasive overtones, the value-complexes may be very intricate. The rich variety of intrinsic-value aspects of many experiences defies analysis. But the intricate and subtle intermingling is evidence of organic interdependence.

(4) Our four kinds of intrinsic value not only intermingle often indescribably, but also may succeed each other in an orderly fashion. Consider, for example, sexual orgasm, which often is preceded by the pleasant feelings accompanying the stimulation of erogenous zones, is initiated when desire is aroused and grows in intensity to an impetuously passionate climax, is followed by a feeling of intense satisfaction, and subsides into a feeling of complete contentment in which even all of the previous experience is forgotten. Curiously enough, the more fully one is preoccupied with the end-in-itself, or intrinsic value of an experience, the less it yields itself to recollection. Apparently we remember our desirings more than our satisfactions.

(5) All four of our intrinsic values depend upon the body, and upon its hereditary antecedents, its physiological functioning, and its psychological conditionings. They depend upon the nervous system with its sensory end-organs and the long history of biological evolution during which instruments aiding survival were adapted and readapted relative to means for acquiring food, avoiding enemies and reproducing, including desires for food and sex, as needed, and desires for rest and escape from activity, when needed. Since the experiences of intrinsic value enjoyed as pleasant sensations when eating healthful food, as eagerness when desiring food or sex or safety, as satisfaction when goals are being achieved, and as contentment when opportunity for rest is available, all aided in motivating survival, biological survival itself has depended upon such intrinsic value experiences. Hence, our four kinds of intrinsic value and our bodily nature interdepend, both now in each person and because their interdependence was necessary, apparently, for the survival of the human race. Axiology, in its foundations at least, is a natural science surely as much as any other aspect of biology, physiology or psychology.

Summarizing my remarks about interdependence, permit me to recall that intrinsic values are independent in the sense that each has a distinguishable nature which can be attended to and enjoyed by itself, and that all are dependent upon each other (1) for supplying all the intrinsic values constituting experience, (2) for causing each other to exist, (3) for combining in constituting particular complex experiences, (4) for supplementing each other successively, as in developing orgasm, and all interdepend with biological functionings. Without such interdependence intrinsic values could not be. The foregoing assertions, intended as expressing commonsense views, are proposed here as theses, or hypotheses, which may be verified by experimental testing.

Ethics as a natural science involves more than establishing axiology as a science. For an understanding of ethical experience presupposes also the exploration of: the nature of aesthetic experience and the epistemological conditions inherent in experiencing intrinsic values as if projected into objects, whether things, persons, societies, or ideals; the nature of choice among conflicting desires; the nature of feelings of obligation, duty and conscience which emerge when weighing value options; the nature of self and the fullness of its potentialities; the nature of communication, including communicating about intrinsic values; and the nature of relatively reciprocal relations between selves which contribute to the value experiences of each. All these, too, interdepend with intrinsic values, as well as with each other. So the field investigated by ethics as a natural science is rich with complicated interdependencies, all of which interdepend with our four interdependent kinds of intrinsic values.

Some Implications of the Ecological Revolution for the Construction of Value

THOMAS B. COLWELL, Jr.

New York University

A philosophic interest in Nature and man's place in it is hardly new to the 20th Century, or even to the modern world. Philosophy began with ancient man's crude but imaginative theoretical efforts to explain the makeup of the physical world and to understand himself within its confines. In broadest terms, the entire philosophical enterprise may be seen as a continuously more refined working out of the relationship between man and Nature.

The various views of man's relationship to Nature which developed in the history of thought reflected the unique perspectives and levels of understanding which the knowledge and culture of different historical periods made possible. These views differed not so much over the obvious point that man, physically and biologically, was in fact a part of Nature; nor even, perhaps, over the role of a supernatural governance of the natural-world—though language formulations frequently made both of these matters seem crucial. They differed more fundamentally over man's knowledge of Nature, and over the problems and possibilities which arose in man's use of natural knowledge to develop and further his ends. They differed, in other words, more over the question of what man's undeniable naturality meant and implied in terms of knowledge and the conduct of life, than over *whether* man was or was not a natural being, or whether his naturality precluded or involved forces beyond Nature.

These disagreements over knowledge and value, so characteristic of our own day, appeared throughout the Enlightenment. From Descartes to Mill, philosophers and scientists exuberantly promoted an essentially optimistic empiricism that celebrated the ability of the un-aided knower to gain knowledge of Nature. This empiricism, though sometimes mixed with rationalism and scepticism, was common to all Enlightenment thinkers. It was the heritage of the Copernican Revo-lution, which had freed the individual from the bonds of institutional dogma and accumulated ignorance, and placed him in a new and more active relationship with Nature that made science and modern civiliza-tion possible.

But Enlightenment thought was not nearly so optimistic when it came to the question of gaining moral knowledge from Nature. To be sure, many of the *philosophes*—men like Condorcet especially—saw no reason why the laws governing human nature could not be ascertained as easily as laws governing physical phenomena. Even more emphatic-ally, Spinoza contended that 'the chief good of man is that he should arrive . . . at . . . the knowledge of the union existing between the mind and the whole of nature. . . . In order to bring this about,' said Spinoza, 'it is necessary to understand as much of nature as will enable us to attain to the aforesaid character. . . .'[1]

John Stuart Mill, however, disagreed strongly with Spinoza's no-tion that what is morally good for man can be gotten from a study of Nature that reveals an ultimately harmonious unity which, once recog-nized, will enable us to live in beatitude. 'It cannot be religious or moral in us,' Mill exclaimed

> to guide our actions by the analogy of the course of nature . . . No one, either religious or irreligious, believes that the hurtful agencies of nature, considered as a whole, promote good purposes, in any other way than by inciting human rational creatures to rise up and struggle against them.[2]

For Mill, the derivation of human values from Nature contradicted *human* nature: 'All human action whatever,' he said, 'consists in alter-ing, and all useful action in improving the spontaneous course of nature.'[3] We should not merely study Nature with an eye to following her pattern; the duty of man lies in 'perpetually striving to amend the course of nature—and bringing that part of it over which we can exer-cize control, more nearly into conformity with a high standard of jus-tice and goodness.'[4]

The conflict here between Spinoza and Mill is but one example in the history of thought of conceptions of the man-Nature relationship which are at odds because of values. It exemplifies what has been the fundamental problem dividing most theories of man and Nature: the question of the derivability of moral knowledge from Nature. As far as I can see, the important theories of man's place in Nature come down to some version of the disagreement between Spinoza and Mill: whether Nature contains the normative ingredients for the construction of human values.

Our own position in the matter—I mean the view which best represents contemporary industrial civilization—is clearly closer to Mill than to Spinoza. We agree with Mill that man is part of Nature; and we agree with him, too, that it is trivial, because obvious, to say that man acts 'according' to Nature. In this, man cannot help himself, for 'all his actions are done through, and in obedience to, some one or many of nature's physical or mental laws.'[5] But though part of Nature, man's unique function—his duty, Mill thought—lies in controlling and transforming the natural world, not piously seeking its guidance. How profoundly we believe this today. How could we help but believe it: the entire edifice of our civilization is built upon it. The Baconian conception of science as control over Nature is not only an intellectual presupposition of ours, it is a deeply implanted emotional attitude as well. Who of us could disagree with Mill when he says:

> Everybody professes to approve and admire many great triumphs of Art over Nature: the junction by bridges of shores which Nature had made separate, the draining of Nature's marshes, the excavation of her wells, the dragging to light of what she has buried at immense depths in the earth; the turning away of her thunderbolts by lightning rods, of her inundations by embankments, of her oceans by breakwaters.[6]

Science is a mechanism of discovery and control, there is no question about it. But its disclosures about Nature tell us, in themselves, very little about how we should be moral. Here again we are with Mill and against Spinoza. Science reveals the facts of the world, we say, but not values we can follow. Values are man made, or imported by man from beyond Nature. Mill put it so well when he spoke of our own 'high standards of justice and goodness' to which Nature must be brought to follow. Our science yields knowledge of means, but not of human ends.

Here then is our idea of man's relationship to Nature: man is within Nature as an active, functional being. But his natural propensity is to control Nature through transformative activities whose goals cannot themselves be ascertained in Nature. Man is both within Nature, and without it. His relationship to Nature is therefore distinctively dualistic.

Is our view sound? Is it capable of sustaining us in the difficult future, in the way it has helped us to build up to now? There are many who would argue that it certainly is, and can. Granted, they say, that our civilization has created problems. But are they not all remedial through continued resort to science? Yes, men have different value systems. But will not these achieve a balance among themselves when we gain final mastery over the physical world? Science will never provide instruction in moral conduct, but it can give us the optimum physical setting for the realization of our 'high standards of justice and goodness.'

The tremendous weight of our Enlightenment faith in science makes it difficult for us to answer these questions in any other way. But this faith has rested on accomplishments, accomplishments that, on the whole, have been truly remarkable. Our initial awe over them has given way to sustained admiration, and now to a kind of complacency. So much has happened so quickly that we are beginning to take science for granted. And with that, the great faith in the remedial ability of science hardens into an unquestionable dogma.

I do not mean to suggest that science is not worthy of our allegiance. Rather, our conception of the man-Nature relationship has given us a narrow view of science, which has prevented us from utilizing it in a broader and more humane fashion. What has happened in the modern world is that the great scientific revolutions from Copernicus through Darwin and the atom, have given us the means to dramatically alter the face of the earth in a relatively short period of time. As with all revolutionaries, we have paid more attention to the revolutionary process than to its consequences. But now, one great fact is beginning to emerge: the consequences of the scientific revolution are themselves beginning to assume revolutionary proportions; they constitute a major problem in their own right.

By consequences of the scientific revolution I have in mind not simply bombs, space ships, automobiles, or skyscrapers, taken by themselves. I mean, rather, the total configuration of both physical and social changes in the industrial world which together comprise a new environment, a new setting for the life of all natural things. It is the environmental consequences of the new science which today have assumed the status of a new revolution of both scientific and social character. They are revolutionary not just because they *are* changes: mere change does not make a revolution. What is revolutionary in the new environment of the 20th Century is the potentiality it contains to arrest the progress of science and civilization as we have known them. Again, I am not thinking of the bomb—that is but one element of the new environment, and perhaps no more deadly than overpopulation or some of the various kinds of pollution we already know so well. The whole of modern technological development—progress, we call it sometimes—is producing environmental alteration that in degree and kind is placing an enormous strain on long-standing ecological relationships and natural resources. Many ecologists are warning that we cannot continue to promote the patterns of energy utilization and disposal characteristic of the last two centuries without endangering the delicate homeostatic mechanisms which go to make up the balance of Nature.[7] Thus, our enthusiastic efforts to control Nature have produced an environment which poses a challenge to the continued existence of a science of control. And science, we must remember, is part of this environment. Its procedures and assumptions, operating through specific institutions of culture, are part of the problem.

The revolution of environment, or better, the ecological revolution, is therefore of crucial importance to the future of modern civilization. For whether and in what way we can work out a solution to the crisis in environmental relations will determine our ability to progress as a scientific civilization.

Perhaps it is too much to characterize the ecological revolution as a latter-day Copernican revolution. In any event, the centrality of the ecological revolution stands as a clear call to philosophy to exercise its traditional role of critic and interpreter of scientific and cultural revolution. Perhaps one of the reasons for the irrelevancy of much contemporary philosophy is its failure to perform this role at the level of ecological change.

What would be some of the implications for philosophy were it to take the ecological revolution seriously?

The first would be a recognition that the fundamental problem facing philosophy is one of working out a new conception of the relationship between man and Nature. In an age of piecemeal analysis this may seem a hopelessly broad undertaking. Yet it need involve no surrender of the philosopher's passion for clarity and small-scale precision.

To suggest that philosophy take the man-Nature relationship as its central concern is, after all, only to recommend a new framework—in the way evolution was a new framework—within which philosophers could reconsider their traditional pursuits and activities. If the theme of ecological relations is really a revolutionary one, no doubt certain questions that have bothered philosophers will become even more important, while others will be transformed or simply be laid aside. Similarly, certain philosophical ideologies will undergo the inevitable alterations that stem from any revolutionary encounter. It would be impossible to describe synoptically all such changes here. But certain broad considerations can be indicated.

It seems clear that the question of the nature and ground of human value would become the center of the philosopher's concern, a kind of locus around which all other considerations would have to revolve. This is so for at least two reasons. One of them is that the question of value is at the heart of the man-Nature relationship. We have seen that man's relationship to Nature is problematic precisely because the consequences of his control over Nature conflict with the dominant values which have accrued to his civilization. Search for new values which will define a new relationship with Nature is therefore imperative.

An ecological approach to philosophy not only makes value questions central, it implies also a new approach to the study of value. Philosophy has always thrived on the examples set by the work of the various sciences. In the case of the revolution of environment, philosophy has recourse to a science that has been quietly at work on environmental problems for nearly one hundred years. That science is, of course, ecology.[8] Ecology is a branch of biology that studies relationships between organisms and their environment on a variety of different levels of organization ranging from individual, population, community, ecosystem, and finally biosphere. Ecology is not a generic science, like physics or chemistry. It is not concerned with ultimate properties or forces, with the internal constitution of substances—though it must employ knowledge of these. It is, to use Marston Bates distinction, a 'skin out'[9] rather than a 'skin in' science. Ecology starts with tangible physical organisms whose internal make-up it must leave to the basic sciences, and proceeds to investigate their interrelations with other organisms and the non-living members of the environment. The emphasis, though, is not on individuals, but on groups and communities of organic life: ecology is primarily interested in systems of inter-relationships and interdependencies which ecologists call ecological systems or ecosystems. Both 'community' and 'ecosystem' are focal terms in ecology. The object of study is the community life of organic populations in the context of their ecosystem—i.e. the entire chain of related entities and processes in Nature which regularly sustain them. Man's ecosystem is the highly complex network of environmental activity which contributes to the life of the human community.

One of the advantages of the ecosystem approach[10] in the study of Nature is that it enables us to gain a broader perspective of natural phenomena than is ordinarily the case in many of the highly specialized inquiries of the 'skin-in' sciences. In seeking out ecological systems as means of organizing and understanding the behavior of particular communities, ecologists are striving for unity and integration in a world which spends much of its time involved in the intricacies of specialization. Though they are specialists of a sort too, they come into their own at tying things together in terms of universal patterns of interdependency. Ecologists are the true generalists among the natural scientists.

There is one generalization ecologists have arrived at that is more important than all others for purposes of our discussion of values. That is the notion of the balance of Nature. The balance of Nature is frequently misunderstood as a rigid structural-functional order of the whole of Nature which all phenomena do or should adhere to. Such a view of an evolutionary world is of course inaccurate. The unity of Nature is a precariously achieved arrangement of changing forces. What is constant to this flux is a pattern which all changes seem to follow. This pattern, a pattern which Nature as a whole exhibits (though not necessarily in all of its parts), is that of a self recycling energy system. Natural communities that survive, find ways of returning used energy back into Nature. As Paul Sears puts it:

> Natural communities . . . operate on a current budget of solar energy, deploying it so as to keep the system itself in operating condition, maintaining or even enhancing the capacity of habitat to sustain life. Through variety and complexity, niches are afforded to organisms, visible and invisible, each of which plays its part in sustaining activity. Organic materials produced by green plants out of the raw substances of air, water, and earth are broken down step by step, in elaborate food chains until their components are returned whence they came, once more in usable form.[11]

The whole of Nature, says Sears, can be conceived of as a 'self-repairing, constructive process' which 'represents a type of equilibrium that approximates an open steady state . . . .'[12]

Thus the 'balance' of Nature really has to do with the *way* in which natural processes relate to their environments: namely, through the efficient re-cycling of energy. When a natural community succeeds in realizing this re-cycling, it gains a relative equilibrium or 'balance' in relation to other communities. Those which do not succeed, do not survive.

The concept of the balance of Nature, so conceived, therefore becomes a *normative* concept for the life of natural communities. Of the many things a natural community must accomplish, it cannot fail to achieve balance in the pattern of its energy utilization. This is the first law of the morality of Nature.

It is but a short step from talk of natural communities to our own human communities. For man and his communities are part of Nature, they are also natural. Human life takes place within the framework of the same ecological controls which govern the rest of Nature. It, too, is required to achieve a balance between energy extraction and re-use. Yet man of all the earth's creatures has been the chief perpetrator of ecological disregard. Under the rubric of progress, he is pursuing a fantastic delusion of endless growth, which, in his economies, his obsession with mass-urbanism, the proliferation of his populations, and in the horrendous examples of his technological pollution, is on the way to ruining the world as a setting for human habitation. The record of man's misuse of the natural environment is too well documented[13] in both popular and technical literature to need mention here. Suffice it to say that the ecological crisis of our time is world wide, is endemic to the kinds of industrial systems we have developed, and cuts across lines of economic and political ideology. And it is rooted in a view of the man-Nature relationship which is dualistic in holding that the *means* of technological advance can be derived from Nature, but the *ends* which direct it cannot.

Since the consequences of our technological means have produced the ecological crisis, it follows that the ends we have followed are suspect by implication. The search for a new theory of man's relationship to Nature therefore centers around the search for a new conception of the ends and values which guide the means we employ.

This is the great unanswered question of modern philosophy: the origin and ground of value. We have swung back and forth between the polarizations of subjectivity and objectivity, relativism and absolutism. Our lives are a sometimes grotesque mixture of elements of convention and supposedly timeless verities. In spite of all our technological betterment, we suffer from a deep seated gnawing that human life is but the knocking about of one arbitrary view against another. Today's turbulent expressions of ideals of political and social reform are reflections of this *malaise*. But neither they nor the remedial efforts of the establishment will succeed if they do not correct our dualistic relationship to Nature with its values of aggrandizement.

Philosophy cannot create new values, nor can it solve practical problems of social organization. But as an agency of culture, it can identify the potentialities for solutions latent within cultural settings undergoing crisis, and formulate them in broad theroetical terms capable of organizing and encouraging inquiries in more specialized disciplines and in practical fields. Such, at any rate, is the opportunity afforded philosophy by the ecological revolution. Ecology provides a model to philosophy and to the other human sciences of a new way of viewing the interrelationships between the phenomena of Nature. Central to its perspective is the idea of ecosystem analysis and the concepts of the balance of Nature. The balance of Nature provides an objective normative model which can be utilized as the ground of human value. It is, of course, no Platonic absolute; nor is it an empty formalistic principle, in a Kantian sense. It is simply a generalization of what has been observed to be a relatively constant pattern in the behavior of natural communities. Like any scientific generalization, it is subject to change. Nor does the balance of Nature serve as the source of all our values. It is only the *ground* of whatever other values we may develop. But these other values must be consistent with it. The balance of Nature is, in other words, a kind of ultimate value: it performs the organizational and governing function of an absolute without at the same time possessing absolute ontological status. It is a *natural* norm, not a product of human convention or supernatural authority. It says in effect to man: 'This much at least you must do, this much you must be responsible for. You must at least develop and utilize energy systems which recycle their products back into Nature. Whatever else you attempt must be consonant with this fundamental requirement.'

The answer to the value question, then, from an ecological point of view, is this: human values are founded in objectively determinable ecological relations within Nature. The ends which we propose must be such as to be compatible with the ecosystems of Nature. This will not restrict creative disagreement about specific values, but will provide a naturally defined boundary (*viz.* the balance of Nature) within which such disagreement can take place. Thus the construction of value may be said to be what some naturalists have called an 'objectively relative' process. Relativity obtains within the inner limits of human affairs, in the countless matters of individual taste, choice, and obligation. But if pushed or challenged beyond cultural relativity, as is usually the case in conflict or crisis, values meet the objectivity of basic ecological limits, and these provide barriers against the open end of relativism. This is not to say that individuals' lives are lived in arbitrariness until a time of crisis, only to be rescued by reference to ecological sanctions. It is simply that the area for our individual movement in value creation is limited by ecological considerations. Just as we recognize certain social restrictions in individual activity, so too we must recognize that the idea of a moral *laissez faire* is an atomistic vestige of the past. Human life is both social and natural, and hence takes place within a framework of limitations. Much of the irksomeness voiced against the idea of limitations on the individual has come because so many limitations have reflected the imposition of arbitrary human design, and have not been based on sound ecological limitations. The picture of a human society based on ecological sanctions is not one in which freedom is reduced; on the contrary it represents the only basis on which genuine development of the individual to the fullest is possible. It is not surprising to find that we have the strongest protestations against the loss of individual liberties in modern industrial societies which on the whole ignore ecological controls, and which in practice are committed to an open-ended moral relativism.

When we turn to the concept of ecosystem analysis, it is perhaps easier to see what it means to say that human values have a root base in ecological relationships. For ecosystem analysis is the study of the complicated networks of ecological chains and variables that function in environmental processes. From the ecosystem point of view, what is important to human understanding is knowledge of the myriad ways in which man's activities depend upon environmental variables—variables such as size, density, temperature, noise, configuration, proximity, color, and many more. These are variables of the physical environment, and for the most part they have been neglected. We have much descriptive knowledge of the size of things—the size of our cities, populations, and the minute dimensions of the millions of mechanical devices we have produced. But we have hardly touched questions of man-in-relation-to the size of this or that. We have no knowledge—only opinion—concerning the desirable size of the population of a city, say; or in education, how small a small class is, or whether a small class is more desirable than a large class. We don't know about these and countless other ecological variables because we don't care. And we don't care because our science and our civilization are not used to looking at things ecologically. Our anti-ecological bias is best seen in the education we all receive in one shape or another. We are brought up to regard man as the sole actor in history, with our modern age the culmination of the mighty drama, in relative isolation from the influences of environment. History is presented as primarily the social record of man, with only incidental reference to environment. The bifurcation implicit in this goes a long way to account for the perpetuation of the ecologic crisis of our time.

When the ecosystem approach is translated into philosophical terms, the importance which modern philosophy has attached to the problem of knowledge—i.e. to the possibility of its attainment—would be replaced by theories and techniques which enable us to make the requisite distinctions and identifications among interacting processes and gross, integrating systems of relationships. Knowing would become a matter of finding ways of reporting and formulating reciprocal trans-actions[14] between related natural entities and activities, man being one of these. And there would be much for philosophers interested in language analysis to do in all this, because many of the terms employed in the ecological approach—terms like 'Nature' itself, 'environment,' 'community'—are badly in need of linguistic clarification. As regards moral knowledge, the standard objections against the derivation of values from Nature loose their force when the ecosystem approach to values is considered. The moment man-in-Nature (instead of man *and* Nature) is made the subject-matter of moral inquiry, value questions are inescapable. Integrated ecological investigation is concerned not merely with the descriptive properties of environmental variables. The very question at issue is how the ecological population or community is affected by the variable in relation to the normative pattern of the ecosystem to which it belongs. The outcome of judgment here is only partly descriptive; in a more fundamental sense it has to do with the relative impairment of an organism or community in the context of the norms of the ecosystem. When an ichthyologist studies a fish kill resulting from the misuse of pesticides, his scientific judgment of the relationships upon which the occurrence depended clearly carries a normative force from the standpoint of the fish and their ecosystem. I can see no difference between this kind of ecological judgment and a similar one concerning man. In fact, in some areas of scientific investigation where we are already employing ecosystem analysis, and perhaps in some kinds of common-sense activities, we are engaged in the construction of values much of the time. The argument that, since man is himself a part of Nature, his inherent subjectivity vitiates all attempts to derive values from natural processes, seems to me labored. The presence of subjectivity in normative behavioral study is not a deterrent to scientific determination, but a positive boon, *provided* the results of inquiry have the opportunity of being tested in concrete social situations. The paucity of such opportunities, rather than the theoretical arguments advanced by philosophers, is the main reason for our reluctance to think about the plausibility of deriving values from Nature.

In this paper I have tried to suggest some reasons for thinking that an ecological approach to human values offers a basis for contending that morality has its ground in Nature, providing us thereby with the philosophical foundations for a new theory of man's relationship to Nature capable of redirecting the vast thrust of our civilization along more stable ecological lines. This theory constitutes a synthesis of the two paradigmatic theories of the man-Nature relationship examined here, those of Spinoza and Mill. Man's penchant to amend Nature, so dear to Mill and ourselves, is preserved, though recast in an ecological framework where the sanctions of ecological systems and ultimately the balance of Nature provide the ground for the values which direct man's amendatory activities. In the end, Spinoza was right: the good for man *can* be found in Nature, though in different ways than Spinoza thought. For centuries philosophers have looked to Nature as a source of value. Now, at a time in history when the solution of practical problems requires more than ever before a viable approach to value, we have in the ecological revolution the means of realizing this dream of centuries. The solution of the practical problems of our environmental crisis lies in practice itself. But practice alone will be blind without first a change in our 'conceptual environment,'[15] which is also a part of Nature. In the alteration of our conceptual environment, philosophy has a major role to play. Whether or not philosophy plays it, the task urgently waits to be done by someone. We are on a collision course that is far more than a conflict of political and economic ideologies. It is the mad scramble by human beings, following outmoded ideas of their relationship to the earth, for control of the natural resources of the planet. In the broadest sense, the problem is an educational one—or more precisely, one of *re*-education. Only as we find ways of going through the very difficult undertaking of divesting ourselves of our dualistic notion of the man-Nature relationship, and of learning to live in the world on different terms, is there hope of avoiding ecologic disaster. Perhaps then we may find it in us to truly love Nature and our fellow man, as Spinoza wanted us to, and as only a few of us so far have been able to do.

Notes and References

1. Spinoza, *On the Improvement of the Understanding*, in John Wild, ed., *Spinoza: Selections*, New York: Charles Scribner's Sons, 1930, p. 5.

2. J. S. Mill, 'Nature,' in J. H. Randall, Jr., Justus Buchler, Evelyn Urban Shirk, eds., *Readings in Philosophy*, New York: Barnes and Noble, Inc., 1950, p. 57.

3. *Ibid.*, p. 69.

4. *Ibid.*, p. 70.

5. *Ibid.*, p. 69.

6. *Ibid.*, p. 52.

7. *Cf.* LaMont C. Cole, 'Can the World be Saved?' *The New York Times Magazine*, March 31, 1968, p. 35.

8. Good introductions to ecology are: Eugene P. Odum, *Ecology* (New York: Holt, Rinehart and Winston, 1963); Marston Bates, *The Forest and the Sea* (New York: New American Library, 1960); Paul B. Sears, *Where There is Life* (New York: Dell Publishing Co., Inc., 1962). Works which stress human ecology include: W. L. Thomas, ed., *Man's Role in Changing the Face of the Earth* (Chicago: University of Chicago Press, 1956); Paul Shepard, Daniel McKinley, eds., *The Subversive Science* (Boston: Houghton-Mifflin Co., 1968); Raymond F. Dasmann, *A Different Kind of Country* (New York: The Macmillan Co., 1968); Jack B. Bresler, ed., *Environment of Man* (Reading, Mass.: Addison-Wesley Publishing Co., 1968); *Joint House Senate Colloquium to Discuss a National Policy for the Environment*: Hearing Before the Committee on Interior and Insular Affairs, U.S. Senate, July, 1968 (Washington, D.C., U.S. Government Printing Office, 1968); *Ecological Research and Surveys*: Hearing Before the Committee on Interior and Insular Affairs, U.S. Senate, on S. 2282 (Washington, D.C.: U.S. Government Printing Office, 1966). The two latter Hearings are mines of Information on Ecology and the Ecological crisis.

9. Marston Bates, *op. cit.*, pp. 16–7.

10. A very able statement of ecosystem analysis and its application in human ecology and the social sciences in general, can be found in S. Dillon Ripley, Helmut K. Buechner, 'Ecosystem Science as a Point of Synthesis,' *Daedalus*, **96**, No. 4 (Fall, 1967), pp. 1192–9.

11. Paul B. Sears, 'Utopia and the Living Landscape,' *Daedalus*, **94**, No. 2 (Spring, 1965), p. 485.

12. *Ibid.*, p. 484.

13. *Cf.*, for example, Raymond F. Dasmann, *The Destruction of California* (New York: The Macmillan Co., 1965); Barry Commoner, *Science and Survival* (New York: The Viking Press, 1966); Robert and Leona Train Rienow, *Moment in the Sun* (New York: The Dial Press); Gene Marine, 'America the Raped,' *Ramparts*, Part I: **5**, No. **10** (April, 1967), pp. 34–45; Part II: **5**, No. **11** (May, 1967), pp. 40–8; Fairfield Osborn, *Our Plundered Planet* (Boston: Little, Brown and Co., 1948); LaMont Cole, *op. cit.*, *passim*.

14. I have in mind the Dewey-Bentley sense of 'transaction,' which lends itself especially well to ecological thinking. Cf. John Dewey, Arthur F. Bentley, *Knowing and the Known*, Boston: The Beacon Press, 1949.

15. I am indebted to the stimulating article by Ripley and Buechner (*op. cit.*, p. 1196) for this phrase.

Some Thoughts on Scientific Axiology: Its Metaphysical Basis and Prerequisite Variables

NORMAN F. HIRST

Semiotic Systems Tracor, Inc., Austin

The mere menton of scientific axiology is probably sufficient to inspire a long and heated debate. Some eminent scholars are of the opinion that there can be a scientific axiology. Other equally eminent scholars are just as convinced that there cannot be. We obviously side with the former; else we wouldn't be writing on this subject. However, while such debates can be both interesting and profitable, we would prefer not to engage in them. Rather, for our present purposes, we think there is more to be gained by continuing the search for such a science. Success, if it is ever achieved, can be the final arbiter.

By science we mean simply the use of formal notions rather than ordinary intuitive notions at key points in the course of inquiry. Whether or not an inquiry is empirical, and in what way it is empirical, can be left open except for the following remarks:

1. We assume that all knowledge, even metaphysical knowledge, has its *roots* in human experience.

2. The reason for the replacement of intuitive notions by formal notions is to insure a common and decisive confrontation between theory and relevant experience.

Regarding the second point, our concern is whether the texture of the theory fits the texture of experience. This fit need not be in terms of predictability nor even in quantitative terms. The laws of classical dynamics do not in general enable us to predict what motions will actually take place. Rather, they give us the conditions which must hold if certain desired motion is to occur. We see no reason for equating empirical and quantitative unless the claim explicitly made, as it is in some physical sciences, is that the texture of the relevant experience is that of finite arithmetic.

All that seems to be required for a science is that there is an isolable, coherent, aspect of experience in which there are 'organizing principles.' An organizing principle is a formal principle. It is concerned with the form and order of an aspect of experience. It does not determine the concrete outcome of that aspect of experience. Structurally, an organizing principle is a uniform constraint on a set of variables. As examples, consider the Hamiltonian or Lagrangian in classical dynamics. These are particularly good examples since they are also examples of extremum principles, and we feel that extremum principles have an essential role in scientific axiology because the 'best' is an optimization of contrasts. If more familiar and simpler examples are desired, consider the conservation of energy principles.

As we know, organizing principles such as those mentioned are not immediate deliverances of common sense, they are not intuitive notions. (Though in the case of conservation of energy, it has become so commonplace that one might be tempted to think otherwise.) Similarly, we suspect the organizing principles of value will not correspond in any direct and simple way to intuitive notions. This is where most attempts to formalize value theory fail. They are, much too much, attempts to formalize directly our intuitive notions—usually in the form of trying to cast our intuitive value language into a precise formal mold. We believe all such attempts are doomed to *ultimate* failure. They may, however, produce interesting interim insights.

Now it would seem that the task of building an axiological science must begin by finding those key points at which we must replace our intuitive notions by formal notions, and by finding those variables which are to enter into the organizing principles. While it is true that these are two of the early steps, it appears to us that a more fundamental step must be taken first. It is a metaphysical step.

Western thought has so far been largely dominated by the habit of resolving wholes into their ultimate and unchanging parts arranged in external configurations. By external configuration we mean a configuration defined as relationships which require no change in the terms because of the relationship. Indeed, there could be no change in unchanging parts. Those aspects of experience singled out by this type of structure are the factual aspects. This approach can never isolate the structure of value. Value is a function of the quality of experience. The structure of value is concerned with how the parts, that is experiencing individuals, change one another's experiencing by 'social' interaction.

If we are to discover the rationale of value we must develop new habits of thought. In particular, we believe we must look to process, organismic metaphysics, and that we must direct our attention to the logic of 'social integration' or the formation of 'societies' in something close to the Whiteheadian sense.

Specifically, we believe that there is an intimate connection between process and value, and between organismic togetherness and the structure of value. Value is the goal of process, process is the means to value. Process allows for the successive realization of mutually exclusive values. It also allows for progressive growth. The growth from lower to higher order societies brings in the realization of higher values, in addition to the successive realization of exclusive values at each level of value.

Many details of our metaphysical view can remain open for the moment. We want, however, to emphasize and to develop the following points. We will have several categories of existence. The ultimate category, the final reality, will be bursts of experience, actual occasions, or events. This category is final only in a functional sense. That is, all explanations must ultimately reduce to the fact that some actual occasion made this choice rather than that. Of course, at a less ultimate level we may be able to go a long way towards explaining the rationale for its choice. But ultimately, it is actual occasions that contribute the definiteness of the real. The universe is the gift of finitude. Out of the infinite manifold of possibilities, a world must be constructed by an addition of choices upon choices. The choices are made by the coming together of definiteness in the actual occasions.

On the more formal side, we assume that 'modes of togetherness' are the ultimate logical notions. The more usual basic logical notions such as 'and,' 'or,' 'not,' 'implication,' etc., are special cases of external modes. As such they are relevant to *fact* inquiry only; facts being derivative abstracts from the ultimate togetherness of the actual world.

Since we wish to work with the most general modes of togetherness, we are inclined to favor some form of combinatory logic. We suspect that even the rather strange combinator known as the 'infinite cancellator' may play a basic role in our theory.

We believe the seat of value is the actual occasion; in particular, generic value is the esthetic quality of experiences. The measure of generic value is an esthetic measure. It is the aim of the early stages of concrescence to integrate the elements of experience so as to satisfy an extremum principle involving the esthetic measure. It is in this way that that actual occasion both achieves its own satisfaction and aims at the relevant future.

We realize that many scholars consider the equating of esthetic and generic value to be a commission of the naturalistic fallacy. We agree if esthetic is taken in its normal meaning.

Briefly, we are trying to formulate those organizing principles which delimit, but do not determine, the emergence of organismic form. Our point is that form emerges so as to enhance the quality of experience. However one might refer to it, we subsume it under the term 'esthetic.'

Esthetics in the normal meaning is concerned with what makes beautiful things beautiful. What makes them beautiful is that, in one way or another, they exhibit those same principles that delimit the emergence of form within the developing life of the experiencer.

The various value disciplines can be seen as being on a par with one another, each of them being a particular application of a set of general laws. To confuse a particular application with the general law *is* a fallacy. However, the stubbornness of the naturalistic fallacy may reflect an important truth. Namely, we suspect the application of the general organizing principles of value to esthetics, in the normal sense, will be relatively direct in comparison to, for instance, ethics which will require the construction of derivative primitives.

The esthetic measure is the first critical combination of variables needed for scientific axiology. We are not prepared to say in any definitive way what those variables are, nor what combination of them makes up the esthetic measure. However, for intuitive insight, Birkhoff's remarkable work is certainly worthy of consideration. Let us assume that the esthetic measure is the density of order, i.e.

$$M = O/C$$

where M, O, and C stand for measure, order, and complexity respectively.

The strategy for increasing the esthetic quality of experience, under this measure, is to arrange for an increase of order and a decrease in complexity. That this does in fact occur we will illustrate with the following discussion.

For our example, we will consider the development of a human life. In so doing, we are going somewhat contrary to what is often considered to be good practice. In the metaphysics which normally dominate western thought, man is somewhat of an abnormality in the scale of things. In our metaphysics man is continuous with the scale of things, except that most universal traits are, in man, highly developed; traits such as 'minding' and 'appetition,' for example, which are at a very low level in inorganic nature, increase through the scale of social complexity from the nexus of atoms, through molecules and cells, to their highest development in man. (Minding is my wife's term for the concrete ordering process which provides meaningful patterns of order and combination to feeling. 'It is that which allows a flower to be a flower and a man to be a man, and provides continuity and purpose to both.') Thus, it is man, himself, who provides the best examples of the full range of universal traits highly developed and integrated.

We consider the life of a human to be a sequence of events, moments of new experience from birth to death. (Some claim these moments are about 1/10 of a second which is probably about right; roughly 2.05×10^{10} experiences from birth to retirement.) The human being can also be considered a personal society, as well as actual occasions within a higher order society—society in the normal sense of the word.

In discussing the esthetic measure of geometric shapes Birkhoff makes a great deal of axes of symmetry. This is an important clue. We will define the order of an experience to be the number of separate transformation groups which can be applied to the experience.

Unfortunately, time does not permit a full and detailed treatment of our theme. Briefly, perception is constructive rather than passively receptive. Human perception and development begins with the establishment of a repertoire of transformation groups, or schema, in the motor system and develops to the transformation groups of the higher mental processes. The higher mental processes give us transformation groups over and above those required to merely function and survive in the world. They are to be expected given the influence of a general drive towards increasing esthetic experience.

Thus, it certainly makes sense to say, with Robert Hartman (*The Structure of Value*), that a thing's value is equal to its number of attributes. This is certainly the beginning of the truth, if we remember that 'attributes' is a way of denoting those transformation groups utilized by the nervous system in developing our experience of the thing. As a first approximation, and with fixed complexity, a thing's value is proportional to its number of attributes.

Now let us assume that man has developed, as fully as possible, his potential for creating order in his experience. His next step must be

K

to decrease complexity. He does this by entering into a higher order society.

As we said, we man 'society' in the Whiteheadian sense. That is, a society begins in the formation of a nexus.

> . . . a nexus is a set of actual entities in the unity of the relatedness constituted by their prehensions of each other, or—what is the same thing conversely expressed—constituted by their objectifications in each other. (*Process and Reality*, 14th Category of Explanation.)

The nexus becomes a society if in addition,

> (i) there is a common element of form illustrated in the definiteness of each of its included actual entities, and (ii) this common element of form arises in each member of the nexus by reason of the conditions imposed upon it by its prehension of some other members of the nexus, and (iii) these prehensions impose that condition of reproduction by reason of their inclusion of positive feelings of that common form. (*Process and Reality*, pp. 50–1.)

To put it simply, the society reduces complexity by serving as a filter, through time, of the elements in experience. Or, as Burgers puts it so nicely (*Experience and Conceptual Activity*, p. 59)

> The realization of values in a conception becomes more rich and the satisfaction attained more intense when the conception has at its disposition prehensions of certain forms of order already recognized in the experienced data. This is an obvious generalization of what we observe in the conceptions arising in the human mind. The required prehensions can be obtained if the process in which the conception arises belongs to a structured society.

Thus he concludes

> The creative urge in the universe promotes the emergence of structured societies of manifold types and of great complexity in order to reach more intense satisfactions.

and

> Values are realized in the universe by the grouping of processes into societies and of societies into more extensive societies of elaborate structure. The societies must have a certain persistence and possess a sufficient measure of stability against changes of their environment since otherwise the values would be lost with each such change. There will never be an end to the emergence of new societies.

In conclusion, this paper is, at best, a very brief summary of certain key points in our continuing research towards a scientific axiology. We do not feel any final commitment to some of the statements made at this time. In particular, we are considering various candidates for notions of order, complexity, and esthetic measure. A formal and adequate theory of order appears to be a key problem, not only for axiology, but for the foundations of such sciences as biology and psychology as well.

Also, we are mindful of the fact that any adequate theory must account for such effects as the mere repetition of order becoming a negative, rather than a positive, effect. We suspect this is due to the requirement of change to realize mutually exclusive values. The exact point at which repetition becomes boring probably depends on the time constants of the individual experiencing organism.

Whatever changes we may encounter as the work progresses, we do not anticipate any significant change in what we consider to be the key points. In summary they are:

1. That a scientific axiology is possible.

2. That science means no more, nor less, than the replacement of intuitive notions by formal ones.

3. That discovering the rationale of value requires a basis in process organismic metaphysics.

4. That expressing the rationale of value requires the replacement of 'normal' logics by combinatory logics.

5. That value evolves in experience according to extremum principles of esthetic measure.

The Serial Order of Values: An Argument Against Unidimensionality and for Multidimensionality

PAUL GRIMLEY KUNTZ

Emory University

We philosophers are still, most of us, under the spell of Plato. Since Plato in the *Republic* arranged everything under the form of the good in linear order we have sought the order of a line. '*Noesis* the highest, *dianoia* is the second, *pistis* the third and the last is picture thinking (*ekasiá*) and they are ordered according to the degrees they participate in truth ... *I understand and concur and I order them as you say.*' (*Republic* VI, 511, E)

The key to understanding the allegory of the line is to understand the relation 'higher than' or 'better than.' Plato had many shades of meaning when he arranged methods and things in four stages of progression, and the many meanings of 'higher than' go far beyond the order of value. Among the many interpretations are 'more real than,' 'more clear than,' 'logically more general,' 'principle or cause of,' but many stress the allegory of the line as a value ordering of the world and 'under the form of the good' the higher is more beautiful and morally superior to the lower.[1] This no one denies of Plato's theory but only some put the stress there.

The bold speculation of Plato is that presumably all that falls under the good can be ranged in a single scale. This means, in our language, that all values are commensurate. There is a 'common scale' by which we can grade any two values of different rank so that the one is higher than the other or the second is lower than the first....[2] We may have dropped from our inventory of operant ideas the correlation of the better and more beautiful with more true and more real: the key correlation in the great chain of Being, along with the doctrine of perfect being or God at the top establishing the plenitude and continuum of the metaphysical hierarchy, but my argument is that we retain in 20th century thought the hope and trust that values fall in a serial order. This is the spell of Plato's Line.

Although I support the presumption of orderliness of some sort as a necessary condition for the development of a science, I would like to question whether it is necessarily a serial order. The model of the line has such hold upon our imagination that even if we grasp theoretically the possibility of an infinite number of orders, still a philosopher tends to seek a linear or serial or one-dimensional order. A good example of this is Josiah Royce. 'In so far as we take account of order, we not only gain a theoretical control over our knowledge of the facts, but prepare ourselves for forms of practical activity which are made possible through the recognition, the definition, the production, and the control of order.' It is obvious why one would like to discover a serial order. It is intellectually thrifty (economic) in the sense that

> from a knowledge of part of the system which possesses it, we can infer what is true about other parts of the same order, and, upon occasion about the whole of the order. The general concept of material order, and of the correlation of series, has shown us how, wherever series are known to us and can be systematically correlated, we can constantly make use of some of our knowledge about the facts with which we deal to infer properties without which the advance of our knowledge would be greatly impeded.[3]

Although most order sought and found by the exact sciences is quantitative, and many interpretations of science stress the quantitative order, order itself is not so narrowly conceived. '... This way of viewing the tasks of the intellect is as unjust to the logic of the exact sciences as it is unable to define the actual range which the conception order has in the guidance of our practical, and, above all, our ethical life.' (p. 221)

Quantitative types of order are not the only exact types of order. Mathematics is not limited to quantitative orders and there are other types that are not defined in terms of quantitative relations. Royce illustrates his point by 'projective geometry' and 'descriptive geometry' which are developed without the idea of measurable geometrical quantities.

> Their source lies not in our power to measure, to weigh, and muscularly or mechanically to manipulate solids, but, ... in our sense of sight, in our power to notice the orderly alignment of points

and sets of points and in the orderly intersections of systems of lines, as such intersections appear in the field of vision. This non-metrical or ordinal geometry may, therefore, be called 'visual geometry.' In fact the eye gives us a certain knowledge of order, distinct from . . . various operations of measurement and metrical comparison. (p. 222.)

Many orders have been discovered prior to measurement, such as the movements of heavenly bodies. Therefore Royce prepares for a consideration of the moral order by stressing the general discovery of order apart from quantitative order which is only a special instance.

'The one great task of the intellect is to comprehend the orderly aspect of the real and of the ideal world.' Order is at the basis of our inquiry into 'a justly organized moral and social order' as well as into the order of the heavenly motions. When Royce stresses order in both realms he harks back to the use of the heavenly order as a model for the ideal moral order. The connexion between the two orders is by no means clear and Royce admits that the bridge is yet unfinished.

> The future must and will find such a bridge. Then exactness of thinking will become consistent with the idealizing of conduct; the realm of the Platonic ideas that are to guide man in his search for wisdom will be conceived, at least in part, in terms of an order which will not be 'ageometrical'—not foreign in type to the sort of order which the geometricians, especially in the non-metrical part of their work, have long had reason to study. It only remains now to mention some ethical and social relations among human beings which are of importance in enabling us to infer from known facts about given human individuals what the duties, offices, and social rights and positions of other individuals either are or may become. (p. 223.)

After so broad and generous a preamble to a science of value, specifically moral value, Royce's examples of moral order are nearly all limited to serial order.

> Among the moral and social relations of human beings there are a number of dyadic relations well known to us as furnishing a basis for serial order, and as being useful in both the lesser and greater matters of social life. Thus the relation of superior and inferior in cases where authority is concerned enables us to define serial order. If A commands B, and B commands C, and if orders can be transmitted from pair to pair, then in general, or under more or less precisely defined conditions, the commands of A may pass, as we often say, indirectly, through his subordinate B to B's subordinate C. In such cases it may be as well for A to transmit his commands through B to C as to express his authority directly. How far such a series may extend and how many terms it may have will vary with the type of authority in question, with the range of its application, and so with the numbers of members who constitute the series. But as

> far as the order goes, its essential characteristics are the same as those
> exemplified by a selected series of ordinal numbers, such as 3, 4, 5, 6.
> The usefulness of the idea of order is strictly analogous in the two
> cases. (pp. 223–4.)

Royce illustrates the moral order by a military chain of command,
by the transmission of messages through the post office, by the pay-
ment of a bill through banks, etc. An individual link in such a chain
can know that the results of his work are not his alone, but issue from
the related work of many other individuals. Royce expresses loyalty to
such an order and not only admires it for efficiency but for establishing
community.

> Order, therefore, or at least possible order, is the condition upon
> which depends the existence of anything lovable about our social
> system. If each acts only as an individual, the mere fact that he
> happens to be benevolent does not render his benevolence other
> than capricious. Loyal activity, on the other hand, is always orderly,
> since it involves acting in ways that are determined not merely by
> personal desires, or by the interests of other individuals, but by the
> relations in which one stands to those other individuals. (p. 227.)

The meaning of a loyal act is one which the community, not merely
the individual, requires.

Royce selects only one-dimensional or linear serial orders to illustrate community. Are all social relations those of subordination, in
which the loyal act is of obedience to superior authority and carrying
out of commands? Are all the dyadic relations asymmetrical in which
one person commands and another obeys? The linear model thus set
up is indeed also transitive, and when the system works because *A,*
say the philosopher king, decides what is the highest value, then the
decision controls all those subordinate to him, and we can predict,
finally, that to the last member, one who obeys the next highest, but
who commands no one lower, call him lowly *Z,* at the bottom of the
totem pole, all follow the leader. That an American philosopher
should emphasize only a Prussian conception of moral order, and this
American philosopher who studies cooperation among miners in working
the cradle in California gold fields, is one of the curiosities of intellectual
history. The extent to which Plato has cast a spell over succeeding
philosophy I cannot here establish, but the model of Plato's line seems
here to exclude criticism of one and only one kind of order and consequent consideration of symmetrical as well as asymmetrical relations.
We must also consider whether the moral order is like the whole number
series without gap, or perchance like the series of prime numbers. I am

expressing the strongest doubt whether values are in an order '*strictly analogous*' with ordinal numbers, say 3, 4, 5, 6. Do we really have a quantitative unit between two values when we have a relation expressed 'successor of by one?' And must the social order be automatically transitive? May not someone in a linked chain of acts use independent judgment and decide that the leader in authority blundered and the unfortunate consequences of error must be prevented from further damaging results? There may not be anyone wise and benevolent at the top of the chain of command and rather than eliciting loyalty and love, the subordinates may be driven to rebellion and hatred.

In spite of these rather harsh criticisms of Royce's attempt to found a science of moral value, it seems correct to say that wherever there is order, there can be a science. And there seems to be an ordering relationship among all values, not only moral values, say the general 'better than' or 'higher than in value,' and that therefore we can have systematic knowledge of values. Presumably we can find regularities and state laws. Such is still the major assumption of those who work in this field. For example, Robert S. Hartman states in the first paragraph of *The Structure of Value* that he endeavors to 'introduce orderly thinking into moral subjects.' By this he means the discovery of axioms or principles of value, and this is orderly because 'it understands a procedure which accounts with a minimum of concepts for a maximum of objects.'[4]

The four papers by Gill, Bahm, Hirst and Colwell are deeply in the spirit of Plato, Royce and Hartman. That is, there is deep agreement that what we seek is objective and public knowledge of the order of values. Each has some characteristic model of order developed in some science that he uses as an example of objective knowledge. This much agreement lays a basis for fruitful discourse between the authors about their differences. With so much in common I should not expect sheer polemic and outright rejection of alternatives.

The four papers disagree about the model of order and the science used as an example of objective knowledge. Gill uses mathematical logic most explicitly as a model of clarity and unambiguity in its propositions. Bahm less explicitly uses psychology; I believe, because it contributes to the adequacy of our view of man's manysidedness. Hirst uses philosophical cosmology (particularly Whitehead's philosophy of process) because its stress on the organic categories gives process the inter-relatedness of a nexus. Colwell uses ecology most explicitly because this enables us to overcome the nature-man dualism that misled us in thinking of man only as an agent in history detached from his natural environment.

These differences are not, as such, contradictions. They may be contraries of which both may be true (or both false) but hardly at this stage can we say that if one is true, then the other is false. Perhaps better we may say that the differences are of the complementary and supplementary sort. That is, in developing a science of value we need both clarity and adequacy and we dare not purchase either at the price of the other. At least the choice may not be made with a good conscience because we need them both in our quest for knowledge. Nor, we may add, dare we purchase the knowledge of social interrelatedness by ignoring the problem of the natural environment or so stress environment that we forget human society. The second pair of opposites is like the first.

Yet there is a hard choice between exclusive alternatives and one point at issue in these four otherwise complementary and supplementary papers. This is the issue raised by Plato and Royce: are values ordered in a line or series of one dimension? I believe I can show that Gill adopts this model of order, as did Royce, from mathematical logic. I believe that although Gill's paper is the clearest it adopts the wrong model of order. Although the other papers are less clear, I believe what they point to is a many-dimensional model of order. And in this choice of a complex order I believe that Bahm, Colwell and Hirst are clearly right.

I am sorry to set one paper against three, for it might suggest that the minority should capitulate. But there is no virtue whatsoever in democratic voting among authorities who can argue and provide evidence. The majority rarely innovates in science or art or philosophy.

I have used 'science' in a very broad way, and only one paper seems to use science in the sense of a natural science (although Bahm claims ethics is a 'natural science'). (p. 237) This is Colwell's and the science in his case is ecology, a very broad and interdisciplinary approach to plants and animals in their environment. We shall not then have to consider whether our proposed science of values resembles biology or chemistry or physics.

Gill explicitly commits himself to the serial-order of values. When he says that between any pair of elements it is possible to decide, I take this to mean that given a difference between the two such that 'better than' holds in some definable respect, either X is better than Y or Y is better than X. If this is the case then it follows that '*A decision having been made, the objects can be ordered.*' That is the 'molecular units can be arranged in a sequence ... with good on top [and] evil on the bottom. 'Better than' is an *asymmetric, non-reflexive, transitive order-ing relation....*' (Gill, p. 226)

One must agree that when X is better than Y, and Y is better than Z, then X is better than Z, and so on beyond one 'skipped inter-mediary,' as William James called the middle term in such a chain of terms, which must have at least three terms but which has no upper limit.

As Gill develops his elements into what he calls 'a partially ordered system a lattice' (p. 226) he discovers one 'single idea which covered them all,' namely *life*. (pp. 228, 233) The extensional list is '*health, wealth, happiness, fame* [otherwise called *approval*] and *power*.'

There are indeed qualifications of the theory and allowances for alternative orderings and I mention that this is only what most people affirm and an ordering to reveal 'hidden structures' (p. 233) but the definition of the good in this linear order is finally affirmed unambigu-ously: 'the good can be defined. If, in the primitive term *life*, possi-bilities and consciousness are included, then *the good is life affirma-tion*. We have seen that 'good' yields an ordering. Complex situations can be arranged from the best to the worst. The resultant lattice, when the detailed work has been done, will be in the mathematical sense of the words, a *value theory*.' (p. 235)

Can a reader be sure what Gill's lattice is? Is it that 'wealth' is better than mere 'health' and 'happiness' is better than mere 'wealth,' and 'fame' is better than mere 'happiness,' and 'power' better than mere 'fame?' We may certainly provide arguments for each step, but does the argumentation lead us to grasp the otherwise indefinable good which Gill equates with 'Life'?

The method used by Gill seems not to be the discovery of a linear order but a Socratic quest for that which is completely and harmoni-ously good, or good without omission of any aspect or internal conflict. We may call this the complete or absolute good. Therefore I say that it does not follow from his argument that we have anything like a linear order. For this precise reason: if life that has health without wealth is deficient, is this as true as life that has wealth without health is deficient? The relation between health and wealth seems to be not asymmetrical but symmetrical. Each is necessary to complete the other.

I do not disagree that 'almost everyone desires physical health' and that 'it includes the psychological' as well, and that other objects of the good life, such as happiness, fame and power, 'lose their appeal' if health is lacking. I do not disagree that those who do not care to be healthy are 'very sick [souls] indeed.' Further, it cannot be the complete definition of the good life.

But can't it also be said of wealth that almost everyone desires wealth, a degree of potency sufficient to obtain what one needs. We should then not identify wealth with money and property alone, but include the psychological sense of strength to work and get food, clothing, shelter, transportation, entertainment—all the items of our budget. And is it not also true that other objects of the good life lose their appeal if wealth is lacking? And is it not true that those who do not care to be wealthy, in the above sense, are very sick souls indeed? But having sufficient to satisfy needs is not the complete definition of the good life.

Now I do not see a rank-ordering of health to wealth or wealth to health emerge. What I see could rather be called mutual interdependence, to use the language of Bahm's organicism. That is, if part of a healthy life is satisfying needs, then wealth is required for health. And if wealth is strength to work and obtain money for necessities (and luxuries too?) then health is an aspect of this human power called wealth. Therefore my answer to such a question as grading health and wealth by the gauge of 'better than': 'Is health better than wealth?' or 'Is wealth better than health?' We should answer that the questions are badly formed. And if both are aspects of the good life, is this not what Gill is telling us?

There is, I say, a deep conflict between Gill's logical formalism and his handling of concrete values. In his logic 'opposite' has the precise meaning of '*a concept and its complement exhaust the universe of discourse.*' (pp. 227-8) This can be expressed in spatial terms, given an area all things enclosed by a line are 'in,' and whatever isn't in is 'out,' and all things are either in that area or outside it. In and out exhaust the universe of discourse. But there is no sharp line dividing health from disease, wealth from poverty, beauty from ugliness, and I imagine fame and power also, although Gill neglected to give an account of them. When terms are so closely related as to 'require each other' is the opposition one of a sharp break and mutal exclusion?

Gill merely quotes a phase of Bosanquet on how art includes some ugliness as well as beauty. 'The ugly,' says Bosanquet interpreting Schasler, 'essentially enters into all beauty whatever; and more than this, is the active element or dialectic negation ... impelling to the creation ... of beauty in its various forms.' The ugly, and the false and the evil, are 'essential manifestations of freedom and therefore not to be held deplorable phenomena. . . .' The ugly does not remain ugly when it enters into relationship. There is always the kind of opposition as between male and female. That is 'such sharply opposed forms of the beautiful contain elements which a little dislocation would make ugly.' Opposition of this sort might be called tension between elements of a whole, making the work better so long as they do not 'destroy . . . the harmony of the system to which it belongs and becomes caricature.'[5]

If this dialectical meaning of beauty and ugliness has meaning, and I believe it does, the statement is hardly a theorem in a linear logic of axioms and terms. Bosanquet would be the first to point out that the process so described is not linear inference or strict deduction at all. It is concrete and deals with action and reaction of the mind in which excess provokes its opposite, as somehow anarchy invites tyranny, or disorder invites order imposed by force and maintained strictly to counteract the lack of sufficient order.

In making a transition from Gill's paper to Bahm's paper one notes that each tries to sum up the good life in a set of heads. In each case there is a packet of abstract nouns. Gill thought he had 'boxed' the good with health, wealth, happiness, fame and power. Bahm has a list of four: 'pleasure, satisfaction, enthusiasm, contentment.' But whereas Gill is looking for a unitary definition (Bahm, p. 243) Bahm affirms these four as irreducible modes of defining the good.

Whereas Gill's search was for clarity, Bahm seeks adequacy ('an adequate theory of ethical practice,' p. 237). He therefore protests, most reasonably, against the reduction of intrinsic values to one and only one kind. Since Gill regarded all values as aspects of life, I wonder whether Bahm would regard Gill's theory as a reductionistic exaggeration of one dimension. And would Gill care to show how Bahm's pleasure, satisfaction, enthusiasm and contentment are aspects of life?

In analyzing Gill's supposedly linear logic and arrangement of values on a scale constituted by the ordering relation 'better than,' I discovered in his thought the organic pattern of interdependence. The kind of order Bahm finds in the moral life is this interdependence: 'Intrinsic values interdepend . . . each is partly independent and partly dependent upon the others.' (p. 238) I believe that the relationship between health and wealth is one of this type. That is, although we can find examples of health without wealth (particularly in the young being trained for work) and wealth without health (particularly in the old who can work no more), these states cannot be long maintained because one requires the other. I certainly agree with the general pattern of Bahm's organic thought that the four ways of reducing all value to one produces an inadequate understanding of the good, and its opposite, evil. All the evils we seek to avoid are not summed up in any single concept, be it pain, frustration, apathy or discontentment. (p. 238)

Bahm has aptly illustrated 'experience as whole' as having many aspects, and an aspect of the whole life is sexual life which can be read hedonistically as pleasure, voluntaristically as achievement, romantically as 'impetuously passionate climax' and spiritually (as by Hindu Anandists) as complete contentment. (p. 242)

What Bahm has not done in this paper is to show how 'obligation,' which he calls the indubitable 'key concept' of ethics, enters into our choices of 'greater . . . over lesser good.' (p. 237) Neither Bahm nor Gill gives an account of such obligatory relations as promising, telling the truth, being loyal to the social order (Royce's summation of all community values to which the individual ought to be loyal). Could it be that Gill and Bahm might be regarded as too naturalistic, too much stressing the biological basis? (Bahm, p. 242) 'All four of our intrinsic values depend on the body, and upon its hereditary antecedents, its physiological functioning, and its psychological conditioning.') If Gill's attempt to fill an obligation is by Schweitzer's 'reverence for life,' would Bahm's be an obligation to live a rich, many-sided life in a universal community in which each man could justly claim as rich a life as he is capable of living?

With these implicit criticisms we pass to Hirst's analysis. Whereas Gill sought clarity by logical construction and Bahm by consideration of the whole of man's physical and psychological life, Hirst seeks, on the basis of Whitehead's cosmology, to state the network of social interrelatedness. His stress is consequently on 'modes of togetherness' or on society. (Hirst, pp. 261, 263).

Although Bahm depends on intuitive notions of the dimensions of the good life, Hirst would substitute formal notions. 'The reason for the replacement of intuitive notions by formal notions is to insure a common and decisive confrontation between theory and relevant experience.' (p. 259) There should be a fit between the structure of the theory and the structure of experience. A science by its nature seeks 'the form and order of an aspect of experience' and upon finding order to state this order in 'organizing principles.' (p. 260)

What kind of correspondence does Hirst expect his theory to have to experience? I suspect in disowning 'any direct and simple [correspondence] to intuitive notions' that he parts company with Bahm.

There is a kind of hierarchical order of values, beginning at the top with an 'extremism' principle, 'the "best" is an optimization of contrasts.' (p. 262) Perhaps there is here a point common with Gill's stress on some unity of opposites and Bahm's stress on adequacy. Perhaps underneath the divergence of method and language is conceptual agreement.

'Value is the goal of process, process is the means to value. Process allows for the successive realization of mutually exclusive values. It also allows for progressive growth. The growth from lower to higher societies brings the realization of higher values, in addition to the successive realization of exclusive values at each level of value.' (p. 261)

The crucial question of Hirst's inquiry (and mine also) is how to measure values if the measurement by quantitative scale is not possible. (p. 260 'We see no reason for equating empirical and quantative....') Hirst makes a Whiteheadian move of looking to a mathematical formulation of aesthetic value. What he adopts is Birkhoff's law that measure equals order divided by complexity, or $M = O/C$. Although Hirst is not able to state the variables of scientific axiology, this measure of experience is proportionately large when we increase the degree of order or decrease the degree of complexity.

What is the order of a life? We are given several ways of conceiving it. One is to increase through the scale of complexity in an evolutionary way to the most complex that is also proportionately more highly organized than the simple molecule or cell. Mind is necessary here to provide purpose that binds together the lowest with the highest and all intermediary steps (apparently the physical succession in space–time of events leaves things unrelated and lacking what Whitehead stressed as 'personal aim' in such a society as man's life) (p. 263). Another way of conceiving order is measuring the order by 'the number of different transformation groups which can be applied to the experience' (p. 263) Hirst postulates some rough equivalence of these two formulas in that mental life provides more 'transformation groups' than are 'required to merely function and survive in the world. They are to be expected given the influence of a general drive towards increasing aesthetic experience.' (p. 263) And there is also some kind of rough equivalence to Robert S. Hartman's theory 'that a thing's value is equal to the number of attributes.' (p. 263)

I am puzzled that Hirst should entertain a quantitative measure (the number of attributes) after having abandoned the hope of any quantitative ordering of values.

But this increasing richness must be balanced by decreasing complexity, and this step defines 'a higher order society.' (p. 264) Although we worked with the arranging of different 'orders' hierarchically, a serial order established by the relation 'higher than,' the social order so ranked works with a different concept of order, not defined, and the author is seeking such a definition. This is interesting because a serial order is defined in the theory of relations as a relation that is asymmetrical, transitive, and connected. (Whitehead deduces non-reflexivity.) But evidently Whitehead's definition of social and personal order in *Process and Reality* does not satisfy Hirst.

I think he strives to avoid a paradox produced by $M = O/C$, namely that a perfectly blank sheet of paper, with sheer identity of quality throughout, as seen by the naked eye, is aesthetically superior to any printed or painted or decorated page. Hirst insists that 'the mere repetition or order becomes a negative, rather than a positive, effect.' (p. 265) Burkoff's formula seems a version of the old law of unity and variety. Not so unified as to bore us, nor so various as to confuse us. The best becomes then the maximum variety that can cohere harmoniously or the maximum unity that can be diversified for interest and contrast.

Can our theory of values based on aesthetics alone provide any account of obligation, justice, responsibility, loyalty and the peculiar relations of a moral sort that bind men together in society? I fail to see any attempt on Hirst's part to provide a transition from the aesthetic to the ethical or even to recognize that most theorists have difficulty with such aestheticism as Whitehead's.

There is another paradox in Hirst's use of $M = O/C$. Presumably we could get the identical M for quite a different number of proportions, indeed for an infinite number, just as there is an infinite series of proportions equal to $1/2$: $2/4, 3/6, 4/8, 5/10$, etc. What has never satisfied me with a formal geometrical approach to aesthetic objects stated arithmetically is that they all ignore so much that we experience. From the golden section down to dynamic symmetry and aesthetic measure, all of them are incapable of stating discriminations we make and stating which are most significant. Even more so, the use of such an over-simplified formula as a help to conceiving of levels of social progress seems to invite criticism on the grounds of inappropriate, if charming, simplism.[6]

I wish Colwell were right that philosophy could be read as 'a continuously more refined working out of the relationship between man and Nature.' (Colwell p. 245) As a matter of fact every ecologist I have talked with has protested against the long Neo-Platonic interlude between the Pre-Socratics and the rise of modern naturalism.

During this interlude the emphasis on spirit divided man from the other animals and from the environment.[7]

Colwell is certainly right that in our age a new problem has arisen because of man's growing knowledge translated into control of the environment of man and of all other animals. (p. 247) We are most certainly lacking in piety of seeking nature's guidance. In resolving the conflict between Spinoza's value-naturalism and Mill's value-transcendentalism Colwell seems right in picturing 'Man ... within Nature as an active, functional being. But his natural propensity is to control Nature through transformative activities whose goals cannot themselves be ascertained in Nature. Man is both within Nature, and without it. His relationship to Nature is therefore distinctively dualistic.' (pp. 247-8)

The intellectual crisis thus envisaged is that at the same time that men through science have vastly increased their power, at the same time we are aware of 'different value systems' between which the sciences do not help us discriminate. If science only provides 'the optimum physical setting for the realization of our human purposes,' what *should* there be? Colwell mentions 'justice and goodness' and we have already confronted attempts to pull together four different definitions of goodness (Bahm's paper). There are notoriously antithetical ideals of justice such that what is just by one definition is unjust by another. Colwell expresses a hope about different value systems: 'But will not these achieve a balance among themselves when we gain final mastery over the physical world?' (p. 248)

The key idea of the order of nature approached ecologically is that of balance. Colwell would wish for man to develop balance among values just as nature is a set of mechanisms that maintain balance. We have such a balance in the cycling and recycling of water, in the production of carbon dioxide, used by plants in photosynthesis, and the production of oxygen which animals use but cannot produce, in the processes of decay whereby animal and vegetable wastes are rendered useful for plant life, etc. Certainly we cannot disagree that man's scientific and engineering processes are having the consequences of producing too much waste in air, water, and soil for natural processes to handle. Waste no longer can decay in Lake Erie because the oxygen content has become too low. Our human population is increasing so dangerously fast that we are poisoning the environment. (p. 249)

Why is pollution wrong? Is it that any order, as Royce would argue, is to be loved, and destroying the balance of nature, 'endangering the delicate homeostatic mechanisms,' is the root evil of disloyalty? (p. 249)

Or is pollution wrong because life as such is valuable and the root of all values, as Gill argued, and to render life impossible is to destroy that whence all values draw their support? Or is pollution wrong because the use of knowledge in these fouling ways renders further knowledge impossible? (Colwell hints at the suicidal nature of the revolution: 'And science, we must remember, is part of this environment.') (p. 249) Or could pollution be wrong because it produces what is unredeemed ugliness, smoggy darkness instead of sunlight, junk yards full of scrapped automobiles, dead trees and missing birds, a silent and a budless spring? Or is pollution wrong because man on the highest level of nature has responsibility to a principle of order beyond nature, and a responsibility for other forms of life over which he exercises such vast control?[8]

I certainly agree with Colwell that the balance of nature is a normative idea and not merely descriptive. It does seem that by use of it we glimpse an all-comprehending idea, binding individuals into communities as they belong together in interdependency. (p. 250) It seems right to see the human appropriateness of this ideal in that it is not rigid but flexible thus allowing for much freedom within the system. (p. 251) The notion of an optimal population sets a limit to the 'delusion of endless growth.' (p. 252)

But have we found in the interdiscipline of ecology a scientific basis for all value? Have we found what Colwell calls 'a *natural* norm, not a product of human convention or supernatural authority'? (p. 253) Is the balance of nature a sure answer to the philosophic quest for 'the origin and ground of value?'

In answering these questions I fear Colwell's hopes have quite outrun his knowledge. He knows that 'we have no knowledge—only opinion—concerning the desirable size of the population of a city, say; or in education, how small a small class is, or whether a small class is more desirable than a large class.' But we can know about these things if we would but care sufficiently. (p. 254) Colwell's solution is that we can develop scientific answers to the question of optimal population by knowing more about the ecological variables. I gather that although science of the past has been value-neutral and not guiding man (pp. 246-8) the sciences of the future, as aspects of ecology, the super science, will give man the ground and basis of values. 'As regards moral knowledge, the standard objections against the derivation of value from Nature lose their force when the ecosystem approach to values is considered. The moment man-in-Nature (instead of man *and* Nature) is made the subject-matter of moral inquiry, value questions are inescapable.' (p. 255)

This is a fascinating idea, that man's distinction between fact and value has been not merely produced by man, but produced as a by-product of the false metaphysical opposition of man (and therefore values) to nature (detached from concerns and therefore value-free). Or more broadly, a judgment of fish-kill due to pesticide has 'a normative force from the standpoint of the fish and their ecosystem.' (p. 255) I should think that the ichthyologist who 'truly love[s] Nature' would make statements of normative force out of concern for fish as such.

We have been carried by Bahm, Hirst, and Colwell far beyond the attempt to locate all values in a strict linear series. But still all these efforts have tended, in various ways indeed, to demonstrate a systematic unity of value.

Must we agree that normative ethics is well done when it is done in the context of natural science? I believe not, for except for Colwell's ecological approach to man in his environment, I see no coherent account of what Bahm says is the key concept of ethical theory, namely, obligation. Colwell gives an account of 'ecological sanctions' that do, if I follow him, establish an obligation to preserve the balance of nature. Colwell has considered the terrible potential of man to pollute his environment and destroy the habitat for every species including man ... But the other three accounts have little concern for inter-human relations. Each of them deals with the human individual and the whole of mankind, with no account whatsoever of human institutions.

I find it highly paradoxical that the paper dealing with the environment should be the paper dealing most seriously with obligation. For obligation is generally a relation between persons and we rarely use the concept between aspects of nature. But surely the reason is that in Colwell's case reflection is prompted by sensitivity to a great wrong. Colwell's paradigm of moral knowledge is: pollution ought not to be. I believe the contrast and comparison reveals too many dimensions to reduce all values to a lattice, to use Gill's term for Plato's line or Royce's chain series.

If I am dissatisfied with the serial model of an order of values, what model do I recommend? I can get no further here than John N. Findlay's summation of 'the Systematic Unity of Values.' As we develop the ability to take different points of view we rise above the idiosyncrasy of our individual personalities and become what he calls 'universal persons,' judging what anyone desires and needs and what desires can be satisfied together without contradiction and mutual confusion.[9] We then envisage no single linear order from high to low, but rather a constellation, or rather 'stars in the firmament of value.' (p. 21)

We generate

> a whole order of impersonal goals, of heads of value and disvalue. If we seek only to desire what could be desired whoever we might conceive of ourselves as being, and we seek to do this with comprehensiveness, consistency and indifference to content, then we shall find ourselves forced to set up all the higher order goals of happiness, freedom from frustration, power, liberty, success, justice, moral zeal, dedicated love, scientific and aesthetic detachment, which are admittedly the worth while things in life, as their defects and contraries are admittedly its real blemishes. (p. 17.)

A major step towards liberating us from the spell of Plato's linear one-dimensional order is Nikolai Hartmann's *Ethics*. (In Part II, *The Realm of Ethical Values: Axiology of Morals.*[10])

It is inevitable that we talk of 'higher and lower values' because we grasp values in grades, so related to each other that we think of them in a series. This is, says Hartmann, the only way to grasp the manifoldness of values. (p. 44) But we should not think of an *a priori* serial ordering because whatever ordering we achieve is influenced by time and circumstance. (p. 45) Thus although Socratic ordering of values stresses the positive relation of values and intellectual attraction, the Christian scale stresses 'the factor of [man's] weakness, the being under the spell of lower powers.' (p. 46)

The realm of values is antinomic. Values lie in opposite directions and we cannot be both innocent and sophisticated, both simple and complex, etc. We must choose between them even though they should be combined. It is inevitable that we are involved in guilt because we have always inevitably sacrificed some value or other. It should not be so, but it inevitably is. The absolute good or the perfection of God is an unattainable ideal, something that we cannot possibly achieve.

Are the higher values the more general such that the scale is one in which we may deduce the lower from the higher? This is another traditional error, suggested by Plato's allegory of the line. In fact, says Hartmann, this is the prejudice of Plato's Idea of the Good. Kant tried to deduce all ethics from the categorical imperative. (pp. 48–49) Hartmann is stressing the doctrine that the higher values presuppose the lower values and depend upon them. This we have seen well stressed in all four of the papers criticized above.

'A further prejudice which slips into the thought of an ordered graduation is the notion of simple valuational scale which ascends in a single series.' Values are in fact heterogeneous: the ranking in order of subsumption is one order and that of higher and lower is another. Different orders do not necessarily coincide, and therefore we have 'a plural dimensional order.' (p. 50) '... The manifoldness of values is too great to embrace in a linear arrangement the intervals corresponding to the differences of content. The values would need to overflow continually into one another, which by no means corresponds to their actual and often very abrupt articulation....' (p. 50) There are not only vertical orderings on levels but horizontal relations between values on any given level, for they are differentiated laterally! Although on the same grade, values may be of quite different value materially. (p. 51)

Is the higher value necessary and the lower value contingent? This is another prejudice Hartmann attacks. Hartmann's argument is that values throughout have validity and cannot be of graduated validity. (pp. 51–52)

The ought-to-be of values is graduated, and this introduces the question of strength or power of values. Values are of very different strength in determining one's judgment of values.

> Difference of strength, however, is not difference of rank. It might rather be affirmed that the two kinds of gradation are opposed to each other: the higher value may be precisely the weaker, the lower the stronger. Within certain limits this indirect proportionality of height and strength may well agree; the higher values are generally for the most part the more complex structures, the lower are the more elemental. But in strength the elemental is always the superior. In this point therefore there would be a return of the fundamental categorial law in the domain of value—the law that the lower categories are the stronger and more independent, while the weaker and more conditioned are the higher and more complex. (pp. 52–3.)

Another reverse relation that holds is that

> to sin against a lower value is in general more grievous than to sin against a higher; but the fulfilment of a higher is morally more valuable than that of a lower. Murder is held to be the most grievous crime, but respect for another's life is not on that account the highest moral state—not to be compared with friendship, love, trustworthiness. Property is an incomparably lower value than personal benevolence, but none the less a violation of property (theft) is much more reprehensible than mere malevolence. A sin against the lower values is blameworthy, is dishonourable, excites indignation, but their fulfilment reaches only the level of propriety, without rising

higher. The violation, on the other hand, of the higher values has indeed the character of a moral defect, but has nothing degrading in it, while the realization of these values can have something exalting in it, something liberating, indeed inspiring. (p. 53.)

If we would make a more thorough study of the serial order of values we should try, as did Hartmann, to inspect our criteria of the grade of a value. (pp. 54–64) We need also to examine the claims of a value-pluralism *vs.* value-monism. (pp. 65-72) We should also further examine the antinomies and oppositions between values (pp. 75–122). With Hartmann also we should be more specific about the lack of systematic structure, that is the heterogeneity of values and the gaps between areas where the relationships seem clear. (p. 385 ff.) 'Valuational space' is by no means complete and clear and the analogy of geometrical order sometimes blinds us to lack of clarity. (p. 388) At one point Hartmann points to the analogy of values to the prime numbers. There are surprising gaps between 1, 2, 3, 5, 7, 11, 13, 17, 19, 23, 29, 31, 37, etc. Perhaps the most fruitful suggestion of Nikolai Hartmann is that the regularities discoverable between values are of many different sorts (p. 389, a table of three groups of two laws each: the third group contrasts valuational height to valuational strength, briefly mentioned above).

The import of my examination of the serial order of values is that philosophic tradition induces us to ignore complexity and to hope that the orderliness will be simple. It would be a great advantage to have a one-dimensional serial ordering. It would be a great advantage to have but one principle according to which all values could be ranked from highest to lowest. Decisions would be less agonizing. But it seems to be meaningless to grade different kinds of value, aesthetic, moral, scientific, as higher or lower relative to each other. (Findlay, *op. cit.,* p. 6)

There may be many more dimensions than those we have yet considered in this brief sketch. For example, in the most recent thorough study of the ordering of values, R. S. Hartman's *Structure of Value,* the philosopher interprets the dimension of emotional distance.

R. S. Hartman first presents us Ortega y Gasset's 'A Few Drops of Phenomenology.'

> A great man is dying. His wife is by his bedside. A doctor takes the dying man's pulse. In the background two more persons are discovered: a reporter who is present for professional reasons, and a painter whom mere chance has brought here. Wife, doctor, reporter, and painter witness one and the same event. Nonetheless, this

identical event—a man's death—impresses each of them in a different way. So different indeed that the several aspects have hardly anything in common. What this scene means to the wife who is all grief has so little to do with what it means to the painter who looks impassively that it seems doubtful whether the two can be said to be present at the same event.[11]

Hartman's interpretation of the dimension of distance enables us to grade the involvement of four persons:

The wife is drawn into the scene; she is an intrinsic part of it, 'it becomes one with her person.' In our terminology she values it intrinsically. The doctor 'is involved in it, not with his heart, but with the professional portion of his self'; he values it intrinsically-systemically. The reporter 'observes it with a view to telling his readers'; his valuation is extrinsic-systemic. And the painter's is purely systemic, all he sees are 'color-values, lights, and shadows.' Ortega *measures* these aspects of the situation by a common denominator: *the emotional distance between each person and the event they all witness.* (pp. 259–60.)

My conclusion is that we must pay attention to the many dimensions of values and avoid the temptation to make the complex and many-dimensional simple and one-dimensional.[12]

Notes and References

1. The divided line, the briefest of allegories in *Republic* VI–VII, takes only about three pages in Greek Paul Shorey, *Plato the Republic*, Vol. II, William translation, Heinemann Ltd., London, 1950 (originally 1935), pp. 108–17, and cf. pp. XXX–XXXI; F. M. Cornford, *Republic of Plato*, Oxford University Press, N.Y., 1968, pp. 221–3, pp. 224–5; E. Chambry, Ed., Platon, Budé, Paris, 1937, *La Republique*, **IV–VII**, p. 141–3; J. L. Stocks, 'The Divided Line of *Plato Republic VI*,' *Classical Quarterly*, Vol. 5, 1911, pp. 73–89; Ronald B. Levinson, *In Defense of Plato*, Harvard University Press, Cambridge, Mass., 1953, p. 52; J. E. Raven, 'Sun, Divided Line, and Cave,' *Classical Quarterly*, **III**, 1953, p. 32; John Wild, *Plato's Theory of Man*, Harvard University Press, Cambridge, Mass., 1948, p. 196–8; A. O. Lovejoy, *The Great Chain of Being*, Harper, Torchbrook, N.Y., 1960 (originally Harvard University Press, 1936); R. S. Brumbaugh, *Plato's Mathematical Imagination*, Indiana University Press, Bloomington, Ind., 1954, pp. 91–104; Herman L. Sinaiko, *Love, Knowledge, and Discourse in Plato*, University of Chicago Press, Chicago, Ill., 1965, pp. 144–66; H. Cherniss, 'Plato' (1950–1957), *Lustrum*, Bd. 4, 1960, pp. 166–71; Victor Goldschmidt, 'La Ligne de la *République* et la classification des Sciences,' *Revue Internationale de Philosophie*, Vol. 32, No. 2, 1955; *Etudes Platoniciennes*, pp. 237–55; R. L. Nettleship, *Lectures on the Republic of Plato*, Second Edition, 1968 (originally 1897), 2nd Ed., 1906. Ch. XI, 'The Four Stages of Intelligence,' pp. 238–58; W. F. R. Hardie.

A Study in Plato, Clarendon Press, Oxford, 1936, Ch. VI, 'The "Inter-mediates" and the Divided Line,' pp. 49–65; N. R. Murphy, *The Interpretation of Plato's Republic*, Clarendon Press, Oxford, 1951, pp. 155–64; R. C. Cross and A. D. Woozley, *Plato's Republic: A Philosophical Commentary*, Macmillan, London, 1966, Ch. 9, 'Sun, Line and Cave,' pp. 196–230.

2. I. M. Crombie, *An Examination of Plato's Doctrines*, Routledge & Kegan Paul, London, 1962, pp. 112–3, 121–7.

3. Daniel S. Robinson, ed., *Royce's Logical Essays: Collected Logical Essays of Josiah Royce*, Wm. C. Brown Company, Dubuque, Iowa, 1951, all the following quotations from the essay 'Order,' which appeared in James Hastings, *Encyclopedia of Religion and Ethics*, Charles Scribner's Sons, N.Y., 1913, which appears here as Chapter IX, pp. 204–31, s6, 'Order in the moral and social worlds,' pp. 220–8.

4. Robert S. Hartman, *The Structure of Value: Foundations of Scientific Axiology*, Southern Illinois University Press, Carbondale, Ill., 1967, Arcturus Books paperback, 1969, p. 3. One might be a bit amused at a science that is often founded and so rarely developed.

5. Bernard Bosanquet, *A History of Aesthetic*, George Allen & Unwin, London, 1922 (First Edition, p. 892, Second Edition, 1904, pp. 417–9.)

6. H. Osborne, *Theory of Beauty: An Introduction to Aesthetics*, Routledge and Kegan Paul, London, 1952, Ch. VII, 'Mathematical Norms in Aesthetics,' pp. 168–200.

7. Robert Platt and George K. Reid, *Bioscience*, Reinhold Publishing Co., N.Y., 1967.

8. Paul G. Kuntz, 'The Balance of Nature,' *Proceedings of the American Catholic Philosophical Association*, **XLII**, No. **2**, 1968, pp. 58–61.

9. John N. Findlay, 'The Systematic Unity of Values,' The Lindley Lecture, Feb. 22, 1968, The University of Kansas, 1968, p. 12.

10. Nicolai Hartmann, *Ethics*, Stanton Coit, Translator, Vol. II, *Moral Values*, George Allen & Unwin, London, 1932.

11. Robert S. Hartman, *op. cit.*, p. 259.

12. An admirable interpretation of contemporary American values is in John W. Gardner, *Self-Renewal: The Individual and the Innovative Society*, Harper Colophon Books, N.Y., 1965 (originally Harper and Row, N.Y., 1963). He avoids simplistic grading of values and tries to survey many inter-dependent factors. This study is particularly helpful in its analysis of creativity. It is most instructive to see a footnote in Wilbur Marshall Urban's *Fundamentals of Ethics: An Introduction to Moral Philosophy*, Henry Holt, N.Y., 1930, devoted to the commonly accepted American values from *Middletown*. There is quite a gulf between the ranking of values according to philosophic tradition and the values actually held by Americans. It would be interesting to see whether American philosophy is now less remote and other-worldly than it was a generation ago.

Recommended Reading—
Toward a Science of Values

Aristotle, Sir David Ross (ed.). *The Works of Aristotle*, **Vol. 12,** *Select Fragments*. (Oxford, 1952.)

Allen, Durward. 'Too Many Strangers,' *National Parks Magazines*, **43,** No. **263,** (August, 1969), pp. 12–7.

Bahm, Archie J. 'Four Kinds of Intrinsic Value,' *Darshana International*, **V,** No. **3,** July, 1965, pp. 22–31.

Bahm, Archie J. 'Organicism: The Philosophy of Interdependence,' *International Philosophical Quarterly*, **VII,** No. **2,** June, 1967, pp. 251–84.

Bahm, Archie J. 'The Aesthetics of Organicism,' *The Journal of Aesthetics and Art Criticism*. **XXVI,** No. **4,** Summer, 1968, pp. 449–59.

Barnett, Harold J. 'The Myth of Our Vanishing Resources,' *Transaction*, **4,** No. **7** (June, 1967), pp. 6–10.

Bresler, Jack B. (ed.). *Environments of Man*. Reading, Mass.: Addison-Wesley, 1968.

Brookchin, Murray. 'Ecology and Revolutionary Thought,' *Anarchos*, **2** (Winter, 1968).

Brookchin, Murray. 'Post-Scarcity Anarchy,' *Anarchos*, **3** (Spring, 1969).

Brownell, Baker. *The Human Community*. New York: Harper and Bros., 1950,

Cassirer, Ernst. *The Philosophy of Symbolic Forms*. **3 vols.,** Hew Haven: Yale University Press, 1953.

Cole, C. LaMont. 'Progress,' *BioScience*. **19,** No. **8** (August, 1969).

Commoner, Barry. *Science and Survival*. New York: The Viking Press, 1966.

Cumberland, John H. 'Economic Development and Its Long-Run Environmental Consequences,' *National Parks Magazine* **41,** No. **242** (Nov., 1967), pp. 11–13.

Darlington, F. Fraser, Milton, John, (eds.). *Future Environments of North America*. Garden City, N.Y.: The Natural History Press, 1966.

Descartes, René. *Rules for the Direction of the Mind*. Trans. Laurence J. Lafleur, L.L.A. Indianapolis, 1961.

Dewey, John. *The Quest For Certainty*. New York: Minton, Balch and Co., 1929.

Ehrlich, Paul R. 'Eco-Catastrophe,' *Ramparts*, **8,** No. **3,** Sept., 1969, pp. 24–8.

Ehrlich, Paul R. *The Population Bomb*. New York: Ballentine Books, 1968,

Gutkind, E. A. *Community and Environment*. London: Watts and Co., 1953,

Gutkind, E. A. *The Twilight of Cities*. New York: The Free Press of Glencoe, 1962.

Hartman, Robert S. *The Structure of Value* (with preface by Paul Weiss.) Carbondale, Ill., 1966.

Howard, Walter E. 'The Population Crises is Here *Now*,' *BioScience* **19**, No. **9** (Sept., 1969), pp. 779–984.

Jordan, P. A. 'Ecology, Conservation and Human Behavior,' *BioScience*, **18**, No. **11** (Nov., 1968), pp. 1023–29.

Lambert, Darwin. 'Let's Outgrow the Growth Mania,' *National Parks Magazine.* **39**, No. **211** (April, 1965), pp. 4–8.

Leopold, Aldo. *A Sand County Almanac.* New York: Oxford University Press, 1965.

Marsh, George Perkins. *Man and Nature.* Cambridge, Mass.: Harvard University Press, 1965.

Mayer, Jean. 'Toward a Non-Malthusian Population Policy,' *Columbia Forum,* **XII**, No. **2** (Summer, 1969), pp. 5–13.

McHarg, Ian L. *Design With Nature.* Garden City, N.Y.: The Natural History Press, 1969.

Michael, Donald. *The Unprepared Society.* New York: Basic Books, Inc., 1968.

Park, Charles F., Jr. *Affluence in Jeopardy: Minerals and the Political Economy.* San Francisco: Freeman, Cooper and Co., 1968.

Predmore, R. L. 'What Role For the Humanist in These Troubled Times?' *BioScience,* **18**, No. **7** (July, 1968).

Ripley, S. Dillon, Buechmer, Helmut K. 'Ecosystem Science as a Point of Synthesis,' *Daedalus.* **96**, No. **4** (Fall, 1967), pp. 1192–99.

Schweitzer, Albert. *The Philosophy of Civilization.* New York, 1949.

Sears, Paul. 'Utopia and the Living Landscape,' *Daedalus.* **94**, No. **2** (Spring, 1965).

Sears, Paul. *Where There is Life.* New York: Dell Publishing Co., Inc., 1962.

Shepard, Paul, McKinley, Daniel (eds.). *The Subversive Science: Essays Toward an Ecology of Man.* Boston: Houghton Mifflin Co., 1969.

Shepard, Paul. *Man in the Landscape: A Historic View of the Esthetics of Nature.* New York: Alfred Knopf, 1967.

Smithsonian Annual II, *The Fitness of Man's Environment.* Washington, D.C.: Smithsonian Institution Press, 1968.

Teilhard, Pierre, de Chardin. *The Phenomenon of Man.* (Intro: Sir Julian Huxley) New York, 1959.

Thomas, William L., Jr. *Man's Role in Changing The Face of the Earth.* Chicago: The University of Chicago Press, 1956.

Index

Action 55
Actual occasion 261
Aim of Science 72f.
Alienated self 133f.
ARISTOTLE 96, 156, 215
Awareness, in organisms 5f.
Axiology, scientific 259f.
AXTELLE, G. E. 82
AYER, A. J. 124, 213

BAHM, A. F. viii, 237–44, 271, 272, 274, 281
Balance of nature 251f., 279, 280
Behavioral science 81f.
'Big Science' 73f.
Biocultural evolution 159f., 172
BIRKHOFF, G. D. 262, 263, 277, 278
BORN, M. 19
BOSENQUET, B. 227, 274, 275
Brain 45f.
BRAMELD, Th. 82
BURGERS, J. M. 264

CHURCHILL, W. 41
COLWELL, Th. B. viii, 245–58, 271, 272, 278, 281
Commands 21
Conference on Value Inquiry vii
CONDORCET, M. J. 246
Constructs 16
Consummatory act 109f.
Convergence 41
COPERNICUS 123, 248
Criteria for scientific choice 65–79
CUVIER, G. L. 102

DARWIN, Ch. 47, 102, 248
Darwinism 107f., 173
DAY, R. 207

De facto values 22f.
DEWEY, J. 85, 109, 110, 129
DESCARTES, R. 96, 246
Determinism viii, 193f., 203f.
Determinism, hard 213f.; logical 203f.; religious 203f.; scientific 203f.; soft 213f.; statistical 214f.
DEVLIN, P. 207, 208
Dharmashastras 146f.
'Difficult moral choice' 183f.

Ecological Revolution 245f.
Ecology 250f.
Ecosystem 250
EDEL, A. 133, 166
Education 45f., 81f.
EDWARDS, P. 213
EINSTEIN, A. 102
EMMET, D. 160
Emotions 123f., 151f.
Esthetic measure 261f.
Esto values 23f.
Est values 22f.
Ethical rules 145f., 156f.
Ethics 15ff., 120ff.
Ethics, Hindu 146f.
Ethnology 145f.
Eudemonism 21f.
Evaluations 58f.

Fact-value problem vi, vii, 15, 34, 119–75
FAY, Ch. vii, 159–168, 172
FEYERABEND, P. K. 102
FINDLAY, J. N. 281
FLEW, A. N. 160, 161
Formative activity of mind 29f.
Freedom viii, 55f., 193f. 211f., 213f., 128f.

Free will hypothesis 181f.
Free will paradox 204
FREILICH, M. 164
FULLER, L. 154

GALBRAITH, K. 165, 166
GALILEO 47
GILL, J. G. viii, 225–36, 271–77, 280, 281
God 36
Good, extension of 227f.; definition of 225–35; intensional meaning of 229f.
GOTESKY, R. vi, 65–80
GOUDGE, T. A. 162
GREEN, T. H. 96
GRÜNBAUM, A. 218

HANDY, R. 109
HANSON, N. R. 102
HARE, R. M. 124, 127, 131, 137–42, 151, 154
HARRIS, E. E. vi, 95, 106
HARTMAN, R. S. 263, 271, 277, 284, 285
HARTMANN, N. 282, 283
HARVEY, W. 102
HEGEL, G. F. W. 97
HIRST, N. F. viii, 259–64, 271, 272, 276–78, 281
History 46f.
HITLER, A. 96
Homo sapiens 10f., 29f., 83f.
HOSPERS, J. 213
Humanism 49
Humanities 15f.
Human synthesis of values 32f.
HUME, D. 96, 119–31, 159, 169, 170, 213, 225
HUSSERL, E. 57
HUXLEY, J. 41, 108, 160

Induction 97
Interdependence of values 237, 275

JAMES, W. 241, 273
JASPERS, K. 41
Justice, sense of 195f.

KANT, I. 55, 56, 96, 113, 153, 218, 282
KELSEN, H. 154
KEPLER, J. 47
KUHN, Th. 102
KLINE, G. L. 213–20
KOLAKOWSKI, L. 218, 219
KROEBER, A. L. 162
KUNTZ, P. G. viii, 265–86

LASSWELL, H. 82, 83, 84
LASZLO, E. 109
LAVOISIER, A. L. 102
LEAVENWORTH, M. vii, 133–44, 170, 171, 173
LEWIS, C. I. 113

MACGILL, N. viii, 203–14, 217, 218
MACKAY, D. N. 210
Man–nature relationship 246f.
MARGENAU, H. vi, 15–26
MARX, K. 164
MASLOW, A. 81, 82, 163
MATHER, K. vi, 3–14
MAXWELL, C. 102
MEAD, G. H. 85, 163
Measurement of values 24f.
MEICKLEJOHN, A. 231
MENDLEJEFF, D. I. 102
Merit, scientific 67, 76; social 67, 76
Method for education and behavioral sciences 88f.
Method of science 17f., 29
MILL, J. S. 213, 246, 247, 256
Mind 45f.
'Modes of togetherness' 261
MOORE, G. E. 18, 133, 135–37, 139, 142
Moral judgments 99, 122f., 194f.
Morals 98f.
Morphic processes 33
Multidimensionality of values 267f.

Nature 37f., 245f.
Naturalism (ethical) 133f., 141f., 159f.
Naturalistic fallacy vii, 140, 170, 174, 262

Natural selection 109, 162
Natural self 133f., 170
NELSON, L. 175
NEWTON, I. 47, 48, 102
Non-naturalism 133f.
Norms, ethical 16

Observation 100f.
O'CONNOR, J. vii, 193–202, 213, 214, 216
Order of values 267f.
ORENSTEIN, H. vii, 145–58, 171
Organic philosophy of man 41
Organizing activity of reason 101f.
ORTEGA Y GASSET 284
OSCANYAN, F. vi, 15–26

PASTEUR, L. 47, 102
PEPPER, S. C. vi, 107–14
PERRY, R. B. 109
Person 203f.
Phenomenological analysis 61, 62
PIAGET, J. 195, 196, 216
PLATO 53, 96, 163, 267, 268, 270, 271, 272, 281, 282
PLATT, J. R. 41
POLIN, R. vi, 53–64
Politics 98f.
Pollution in Indian ethics 146f.
POPPER, K. 100
Psychology 194f.
Punishment 206f.

QUINTON, A. 160, 161

RAWLS, J. 195, 200, 216
Reason 95f., 120f.
REDFIELD, R. 165
Responsibility 203f., 218f.
RICKERT, H. 57
ROGERS, C. 82
ROSE, M. C. vii, 181–92, 214, 215
ROYCE, J. 268–72, 279, 281
RUCKER, W. R. vi, 81–94
Rule of correspondence 19
RUSSELL, B. 108, 172

SCHWEITZER, A. 234, 276
Science 15f., 21, 40, 48, 65f., 95f.,

Science—*cont.*
145, 193f., 249, 260f.
Science, behavioral 16f.; natural vii, 16f., 98f., 133f., social 17f.; of values 54, 225ff.
SCHLICK, M. 213
SEARS, P. 251
Selection, biological 111f.; cultural 113f.
Selective system 109f.
Serial order of values 267ff.
Social value of science 71
Society 70f.
Species 3ff.
SPENCER, H. 135, 141
SPINOSA, B. 246, 247, 256
STEVENSON, C. L. 120, 124, 127, 129
STRAUSS, L. 145
STRAWSON, P. F. 209, 217
SZENT-GYÖRGYI, A. vi, 45–49

Taxon 3ff.
Technological aim 70, 75
Technology 102f.
TEILHARD DE CHARDIN, P. 41, 228
Theories of intrinsic value 237f.
TOYNBEE, A. 41
Transcendence 56f.

Understanding 30f., 96f.
Unidimensionality of values 267
Unifying conception 34–36
Universal human programme 39–44

Value, analysis 85f.; categories 83f.; deprivation and enhancement continuum 87; dimension of 267ff.; dynamics 84f.; goals 83f.; sharing 85f.
Values, biological 6, 108f.; esthetic 49; ethical 15, 49; human vi., 9f., 67, 253f.; intrinsic viii, 237f.; non-natural and natural 134f.; primary 22f.; recovery of 27–44; social 61; survival 3ff., 107–114
Verification of free will hypothesis 186f.

WALTER, E. F. vii, 119–32, 169, 170, 173

WASHBURN, S.   161
WEINBERG, A. M.   65–79
WHITE, L.   162
WHITEHEAD, A. N.   39, 249, 264, 271,
    276, 278
WHYTE, L. L.   vi, 27–44
WILLIAMS, C.   173

WILSON, W.   96
WISDOM, J. O.   vii, 139–76
WOOTTON, B.   207

YOUNG, J. Z.   122
YOUNG, M.   155